KNOWLEDGE

OF TIME AND SPACE

KNOWLEDGE
OF TIME
AND SPACE

Tarthang Tulku

Dharma Publishing

TIME SPACE AND KNOWLEDGE SERIES

Time, Space, and Knowledge
Love of Knowledge
Knowledge of Time and Space
Dynamics of Time and Space

Typeset in Mergenthaler Trump Mediaeval and Helvetica Light.
Printed and bound in the United States of America by Dharma
Press, Oakland, California.

ISBN: 0-89800-205-2; 0-89800-206-0 (pbk.)

9 8 7 6 5 4 3

CONTENTS

PART TWO: SPACE

Opening Space

Body Space

Allowing Mind

Space Field

Field Dynamics

Senses in Space

Allowing Matrix

Great Space

PART THREE: KNOWLEDGE

PART FOUR: INTIMACY

Inseparable Presentation

Decisive Creation

Intimacy

PREFACE

Time, space, and knowledge together form the ever-present background of human experience. When these elements of existence are brought to the foreground, they begin to reveal vital new dimensions. For many years now I have been exploring these dimensions, for I have found that direct inquiry into time, space, and knowledge opens a creative vision of vast proportion.

The full scope of this vision has been difficult to communicate, and some aspects of it have eluded my attempts to express in words. This book represents my best efforts at this time to set the ideas down on paper. Several of my students have helped to edit this work into its present form. Although much care has been taken, it is inevitable that material is lost in the process; each time a manuscript in this series has come close to being completed, I have had serious doubts about publishing it. Yet in every case, it has seemed that the attempt is worthwhile: Though the books do not completely reflect the vision that gave them birth, Time, Space, and Knowledge communicate themselves nonetheless, inspiring all those who seriously engage the vision.

Since the first volume in this series was published over ten years ago, the vision has touched people all over the world. Study groups on TSK have been formed in many countries. Here and in Russia, throughout Europe and in South America, students of the TSK vision have faithfully traced out the questions raised in these volumes, and have carried out further explorations of the vision for themselves. I think this volume will help in their investigation, for the language is less technical than in *Time, Space, and Knowledge* and more accessible to the general reader.

I plan to continue presenting varying perspectives on themes related to TSK, so I have no real difficulty with publishing material that is in a sense incomplete. Modern scientists or philosophers may challenge some concepts found in this work or note statements that appear contradictory. However, Time, Space, and Knowledge is broad enough to accommodate all interpretations, explorations, and juxtapositions, and I am confident that the reader can find his or her own way into the vision. Inspired by these explorations to develop independent inquiry, serious lovers of knowledge will never be disappointed by the vast dimensions of Time, Space, and Knowledge.

Tarthang Tulku
Berkeley, CA
1989

INTRODUCTION

Time, space and knowledge are the most basic facets of human experience. They are the Being of our being as it manifests in this world. Space allows the world of objects to appear; time makes possible the sequence of events that gives order to our lives; knowledge gives meaning and significance to whatever appears or unfolds. Time and space are the ordinary stuff of existence, which ordinary knowledge aims to know.

Precisely because of their 'ordinariness'—because there is nothing more basic to our reality—time, space, and knowledge can also serve as the gateways to new vision. Knowledge in dynamic interplay with Space and Time can challenge familiar assumptions about self and world, knowing and the knowable. Time can present and Space can allow a new kind of inquiry, revealing Knowledge in a light that illuminates the whole of Being.

The world we live in today is in need of a more comprehensive vision that reveals our true relationship with time, space, and knowledge, for it appears as if time, space, and knowledge are becoming unfriendly towards us. Time seems to move too quickly: When we try to match its rhythm in our lives, we find it difficult to 'find the right time', to 'be on time', and to 'catch things in time'. We are always 'running out of time': We simply do not 'have the time' to do everything that we need or want to do.

Space is increasingly crowded with the abundance of objects modern technology has created, and this in turn is reflected in the crowded inner landscape of our thoughts and desires. While knowledge continues to subdivide, specialize, and proliferate, we appear to be moving toward less certainty rather than more. The light of knowledge as it is projected from the past into the future has somehow grown dim, and is now powerless to illuminate a clear path of action. We no longer see where the arrow of the future is pointing; we do not know the direction of human destiny.

When time is short, space is limited, and knowledge is uncertain, where can we turn? This is a serious situation, for although we can no longer look upon time, space, and knowlege as joyful participants in our lives, we cannot simply turn away from them or 'divorce' ourselves from them. They are an integral part of our lives . . . we could say they *are* our lives.

As human beings, we all participate in the same play; we are all active together. In the course of our lives, we play different roles, developing through space and time. This activity is already the expression of knowledge. Mind engages the quality of knowledge, and we participate in this engagement whether we are aware of it or not. Our lives naturally embody a momentum that unfolds from knowledge as the central truth of our being.

A new kind of inquiry would invite a new appreciation of ordinary existence through investigating experience from the perspective of time itself, space itself, and knowledge itself. Instead of looking *at* objects, we might notice the space in which they appear. Instead of accepting the patterns and positions of the self, we might look at the temporal dynamics of the self in interaction with its world. This shift in attention begins to shift our concern from the content of what is known directly to knowledge itself.

When we shift our attention from *what* is given in experience to the *way* in which it is given, new facets of time, space, and knowledge are revealed. As we learn to look at the indistinct edges and boundaries of what we know, rather than the impenetrable center, our eyes adjust to a different kind of light, and we see much that we had previously overlooked.

New ways of knowing emerge, inviting us to go beyond the structures of thought and the patterns of desire, and discover a far more abundant body of knowledge. Embodied in being, such knowledge manifests spontaneously, without the effort characteristic of thought or the distortion that comes with wanting, and without having to be prepared for in advance. It makes possible action free from obscuration, not bound by judgments and presuppositions about the way things are. It works a change in thinking, character, and being.

The unfolding of this inquiry invites Time, Space, and Knowledge to speak for themselves—not simply as facets of 'our' experience, but as interacting dimensions of Being. When we let old patterns of action, perception, and understanding drop away, *without immediately installing new ones in their place,* we begin to acknowledge the creative play of Time, Space, and Knowledge 'before' all interpretation as well as 'within' all experience.

Although what is said here necessarily takes a specific form, whatever limits that form imposes can be transcended if the presentation is understood as an invitation to Knowledge to speak, using a language shaped by Time and open to Space. This conversation among Knowledge, Space, and Time requires a new way of speaking. Familiar words must be used in unfamiliar and unexpected ways, and long-established concepts must be given back their power to awaken and expand awareness. The reader can and indeed must join in this conversation, which is also addressed to his or her own 'knowledgeability'. For unless there is genuine listening, the voice of Knowledge cannot be heard.

The mind has many patterned ways to prevent this listening and speaking: boredom, easy distraction, bemused reflection, or a steady stream of conceptual insights. Relying exclusively on words and thoughts, judging in terms of previous understandings, accepting uncritically beliefs proffered by others, turning inquiry into game playing, rejecting rigor and precision in the name of 'direct experience' — all these approaches only further habitual and frustrating ways of knowing and being. Even eager acceptance turns out to be a way to adopt another identity or attach ourselves to a school of thought or doctrine. Such an understanding only supports ownership of knowledge and the sterile production of commentaries on what is no longer living.

The best test is this: If what is being read does not emerge as a fundamental theme in the ongoing practice of daily life, the project of our inquiry has not been fully taken to heart.

We can begin our inquiry with a passionate commitment to what knowledge can accomplish. Not content to explore on the level of ideas, we can live out and embody the unfolding inquiry in the way that we now live out ordinary understanding, ready to further knowledge in ways that further human being as well.

Alive to the possibilities of Time, Space, and Knowledge, we can invite the truth of what presents itself to address us with a voice that has long gone unheard, but has never fallen silent. At first we will engage this invitation through language and linear presentations. Later, it may be in discourse with others committed to the same inquiry and actively participating in the ongoing invitation that we hear what has gone unheard. Eventually, we can learn to hear this voice in the sounds that resonate throughout our world. If we are mindful, we can learn to recognize it even in the cacophony of voices that wells up from moment to moment, naming, shaping, judging, and defining conventional reality.

We might say that Time, Space, and Knowledge have their own 'order', which gives rise to a purpose that can in turn be expressed within knowledge, space, and time. There is a 'truth' appropriate to this purpose, even though that truth cannot be specified in any ordinary sense. To misappropriate or deny that 'truth' which comes to our awareness will undermine the vision of our own experience.

The Time-Space-Knowledge vision is one of transmutation. It carries within it the specific energy inherent in transmutation. When this energy is activated, attempts to 'appropriate' the vision or carve it into manageable pieces could turn in negative directions, giving a counterproductive, even explosive reaction. We can safeguard our inquiry by an attitude that is open and vigorous. It is not important to 'understand' all that is said here; it is enough to be open to each question as it arises, and to persevere through uncertainty or discomfort. Difficulties arise only if the material presented is approached merely through labeling, incorporating, and storing away.

The alternative is to investigate the Time-Space-Knowledge vision with active intelligence. Knowledge itself is the best friend of intelligence. It can be our eyes and ears, our leader and our shelter. Human beings have achieved so much with knowledge; now we too can join in the unfolding of a knowing that develops through the activity of time into the openness of space.

Knowledge is not the property of anyone, and this presentation should not be considered exclusive. Others might find a completely different and more effective way of exploring the vision, drawing on a different vocabulary and style and engaging whole new realms of discourse. For knowledge itself is not secretive or reluctant to appear, nor does it disclose itself only to a chosen few. It is only our insistence on limitations that closes knowledge off. Whatever counteracts this tendency toward limits makes knowledge more freely available, bringing benefits to everyone.

If we let the search for knowledge become the play of time and space, we will find that the clarity of inquiry merges with the freedom of time and the openness of space. Time, Space, and Knowledge 'take form' in such a way that no one takes, nothing is taken, and no form is established. As they appear in the light of inquiry, they invite a knowing that deepens and expands in a dynamic of celebration.

For too long we have turned our backs on our human potential, until we have forgotten that there are any other possibilities for being. Now let us turn instead toward Knowledge, as the who of our being and the how of our action, the where of our becoming and the why of our existence. Alive to knowledge, we can commit ourselves to living in accord with the truth emergent in time and space, and discover for ourselves and others the meaning of our full potential.

Let us imagine Knowledge boundless in its prospects, welling forth in waves, resonating throughout the universe, expanding beyond its parents, Time and Space. Let us ask Knowledge to sustain and nourish us, sweeping us up in a beauty that feeds our hidden hungers and shelters our most noble aspirations. As we begin our inquiry, let us imagine that we are donning the silken robe of Knowledge, a coat of many colors—a magical garment that gives us warmth, comfort, aesthetic delight, and a sense of deep refinement.

To all dedicated students
of the Time, Space, and Knowledge vision

TIME

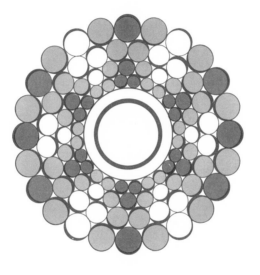

PART ONE

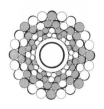

Three Times

PAST, PRESENT, AND FUTURE

Imagine you are walking on a flat sheet of ice, out of the past and into the future. Around you is dense fog and the still of a night without stars. As you leave the lifeless past behind, something at your feet rises up to meet you.

What is this something? Is this the future? What produces it, and what is its substance? Where does it come from? What is it that allows experience to unfold?

Ordinarily we say it is the past that produces the future. And yet the past is dead and gone—from where would it gain the generative power to give birth to the unborn? Then can the present produce the future?

Clearly, the future must have an origin, for the 'from-to' nature of time demands origins. And yet the present is always slipping away. From where could it take the 'substance' needed to give form to the future?

Could it be that we are looking at the present from too narrow a perspective? The present is more than just the dividing point between past and future—it has the other unique aspect of being the only domain in which the self is active. The 'active self' and the 'present' are so interconnected that it might be interesting to ask if this active aspect of the present could be the 'source of' the 'substance' of time as it flows into the future. Could the 'substance' of time be drawn from the active existence of the self, the 'owner' of experience?

This possibility deserves to be explored experientially, although as an account of time's 'substance', it presents certain difficulties. If the 'owner' of experience gives substance to time, how can we account for the temporal origin of the 'owner', or make sense of the 'substance' of time before there is an 'owner'? And how can different individuals, each living out his or her own present, interact to establish the 'shared present' that is the reality of the objective realm?

Perhaps the relationship between future and present is actually the reverse of what we think it is. Since the present as it takes shape in each moment emerges out of the future, could we designate the future as the 'source' of time's 'substance'? Actually this would seem impossible: Since we deny the future the status of being real, how can it serve as a 'source from'? But the present could hardly come to be as a specific 'environment' for being if it were not for the ongoing momentum through which it 'continues' into the future. Just as an echo conditions and confirms the 'being' of a sound, so the future conditions and confirms the being of the present.

This consideration seems to support the reality of the future, for we normally hold that what is real can be conditioned only by what is also real. Moreover, it speaks in favor of the future's undeniable link to the present. But there seems nothing more to be said about what the future is, or how it might provide the 'substance' of time. The future is unknown by nature—the 'x' of experience, *axiomatically indeterminate* in source, location, conditions, and consequences. Looking from the present 'forward', we can speak of expectations or identify a thrust toward becoming, as in a pregnancy approaching its term. But if we try to reverse this temporal flow, there is no possibility for communication.

The future as projected projector of the present cannot be established in advance as valid in its specifics; if it were otherwise, the future would no longer be the future. Untouchable in its actuality, the future 'awaits' present determination.

How then does the *past* relate to the present? To begin with, we would ordinarily say that the past is wholly determined beyond possibility of change. But we also hold that the past is linked to the present by a gathering momentum, an originating sequence that steadily comes to fruition. The past determines what can appear in the present—the content of what can be.

What do we actually know of the past? Although we are firmly convinced that the present is an outcome of prior influences, since the conjunction of past and present seems beyond validation, we can only know 'now' rather than 'then'. Our knowledge of the past is based on inference and on certain key assumptions: that 'evidence' of past events—including memory and physical traces—is trustworthy; that patterns repeat themselves over time; that present 'laws of nature' operated in prior ages as well as this one; that time proceeds in a linear fashion from the past toward the future. Since we live only in the present, no witness seems available who could affirm that these assumptions are correct.

These barriers to our knowledge of time seem intrinsic to the process of knowing. When recollection embarks from the present toward the past, it seeks out a reality that is gone forever. When it returns, present circumstances have changed, so that the body of the known to which recollection is meant to add its content is no longer available in the same way. Having set sail, this ship can no longer return to its point of departure.

We can make the same point in reverse. From the past as it 'originally' was, conditions have spun forward in time, changing what followed and screening 'what really happened' from direct investigation. The past appears to memory within a 'field' of later fabrication, responding to a momentum whose rhythm reflects what was once not yet but is now no more. In such circumstances, what shared truth can be expressed? How can past project an accurate reflection into the present, or present return to the past?

The present analysis also takes place 'across' time, and in this regard is typical of any attempt at explanation or explication. Whatever 'conclusions' we reach in our inquiry at once slip into the past, inaccessible to direct experience, even as conclusions. Any conclusion explains what appears in terms that parallel in reverse the process that produces the conclusion. Its explanations point toward 'derivation' and thus point at once toward the unknown that once was. Bound by the specific dynamic of analysis, no derivation can be brought forward into the present for direct knowing.

If we could know in a way that did not depend on derivation, we might find that there is no necessity to validate the past as the 'source' for the content of appearance. Such a 'source from' may be a present construct: the present presenting itself as derived. A determinate past indeterminately linked to the present may be an *inference* based on the *sense of past* that operates 'now'.

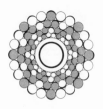

Three Times

BODY OF TIME

In the intimacy of present contact, experience speaks of inspiration. A movement of the spirit activates direct knowledge, giving the given and granting what we take for granted. As time unfolds across past and present and future, this originating inspiration takes on content and significance. The creative surge of what we embrace in the present is the outcome of a momentum that gathers toward specificity. Past and future intervene in present becoming, giving momentum expression.

Inspiration is without distinctions, making all seem possible. Yet experience of all that is possible does not appear all at once, nor does the present harbor all possibilities as actual. Qualities and characteristics 'measure out' experience, allowing description and comparison. They enable us to present the present to our own knowing. Yet these most vital aspects of experience seem to have their source not in the present, but in the past and future. Perhaps *the future gives the present form,* allowing it to emerge, while *the past gives it substance,* like an object casting its shadow.

Together, past and future filter the range of all possible events, shaping the indeterminate impact of inspiration into the actual. The present comes to be as what has emerged from a specific past and continues toward a specific future. The source of what is lies in what we understand to have been and expect will be.

These determining attributes of past and future 'coexist' with the unknowability of past and future as such. Though time 'flows' constantly from one to the other, past and present and future seem like three independent domains or 'fields'. Perhaps, however, what appears disconnected on the surface is linked underneath, like the caps of waves on the ocean. If so, a unifying 'body of time' would account for the appearance of the three times. Is there a way to explore whether this might be so: to investigate the interconnections among the three times?

One approach might be to describe the three times as 'gone', 'becoming', and 'not yet', but these designations do not tell us very much about the nature of time. How does present shift to past; how does future open into present? Is the movement sudden or gradual? Are there clear borders and transitions?

Suppose that we pushed past and future to their furthest limits— the beginning of the beginning and the end of the end. In the sense that these two extremes are unknowable, they are identical. We might speculate that this identity 'extends' further; that at their extremes past and future meet. Is there a way to prove or disprove this hypothesis?

Taking a third approach, we could focus on the difference between the present on the one hand and the past and future on the other. The present in its immediate intimacy could be understood as the direct presence of space. The past and future, however, cannot be found within space. They stand outside the gate of being. But what exactly does this mean? What distinctive qualities do the past and future have that set them apart from the present—and from each other?

The qualities of the past and future can in some sense be experienced, even if these times are not directly accessible. Each 'field' of time has its own impact on awareness, and the degree of impact changes constantly in accord with our participation. Someone with natural sensitivity or meditative training, or someone caught up in an intense experience may be able to challenge the parameters of such participation, opening alternatives.

How do awareness and the senses gather together in past or future? Are they sharp and vivid, clear and effective, or are they fuzzy, dull, and dreamy? What is the impact and the 'feel' of space in the three times? Can we restore the immediacy of the present to memories that have passed, or bring that immediacy to what has not yet arrived? Could close investigation or experiential exercises open past and future to being? Can we lead awareness to this point? What do we 'know' of the relationship between our awareness and time?

The structure of our mental faculties leads us to impose on time a particular 'order' or design. We view time as being one-dimensional, like a rope stretched taut between an imagined point of origin and another, similar point of termination.

In one sense we locate ourselves at some point along this rope or line, which we designate as the present; in another sense, this location is really no location at all, for the present is simply 'where we are located'. Invariably all the past is behind us and all the future ahead of us.

In *occupying* this nonlocated present, we are cut off from the flow of time. An indication of this 'being cut off' is our limited ability to contact what happens in time. The past is available through being stored in memory; the future through inference. Neither tool is very reliable or accurate: They represent only incompletely the countless transitions that time presents.

The limits that time presents form the truth of our existence. Although we claim to 'have' time, our claim of ownership rings hollow. We are always rushing, always short of time; and if the rushing stops, we are left feeling empty and without purpose. Emotionality and confusion eat up the little time we have; if maturity brings a deeper understanding, it may well come too late.

These limits may not be natural to time at all. If the whole of space, immeasurable both in scope and content, is encompassed within this very moment in time, these limits may be imposed on time from 'outside'. Within the vastness of space, what is known to our awareness is a sharply limited aspect of knowledge as a whole, like a narrowly focused beam of light that leaves the surrounding darkness intact. If the reach of space and the range of knowledge are so vast, can time really be restricted?

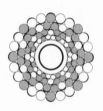

Three Times

PASSAGE OF TIME

W hen we walk from here to there, it 'takes' time to do so. We know *how much* time by reference to other events that also take place in time, such as the movement of the hands of a clock. Since time measured in this way is 'objective', we consider it almost absolute, but in fact such a measure is meaningful only because it is related to other events that concern us. For example, the span of a day is marked by the passage of the sun across the sky, light giving way to darkness. There is the time between one breath and the next, or the time between one stage of life and the next.

In measuring the difference between the blink of an eye and a billion years, the point of reference is human experience, indissolubly linked to the physical realm and to embodiment. Time in a nonphysical realm might be very different, since experience and the basis for measurement would be inconceivably different.

Time as it existed before human beings appeared is also a matter for speculation. Our way of measuring assimilates that time to our own, positioning 'our' time on a continuum with 'all' time. But without human beings to provide a basis for measurement, earlier time might well have been quite different from our own.

We tend to believe that the presence or absence of human beings would not affect the flow of time, which remains uniform and objective. But this assertion is based only on our convictions regarding time. The knowing we call on to witness time's uniformity arises *within* the framework of time. Presented in time, knowledge accords with the possibilities that time presents.

Our usual picture presents time as unfolding along a horizontal line drawn from past toward future. If we think of this line as representing the history of the universe, a point near the beginning would represent a time when the universe was younger than at present. Furthermore, an object that came into being at that point would be older than something created at a moment closer to the present.

This model could easily be replaced by others: We might look at time as unfolding vertically instead of horizontally, or in layers or cycles, or even through oscillations in place. But each of these models would maintain the key elements of continuity and flow that allow us to speak of 'older' and 'more recent', and to understand what is closer or more distant in time in terms of a ratio.

Based on continuity, we understand the progression from event to event as we would understand the flickering of a candle flame: variations in one steady event. It is helpful to see that in such an understanding, there is no basis *in time itself* for distinguishing past from present and future: no distinctive disconnection. Indeed, if there were a disconnection, what had been disconnected would have to be rejoined for the flow of time as we experience it to proceed. Who would be the joiner, and 'when' would the joining take place?

The passage of time would not make sense unless time exhibited continuity. The senses report a continuous unfolding of events, and the mind moves in its own continuity of thought and perception. As we walk from this place to that, we may be daydreaming and unaware of what is happening; still, we are certain that time continues to unfold.

The continuity we experience and accept is linked to the basic sense that we are 'here' in space and time, for the specific territories of experience are carved out by a fundamental rhythm that situates and positions. Whatever distinctions we maintain, specific 'dynamics' and 'mechanics' determine an underlying structural unity. Past, present, and future share the temporal order; points located in space share 'locatedness'; the knowledge that knows shares a particular 'body of knowledge' based on the time and space available.

Each point, whether understood in terms of time or space or knowledge, is viewed in multiple dimensions that express a whole. This is one reason it is so difficult to conceive of a time before the universe came into existence, or when the universe would no longer exist. Such discontinuities are not tolerated.

Continuity is likewise bound to the experience of the self. 'My' perceptions, thoughts, awareness, and memories form part of a lineage based on the private domain of the self. If 'my' mental activities were not separate from other people's, it is difficult to know whether we could even be aware of the passage of time as continuous.

The actual experience of the self, however, suggests that continuity itself is not continuous. Instead, continuity depends on mechanisms of repetition and derivation. The separation of time into past, present, and future is one indication that continuity must be referred to such underlying 'mechanisms'.

The present arises in terms of a 'from' and a 'to' that trace to past and future; in the same way, each of the three times supports the others. Without this structure, could continuity manifest? Experience itself might be considered another such mechanism: a way in which time can present itself as ready to be recorded and measured, so that distinctions and comparisons can be made, establishing connections that assure the continuity of continuity. Perhaps the 'existence' of the self is a fundamental mechanism for continuity as well.

Looking directly at such mechanisms, rather than the content they provide for, we see the momentum of 'from' and 'to' at work. One point moves toward all points: A rapid rhythm expresses the dynamic of continuity and unity in the form of patterns that generate a characteristic 'friction'. Appearance arises, the product of a 'field transformation'. The basic mechanisms are confirmed in such a way that their operation is never in question, and the world makes itself available for measurement and specification.

Provided these basic 'mechanisms' continue in operation, even a completely nonstandard 'experience'—for example, an experience of 'timelessness'—will not ultimately disrupt the unity and continuity of our being 'here' in space and time. But if the mechanisms did not function, or if they were not given the same authority, would continuity cease to exist? Could 'events' arise that were 'discontinuous'—that had no place within the temporal order?

Our ability to imagine the unfolding of time is restricted by the scope of our experience. For example, we might be able to imagine the passage of a year, but can we imagine the passage of a century? Could we extend our imagination to a span of time measured in thousands of years? A geologic era? An aeon?

Even if our faculty of imagination falls short, we can hypothetically entertain the notion that an aeon of time might also be considered a single 'moment'. Whether this happened would depend on how time was measured, and this in turn would depend on the activity of mind as shaped by knowledge and experience. The limits on our own experience make impossible an awareness that experiences aeons as moments, but we could imagine a being so different from us in knowledge or experience that measurement on this scale was wholly natural.

Since such a viewpoint is theoretically possible, we are free to work out its implications. Suppose we were to understand the span of time in which human beings have existed as taking up only a single moment. In that case, each 'event' that has taken place 'within' this span will have to be understood as inseparable from every other 'event'. We might say that all events are mutually recorded and preserved: equally exhibitions of one another.

From this perspective, every unfolding drama through the span of human history can be understood as part of an ongoing manifestation that makes no distinction between past, present, and future. In this 'time without distinctions', all events—all shapes and forms, thoughts and emotions, historical happenings—are equally available. Though a particular event may not be visible in space 'here and now', this fact takes on a different significance. The 'here and now' structure no longer specifies a particular moment in time, but rather a variation in a kind of atemporal 'isness'. 'Here and now' is an exhibition consistent with 'this' circumstance and not with others. Ten thousand years ago, one set of circumstances prevailed; ten thousand years from now, a different set of circumstances will operate. But this difference is no longer to be understood as temporal.

This thought experiment suggests that the 'genius' of time in presenting the vitality of appearance cannot be confined to the present. Time's creative force emerges within a unity that links experience across past and present and future. By the same token, change cannot be the essence of time.

The creative, presentational quality of time is bound neither by this moment nor that moment, nor by the transition between moments. Past and present and future may be labels that cover a more unitary sense of time. Looking experientially, we might ask: When we identify ourselves as active 'in the present', are we cutting off time at a deeper level?

No matter what moment we find ourselves in 'now', we cannot escape time. What is this inescapable 'time' that binds us? If we understand it as accessible through the 'present' moment, we must also acknowledge that this moment is linked to other moments 'in' time, whether past or future. Such links suggest that the notion of time as unitary is more than simply an interesting hypothesis. Perhaps all time is recorded in each moment of time, with the specific moment shaped in its particulars by the underlying structure of the whole.

To say that *other specific moments* are recorded in this one may hold too tightly to conventional ways of thinking. But if 'time' is not specific moments of time, it must be an entity separate from these moments. Can we make sense of such a possibility? In doing so, what assumptions about the 'nature' of time will we apply? Can these assumptions be further investigated?

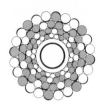

Experience in Time

INTENSIFICATION
OF TIME

W hen time's momentum is measured out as the lifeless ticking away of linear temporality, the intrinsic 'aliveness' of time is channeled into mechanisms for multiplication and duplication. Played out into a world of positions, time sets up boundaries, identities, partitions, and limits, affirming a 'from-to' order that moves away from the centerless center of time's flow. Filtered through such 're-presentations' of knowledge, the creative energy of time disappears from view, and becomes inaccessible.

The 'self' as 'bystander' serves as guardian of this order. When the self 'stands by', it claims the right to possess what time presents, assuring that time's momentum will 'take form' in accord with a specific logic. This logic in turn is informed by a 'logos', coherent and internally consistent, that names and defines, confines and eliminates, establishing a structure based on a center and directions that extend out from that center. For the 'logos' of self and world, *what stands at the center of the structure is experience:* the reality known to the self.

Just as substance at the center makes space dense, so experience at the center makes time tense. The 'denseness' of space and the 'tenseness' of time interact to establish restriction and necessity: the realm of objects and the concerns of a self. 'Tenseness' leads to constricting intensity that allows for no alternatives. It generates tension, which radiates out in all directions as different forms of pain and as a pattern of knowing characterized by reasons and distinctions, excuses and justifications. Channeled into strictly defined lines of force, linear momentum accelerates, creating still more pressure.

The temporal order established by the 'logos' in this way continues to build and intensify. Pressure feeds back on itself, like an echo in an enclosed chamber; the echo grows louder, drowning out other sound. With momentum building unchecked, chaos threatens behind each appearance, manifesting psychologically in confusion and a sense of being lost. Since the 'order' imposed through (the self's) experience is not centered in time's dynamic, it is only superficial. A sea of emotions seethes beneath the surface, occasionally erupting.

When involvement grows this intense, it feeds back into the frozen momentum of first-level time, creating an imbalance that begins to affect the 'structural integrity' of the temporal order. Pressure builds up, becoming destabilizing, even painful. Unless it is cut off through other self-interpretations, identification grows more complete. For example, if the initial response has been 'I am angry', the anger becomes all-encompassing: The self becomes its anger. When identification is total, 'I am angry' is transformed into 'I hate', and energy spills over into action.

In this 'order' governed by such a 'logos', people live for simple reasons, trying their best to satisfy their desires until eventually their life is used up and death brings new transitions. Despite the steady shifting from state to state—a mystery to conventional knowledge—time is oppressive, its mechanical momentum continuing unchecked.

Subjectively, the experience of a 'bystander-self' knowing an 'outsider-world' continues to appear fluid, for it manifests in various ways and embraces various natures. But its inner rhythms reflect only limited patternings. A shape or character is established and moves at once toward duplication. Thoughts repeat themselves endlessly; habits assert their dominance. The structure of repetition catches the self up into a world where space is dense and crowded with objects, and time is either too soon or too late.

The play of events and reactions can seem exciting, even fascinating, but the same positions and interpretations are simply being reenacted. For all the movement, there is no sense of destiny and no purpose. The self jumps from a past that is gone forever to a future that is not yet here. The present serves only as an empty point of reference.

The self finds itself caught up in a situation where it must act within a state of ignorance, unable to ever *know* the past or future, even though it can predict the future, remember the past, and experience the present. Yet even present reality is accessible only so long as it continues to be as it has been. Immediate experience, which the self claims as its own in a special way, is actually an interpretation based on the past—at most a new combination of elements already established.

These limitations on the self's participation in time help account for the specific psychology that we normally understand as the very core of the self. For the 'bystander-self', affirming itself through owning experience, the fundamental 'order' is one of involvement and identification with what time presents. When identification is restrained, the self involves itself with the presentations of time in a distanced manner, keeping time's energy in check. Examples include sensory experience, thoughts, and memories; for example, 'I see' and 'I recall.' On the other hand, when identification is intense, the self draws on time's energy more directly. Increasing involvement manifests in a self-interpretation rooted in 'I am', as in 'I am angry' or 'I am tired'.

The patterns and involvements of the psychological mode could be understood as a standard first-level 'readout' of the 'logos'. Caught up in the measured rhythms through which appearance unfolds mechanically from past to present to future, committed to existence and becoming, the self only skims the surface of time, never touching its body.

According fully with human consciousness, the three divided times distribute experience across time. The entities revealed within time likewise exist in a way that divides their being across time, leaving the wholeness of their being inaccessible. A limited knowing 'reads out' limited ways to be.

The whole of this structure depends on placing the self and present experience at the center of what is real. Could there be another way of knowing and being that returns time to the center; that touches the body of time directly? Could there be a way for fuller awareness to know time anew?

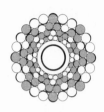

Experience in Time

SELF
AS BYSTANDER

The known world is experienced by the self, which *owns* its experience. For this basic structure to work, the self must adopt a specific position that puts it *outside* experience. Thus, while experience is inseparable from the flow of time, and is in fact the way that the flow presents itself, the self is an 'outsider' with respect to the temporal dynamic.

As an 'outsider', the self occupies the specific role of 'bystander', unaffected by the 'passing' of time. The objects and forms that it identifies and defines are also 'outsiders', but in a different sense: Like rocks in a stream, they are *in* time, carried or carved by its flow, yet separate from the flow itself.

'Outsiders' form the self's 'world', and self and world together comprise the whole of existence. Past, present, and future, considered as static structures, are among the 'outsiders' available to be known; time as an active, dynamic medium cannot be grasped directly, and so is largely overlooked.

This static picture is inconsistent with the scientific model that presents each object and each atomic particle as being in constant flux, shifting and changing, responding to an ongoing momentum of its own. The mind too is always active, never still. Yet motion on the atomic plane is too rapid or too subtle for us to notice, while on the mental plane the role of mental activity in observation makes it difficult to track the fluctuations within the mind itself.

As for the self, it is constantly active: doing, speaking, judging, responding, thinking. In terms of the static view just described, what energy makes this activity possible? The activity of the self challenges the 'bystander' model, pointing directly to time's dynamic as powering the flow of experience, action, and interpretation. Time presents both the self and its experiences, arising together. While it goes against our usual understanding, we could say that *the self and its experiences are an interpretation of time's momentum.*

Reinterpreted in light of this possibility, the prevailing model of 'bystander-self experiencing outsider-world' offers indirect confirmation that the momentum of time saturates both self and experience. Form and identity become the content projected by experience as it draws on time's dynamic, thereby projecting the self into the realm of existence. Existence responds to the transitory nature of linear time by proceeding from one transition to another.

When time's presentation is 're-presented' as the frozen 'order' of self and world, 'outside' of time's flow, the self can appropriate the dynamic of time as the *substance of its own being*. Turning its experience into the vehicle for the temporal momentum, the self shapes the rhythms of time toward establishing its own identity. The 'order' created in this way 'feeds back' on itself. Feeding on time, it reinforces the basic structure of self and world, as the self lives out the role of the 'bystander'.

Aware of this move toward appropriation, we can rediscover the momentum of time accessible within the static structures of experience. Though the temporal order steadily invites us to put time in the background, it is an invitation we can readily decline.

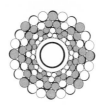

EXPERIENCE
AT THE CENTER

A s experienced by the self, time is varied in its presentations. There are good times and bad times,
times that are rich and times that feel impoverished.
There are times that appear routine, times of rapid
change, and times when the quality of each moment
seems to be determined by the nature of what is experienced in that moment.

Conventional knowledge understands such variation
as merely subjective, 'less real' than the 'objective' time
that serves as the 'background' for experience. Although
the self and its experience stand at the center of the
'timed-out' world of unyielding linear temporality, that
world is presented as existing prior to the individual. The
self shapes its life around its own concerns and wants,
but interprets its experience as evanescent and insubstantial in comparison to the structures of 'public' space
and time. We emerge into the world already 'out of time'.

The self's concerns in the modern world leave us with a perpetual shortage of time. Though our life spans are increasing, the world is evolving in ways that seem to shrink the amount of time available to us. As the world grows smaller and more interconnected, events unfold faster and faster. We find it difficult to be 'on' time or 'with' time; we are always running 'out of' time.

When we are not 'with' and 'on' time, the world tends toward chaos. Our response is to assert more control: to set schedules and rules for ourselves or adopt standards to govern our conduct. We establish systems of morality and codes of conduct, policies and structures, laws, organization, technology, scientific knowledge, philosophical models.

Yet the more we rely on these methods, the more we seem to undermine our own efforts. Faced with the onrushing pressure of time, we fail again and again to accomplish our goals or fulfill our vision. Whatever way of life we choose, whatever values we adopt, dissatisfaction is always after us like a jealous spouse.

Married to our dissatisfaction, we can never quite believe our own assurances that things will improve. Time is automatically against us, taking what we value, refusing to allow positive imprints of real significance. When success offers a glimpse of a different possibility, the result and the sense of accomplishment do not last— time moves on, leaving little opportunity to taste freedom or pleasure or joy.

The pressure of time leaves us feeling constricted and in conflict. Time slips away, eluding our grasp. The more involved we are, the less time there is. And this trend only accelerates: Ten years is a short time, but when ten years have passed, the next fifteen years seem to go by even more quickly.

Having so little time seems a sign that we are lacking or misusing knowledge. Sometimes it is just that knowledge comes too late: At the time we did not understand; now, when we do, the opportunity to act on what we know is gone. At other times the problem seems more basic, related to the way that knowledge interacts with time. When knowledge does not know how time works, we find ourselves disconnected from our innermost beliefs and values, unable to act on what we think we know. Questions lead to confusion or conflict; choice becomes difficult; values themselves prove unreliable. We can only affirm that time is out of our control.

Even if time has seemed to be on our side, alive and dynamic, helping us to succeed in our endeavors, eventually we know that time will turn against us, pointing us toward frustration and disappointment. There will come a time when whatever efforts we make will not be enough: We will no longer have the time to do what we need or want to do. Our awareness of time's influence on our lives may itself discourage us from positive action. Time's transformative energy seems innately aligned against us.

What alternatives are open to us? We can hardly choose to 'opt out' of time, for time is what makes action and accomplishment possible. We could perhaps give up the idea of acting, but this simply means yielding to time as chaos. The resulting disorder is at once meaningless and repetitious. We find that time moves not only forward, but also sideways and back and forth as well.

If we could expand the usual ways in which consciousness operates, we might find that we could contact time more directly. But this possibility makes little sense so long as we hold to the one-dimensional, 'from-to' model for time, for within the conventional 'order' there is no opportunity for a different 'minding'. Yet that model has been adopted for specific purposes. Could it be expanded?

The time we know now, based on the narrow vision of 'from' and 'to', confines knowledge to the lifeless truths of well-worn thought and historical reference and the inferences based on those truths. We experience these limits directly—in the restrictions on our awareness, the defects of our recollection, and the poverty of our imagination.

Seeing time in terms of our own experience and concerns chokes off the dynamic of time in a way that also closes down the vastness of space and blinds us to the scope of knowledge. It is as if we tossed a pebble in a pond and then kept our focus on the point where the pebble entered the water, ignoring the ripples that spread out in all directions.

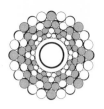

Linear Time

SHAPING EXPERIENCE

The truth of experience seems inextricably inter-
twined with the projections of awareness. As awareness projects forward and outward, it encounters, shapes,
and defines experience. If awareness were different, experience would be different as well. If the change in
awareness were of a sufficient order of magnitude, perhaps it would no longer be appropriate to speak of experience at all.

As an aspect of experience, linear time could be said
to arise as the projection of a particular awareness. The
'reality' of linear time (understood as its claimed independence from awareness) is only an aspect of this projection; while not 'false', it could be described as illusory.

We can trace the projection of linear time to an awareness linked to the 'bystander-self', who owns experience,
gives it form, restores it, claims it, feels it, and 'exists'
through it. For experience to take place at all, the

'bystander' must be active, giving and receiving messages intended to assure that experience will make itself known as anticipated. Each potential experience must be filtered to make sure that it takes shape and form in accord with rules laid down within the prevailing 'order'. With regard to time, the fundamental rule is linearity: One experience must follow the next; two distinct or opposed experiences cannot arise 'at the same time'.

It is *because* this rule is in operation that the distinctions we experience can be approved, confirmed, and recognized as 'real'. We could say that linear time is the 'carrier' for experience, assuring through its specific 'carrying capacity' that experience will be experienced in a particular way.

How do the distinctions that time 'carries' arise? Do they take their shape and form from time as a preexisting structure, or do they generate the experience of linear time as the necessary condition for their meaningful appearance? If we reply that linear time and experience both call on awareness to bear witness to their truth, the same question arises on a different level. Like linear time, the mind 'within' which awareness arises may be a construct: a 'feel' or 'field' that communicates as its message the independent reality of experience and the preexistence of time.

Mind and awareness interact with the three times in many different ways. We find the traces of mind in every aspect of experience: in the senses, in the emotions, in past recollection, in confusion and imagination. When mind is not present, experience is either nonexistent or inaccessible. Yet mind is not easily grasped; like a clever thief, it is always a step ahead of our inquiry, active in a way that we cannot ignore but that remains enigmatic. Moving through time like the wind, the mind leaves no footprints to mark its passage.

In the continuing exhibition of appearance to mind, certain rules apply. The experience available dances in time 'for a time', then disappears, to be replaced by new experience. Yet when it disappears, it has not gone beyond time; in some way it has entered the past, where it remains bound by prevailing temporal structures.

Although mind moves through time with great freedom, slipping from present into past or future and back in a matter of seconds, mind is also the victim of these structures. Bound to the physical body, it moves inexorably toward aging and death. Bound to its emotions, it lives in accord with hopes and fears that play themselves out in the past, present, and future. Acted on by time, the mind can determine time's effects but cannot affect its operation.

Even when it moves through time of its own accord, the mind plays a rather passive role. When something 'comes to mind', a cycle of feelings, thoughts, emotions, and judgments is set off. These events invite mind to *respond* in a way that removes us from immediate experience. We are therefore never truly *active* in time.

Yet mind can play with experience in ways that influence how time manifests. Meditative practice, for example, can foster concentration that condenses or compacts time; the strong determination to accomplish al can have a similar effect. Awareness of psychological subtleties can attune the mind to the active energy and flow of 'events', revealing time conspiring with awareness to create the 'truth' of experience. Greater factual knowledge can link the present to the record of past events and the prospect of future happenings, extracting patterns that add to time an additional dimension. Finally, mind's intentionality makes it possible to act 'into' time, shaping the stream of mental events or influencing what 'takes place'.

These abilities suggest that while time may be the active agent, the self that 'minds' need not be the one acted on. If it is time that reports experience, there need not be a subject of the report, nor even an owner. Participating without being 'subject to', the mind that records experience can function as agent of a more direct awareness, and respond more fully to what appears.

Perhaps we already participate in such awareness, in such a way that we participate in time as well. For instance, the operation of the senses could be seen as passive, each sense faculty recording data within its 'field' and 'reading-out' what has been recorded in accord with the 'order' established by linear time. Yet without the dynamic *'aliveness'* of time, the senses would lack the power to give access to experience. We can cut through the structures of the temporal order to a 'sense intensity' that expresses this 'aliveness' directly. Indeed, each act of experiencing the 'feel' of what is 'real'—even as restricted by the constructs of ordinary knowing—can lead us to the 'aliveness' that time presents.

34

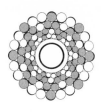

Linear Time

TEMPORAL
ORDER

The characteristics and structure of the known world are founded through a twofold activity of establishing and knowing. The 'bystander' acts on an 'outsider' to establish an object that the subject can successfully know. Consciousness and physical objects, linear time and empty space all arise together, products of the founding momentum of this fundamental activity. The temporal order itself could be said to arise through 'taking' this momentum in a certain way.

The temporal order of both the subjective and objective realms—and their interrelationship—could be understood as expressing the founding 'logos'. Events 'generated' in the objective realm are somehow 'seeded' into the inner, subjective realm.

Once this seed has been planted, a gradual development toward an interpretive order takes place. It is as though the inner dynamic, once activated, projects its temporality into the external timeframe.

This projection is then replayed or re-presented in terms of the governing objective system, establishing structures and entities and the history of their origin. If the object and objective time predominate, history presents conditioning and determinism; if the subject and its time predominate, history takes the form of psychologism and perhaps a kind of nihilism.

In this view, the usual constructs of the linguistic order are reinterpreted. 'Subject and object' are no longer the key actors. Instead there are patternings *presented* by the 'logos' and thus bound to one another: the objective realm, with its history stretching back toward an unknown beginning; the self that organizes and interprets experience, yet remains subject to what experience brings; and the multiple patterns of knowing, reflecting in various ways a structure inherent in both language and experience. Conventional time itself, built up out of 'before' and 'after', 'once' and 'since', 'already', 'again', and 'not yet', is likewise a structure of the 'logos'.

In the interplay of subject and object that the 'logos' defines and that gives the 'logos' form, something is communicated forward, transmitted in such a way that nothing can be lost. This 'something' could be considered the energy or momentum of time—not at the first level of a linear, 'timed-out' order, but at a second level of dynamic becoming. The projection of the subjective into the objective and the reflection of the objective in accord with subjective needs and concerns are expressions of this second-level momentum. From this perspective, the 'logos' and its structures can be understood as the presentation of a second level of time.

Attempting to investigate the 'order' so established by mentally analyzing appearance into its component parts and then reconstructing the whole out of those parts would be self-defeating, as such an approach would already conform wholly to the 'order' being investigated. Thus to investigate the temporal order we need to turn to the founding *activity* of establishing and knowing through which the 'order' arises—returning to the point at which momentum takes form.

In looking at the founding *activity*, we see that activity depends on time, and time is given by the 'logos' of the 'order' in two distinct ways. First is 'objective' time: points that can be divided into past, present, and future. For a point to be established, however, it seems it must be occupied: There must be a presence 'there' to give the point definition. This leads to the second aspect of time: the subjective realm of experience, in which the 'bystander-self' presents itself as the occupant of each point, establishing and determining the presence of the point through its own presence.

Finally, there is the interaction of these temporal realms 'across' time. The objective point occupied by the subjective self does not endure; it immediately 'passes on'. 'Passing-on' presupposes the linear unfolding of objective time, so that one moment can succeed another—a structure that must persist 'over' time in such a way that the 'bystander' can renew its present occupancy from moment to moment.

Through these interacting aspects, time is thrice determined. Shaped into a structured sequence, occupied by a 'bystander-self', permitting only the sequential knowledge available to the 'owner-occupant', time's creative potential is stripped away beyond the point of recognizing that anything has been lost.

Acting within time, the self interacts with this heavily determined structure. The self is 'of' time, 'at' time, and 'on' time. Each specific point in time, each 'now', is 'measured out', and each measure of time has its own reference. The content that time presents is made available to be experienced by the self; the self's experience in turn is referred to the 'objective' temporal framework.

It is here that we might look for active momentum to reemerge. *In experiencing*, the 'bystander-self' establishes and confirms the objective temporal order. It *projects* the duality of subject and object, self and world. If we refer this active projection back to the founding momentum, we can restore to time the creative potential lost when the patterns of the 'order' are firmly set in place.

When time is understood in a more open and less structured way, the structures and characteristics established and known 'in' time 'by' the self are transformed: They become inspired presentations of the 'logos'. The *solidity* of what first-level time presents to experience—together with the structures 'experience' and 'linear time'—are seen as one possible 'read-out' of a more fundamental, second-level dynamic.

By looking past the patterning of existent objects, abandoning reliance on 'outsiders', we can rediscover this second-level momentum as it operates 'before' the foundation of the temporal order—a momentum of 'just interactions'. First-level time in both the subjective and objective realms can be understood as the frozen representation of these interactions, which can now present themselves directly.

However, the momentum of time 'before' all interpretations and positionings is inaccessible to our ordinary subjective or objective understanding. Caught in a 'source from' model, the 'bystander' confronts time itself as another fixed 'outsider': a patterned web that snares and binds. The self has access to its own concerns and constructs, but all other forms of energy—for example, the display of natural forces, or the infusion of a setting with creativity or beauty—trace to a source 'outside' experience. The 'logos' will not sustain a knowing that could acknowledge time's dynamic directly.

Rather than being a power available to draw upon, the dynamic of time appears within the temporal order as a hostile force bearing down on the self—a constant, threatening reminder that the stories and interpretations of the self have no power to affect the objective 'order'. The self participates unwillingly in a 'frozen momentum' that sweeps it inexorably toward death.

This picture is incomplete, even on its own terms. Things exist only in the present, and they are present only because the self is present. Even though it is the product of a preexisting reality, the self is thus also the arbiter of that reality's existence.

Why does the self insist on a reality more basic than itself? Perhaps the answer lies in the dominant role of experience in forming the self's world. When time's energy is available only as the self's experience, how can existence be affirmed unless there is something available to be experienced? Though the power of linear time may hold the self in thrall, the self makes use of that power to assert its own identity. The self appears in a world it did not choose or create, yet does so in a way that enables it to assert ownership over that world.

We can express this complex interaction as follows:

The temporal priority of the objective realm is based on a prior accepting of the existential priority of the self.

Understood in this way, the existence of the objective order is an *interpretation* of time's momentum—consistent with the underlying 'logos'—that arises from the self's *need* to exist. We could compare this interpretation to the traditional view that the world was created to satisfy the wishes or intentions of an all-powerful being: In some of its variants, this interpretation might be said to read the self's need to exist back into the cosmos itself.

Whether understood on the personal or the cosmic level, the interplay of objective existence and a subjective need to exist takes characteristic forms of attraction, intention, and purpose. Experience bears the flavor of incompleteness and insecurity. Based on need, a 'self-centered' momentum is founded. Knowledge is restricted by unfolding patterns that originate in concern and desire. Ways of knowing not linked to this patterned momentum—for example, theoretical insights—prove powerless to affect the order of experience. Even knowledge of 'the right' or 'the good' cannot influence the solid world of 'outsiders' or the problematic existence and activity of the 'bystander-self'.

As the self struggles to make sense of its world, it offers additional interpretive structures. For example, the law of causality tracks aspects of the 'logos' that appear to govern the *objective* order, while logic is put forward as a highly self-conscious structure at work within the *subjective* order.

Other structures trace the consequences of actions in the objective and subjective realms alike, in accord with the law-like development of the initial impulse that mental or physical action sets in motion. 'Artificial orders' may also be put in place; for example, a code of laws, a corporate charter, or the unspoken and ever-shifting customs governing social interaction.

Such models and interpretations represent attempts by conventional knowledge to work out the inner structure of the prevailing 'logos'. Indeed, philosophy, science, law, religion, and the other ordering disciplines created by the human mind can perhaps all be understood as such attempts: secondary 'orders' arising out of and addressed toward the underlying 'order' established by the 'logos'.

More basic than all such interpretive structures and implicit in each of them is the *temporality* of the prevailing 'order'. A fundamental dynamic of succession and development is invariably in operation, governing events and their consequences.

The 'bystander-self' interprets the rhythms of time in a specific way, asserting mind, experience, and time alike as independent 'existents'. These assertions form part of the central 'report' that the 'bystander' delivers: an outcome of the specific project that the 'bystander' assigns itself and then projects 'outward'.

The usual interpretations of time—for example, locating an event in past or present or future—form part of this 'report'. This does not mean that a different 'report' might suddenly place a past event in the future, or allow two events to be experienced at once. The constructs 'event' and 'experience' seem too tightly bound to the structures of linear time for such piecemeal transformations to take place. However, it does seem that time in its relation to experience and the constructs of the 'bystander' could operate quite differently. And if the 'reality' of time is flexible, the 'truth' of time might hold unforeseen potential.

The relationship between self and time is more intimate than we habitually acknowledge. The self is born into a certain situation in time, develops in accord with rhythms that operate within that situation, and leaves the altered situation behind it at death. Shifts in the objective temporal flow affect the self at the innermost level. The times can be pervaded with a distinct mood or spirit that supports certain kinds of activity and ideas while frustrating others. Individuals intent on expressing their own individuality may find in retrospect that their personal choices reflect a social trend that has come and gone with time.

Although we say that the self owns its experiences and acts accordingly, the intimacy between the self and its time allows us to ask whether the self and its experiences are *given together* by the 'logos'. We could compare the 'bystander-self', with its limited ways of knowing and being, to the reflection of an object in a mirror. The reflection depends on an intricate set of circumstances: If those circumstances shifted, what would happen to the reflection? Would it be transformed, or perhaps disappear entirely?

We can also reverse the question. If circumstances shifted in such a way that the object no longer produced a reflection, could the object still be said to 'be there' at all? Correspondingly, if the 'order' established by the 'logos' was successfully challenged, if the 'bystander' no longer arose at the center of experience, would the whole of the 'order' collapse at once? Would the frozen momentum of time be able to flow freely once again?

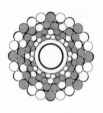

DYNAMIC BEING

In ordinary understanding, time is the 'happening' of what 'takes place', the unfolding of events in a particular sequence in accord with certain fundamental rules. An event has antecedents earlier in time, causes and conditions that must take place for the event to occur.

The present established on this basis in turn founds the possibilities for the future. An underlying logic and structure bind the temporal order to past, present, and future as three aspects of time.

But this seems to leave something fundamental out of account. Time 'flows' or 'passes'; it is vital, and whatever appears in time is linked to this vitality. Objects take form when the particles that compose them 'come together'; life arises when the right genetic material interacts; perception, observation, and the knowledge they bring are possible only through the interplay of knowing subject, known object, and sense faculties. Existence itself is an *activity*.

This 'coming together' and interaction can be understood as a gathering momentum, a dynamic being. The classification into past, present, and future is a very rough approximation of this fluid motion. Of course, we could refine this model; for example, past, present, and future might each be seen to have their own past, present, and future. Such refinements, however, do not address the central point: The momentum of time is more fluid than the interpretive structures imposed on it.

When time is consigned to the background, it serves chiefly as a device for 'measuring out' the passage of events. Yet subject knowing object is an act that communicates energy and movement born of the *dynamic* of time. Time could more accurately be considered a fundamental force, like the force that binds together the nucleus of an atom. Without this force in operation, measuring out experience and bridging one experience to the next, how would it be possible to name or prescribe the qualities that mind and senses rely on to discover meaning?

Knowledge depends on the *act* of knowing, which unfolds in time. Without time, it seems that words could not be pronounced, nor could symbols do their work or physical objects manifest. Without beginning and end, rhythm and momentum, neither the physical nor the mental realms could operate. On one level this is self-evident, but have we really considered or experienced the temporal dynamic?

The force of time manifests in the established 'order' through a momentum whose thrust and directionality are preestablished. Entering into relation with this pre-established momentum activates the potential for roles, models, meanings, value, and purpose. It makes possible units of measurement, transitions, sequence, measurement, and calculation. It provides for birth and death, growth, control, formulation, and responsibility. For the given human subject, time lets information be projected from the objective to the subjective realm. It makes known the unknown and illuminates the known, allowing knowledge to become established and recorded.

Caught in this established 'reality', we respond to what time sponsors in ways that restrict what can appear. What is sponsored is based on programs constructed from previous responses, and these in turn are based on what is contributed to what has already been recollected. Patterns prescribe the possible, confirming a basic agreement as to how space, time, and knowledge interact.

Based on this agreement, we assign names, posting them like signs that identify what is experienced. Completely, specifically, and distinctively we assign meaning or otherwise order experience: We exercise our faculties in a reasonable (permitted) way, responding to what is recorded, naming as unknown what we cannot respond to. Having set up a rational order, we make points and connect them, marking out the motions of the specific.

In this unquestioned interplay, the dynamic of time is closely at work. The player plays through having the play to play with. Energy unfolds into space-existent time-experience. Marked-out points embody, while the movement that 'makes something' of those points finds expression as lower-level knowledge.

As the designs in this pattern take hold, beauty becomes a random occurrence. What is not set in place cannot appear in time or space or be available to knowledge. The momentum of 'what is' controls our responses, yet its dynamic passes us by, not available to be acknowledged. Just as we cannot go backward in time, we cannot know what is not acceptable within the prevailing 'order'. Losing without founding, cut off from the energy that might make transformation possible, we go with what can be—with suffering and joy, hope and fear, and the concerns of the self.

Time of Knowing

INTERPRETIVE
STRUCTURES

The subjective and objective realms face each other like two clocks, each 'keeping' its own time in accord with its own 'order'. Only what 'times itself out' in conformity with *both* clocks—for example, direct experience or action—can be accepted into a co-emergent 'reality'.

Emphasis on 'logos' as an ordering principle might seem to make the subjective 'order' more basic than the objective by making active knowing the foundation for 'reality'. Thus, the positing of an 'independent' objective order could itself be considered a subjective interpretation. Likewise, when time is defined 'objectively' as what a clock measures, it is the knowing subject that offers this definition, having first conceived of the clock, constructed it, and put it into operation.

This analysis, however, forgets that subjective and objective are *complementary* interpretations of the underlying temporal order founded by the 'logos'. Although this 'order' might be described as an 'interpretive structure' imposed on 'direct experience', it is the 'order' itself that allows for such a description. The 'subjectivity' of interpretive structures is likewise an interpretation. As categories available 'within' the order, 'subjective' and 'objective' cannot accurately be applied to the 'order' itself.

When we rely on such ideas as 'subjective' and 'objective', we are following out and interpreting distinctions allowed for and consistent with the temporal 'order'. As the 'order' is 'measured out', language rushes forward to set definitions in place. On the surface we might consider this a matter of falling into 'subjectivity', but this interpretation misses the point: To speak *of* a subjective viewpoint is already to speak *from* a subjective viewpoint; that is, to speak in 'terms' that the 'order' sanctions.

How well established is 'temporal' development? The reality of changes in shape, form, attitudes, and other properties may seem self-evident, but the evidence on which this conclusion depends is based on the prior acceptance of rules and constructs given by the 'order'. Without the distinctions that description, definition, and interpretation provide—for example, in identifying something 'constant' that 'undergoes' change—there would be no way of becoming aware that development or transition had occurred.

When change can be discovered only on the basis of description and similar structures, what is its underlying significance? The rules of grammar and syntax, which allow for (and require) interpretations of the prevailing 'order' in terms of temporality, are simply further reflections of that same 'order'. Demonstrating the 'reality' of temporality through the application of such structures simply means confirming the internal consistency of the 'logos'.

There would be no point in rejecting the claim of temporality, which has very real significance for our lives. On the other hand, why accept this claim as fundamental? To focus on the sequence of changes that we experience in our lives as basic to reality is like investigating the ocean by examining the different shapes taken by a wave, without first having inquired into the 'wetness' of water. Do we understand the 'source' of change? Can we say where the temporality of the temporal order has its origins?

In the course of knowing that language invites, a label is applied to set something in place, so that what is labeled can be set aside. Knowledge is restricted to establishing the appropriate references to the relevant labels. Confined within the structures that language acknowledges and authorizes, knowledge cannot readily go 'beneath' language itself.

For example, an entire range of activity is implicit in every use of the simple and indispensable word 'is'. 'Is' points out; at the same time it establishes existence. In consequence of 'is', a position is set up and at once made final, the more so since it is already assumed in advance. Every time we say that something 'is', even if we are trying to be very precise, we must fight against the weight of this implied activity.

The momentum of the temporal order as a whole is inherent in the words we use. Its inertia restricts knowledge and confines inquiry. Words and their binding structures both mirror and reinforce the prevailing space and time. Carriers of conventional knowledge, they tend toward the re-founding of that knowledge with each repetition.

Yet this does not mean that we should aim to leave words behind, for language is linked to a deeper knowing that can be a precious resource. Its power of analysis can challenge its own constructs and operation, opening to a more fundamental understanding; its power of interpretation can point back toward its own origins, inviting inquiry into naming and knowing; its power of creation can present alternative images and 'orders', countering the inertia of the presupposed.

The communication that language manifests stands in special intimacy with time. On the most basic level, communication is an action within the temporal order. Its rhythms are programmed in advance by sound, which propagates in accord with the rules that govern the physical order. A noise is made and then another; a series of sounds opens into the realm of meanings, and so to language.

As the active expression of language, speech mirrors the energy of time in structured and ordered ways that allow specific kinds of knowledge and understanding.

The outcome is the temporal order of transition, linkage, and succession, with its mechanisms of polarity.

With a different language, we could activate the potential of language as a resource for knowing that went deeper than the structures of the temporal order. To do so, we must learn to restore to words the energy and 'aliveness' of time. Language can 'measure out' or create; it can penetrate the assumptions of presupposed juxtapositions or give them form. Which course it takes—how it relates to the 'logos'—will depend on the intention and the dynamic it expresses.

When we investigate with care, we soon see that many of our concerns are only linguistic in origin. For example, this investigation itself revolves around the terms 'time', 'space', and 'knowledge'. Why were these three factors of existence chosen and not others? How do they relate to one another? It is easy to forget that 'time', 'space', and 'knowledge' are themselves constructs of language. Questions about them refer to nothing substantial.

A similar confusion arises whenever we try to act on the basis of first-level knowledge, for the first-level 'order' unfolds through polar concepts that are mutually interdependent. Language appears to give each member of the polarity a separate identity, encouraging us to give one side or the other greater value or importance, but the two sides are inseparable. When we choose happiness, we are choosing sadness; when we choose knowledge we are choosing ignorance. Each 'opposition' reflects a more fundamental and encompassing 'position'; when we let the 'order' communicated by language guide us toward choosing one side of each polarity, ignoring or rejecting the other, our choice will be incomplete and frustrating.

Language frustrates at an even deeper level by making claims 'about' reality that are actually claims about its own structures. Whenever we try to arrive at meaning or understanding through language, we are caught up in a system that is self-referring. We define a word with other words, turning knowledge into a story with endless episodes. Each episode takes its meaning from others, so that if the link between episodes is severed, meaning is lost. We might say that language is a vehicle in which we can travel endlessly without *arriving* anywhere.

In trying to gain knowledge through language, we are like shoppers wandering down a lane in a crowded bazaar, picking and choosing from the stalls on one side of the lane or the other. There is no shortage of eager sellers: Systems of belief and explanation, models, dogmas, propositions, judgments of all kinds display their wares and vie for attention. But though we buy (and also sell) with abandon, what is really gained? Perhaps some wealth changes hands, perhaps there are occasional bargains, but that is all. It seems it might be better to stop spending our resources in this way, at least for a while. Perhaps if we drew back, we would notice that a 'higher-order' knowledge is the sponsor of the sale.

Is it possible to 'withdraw' from the temporal order in this way? As long as we rely on language, as it seems we must, 'withdrawal' will be difficult, for language confines us to a narrow domain. Even when we take 'escape' from such a closed system as our 'goal', we are applying concepts projected by the linguistic 'order'—echoes of voices that speak on endlessly, constantly verifying approved structures.

The ideas expressed here are bound to language in the same way. The positioning that language communicates and affirms is subtle, and includes even the position that denies or sets out to avoid all positions.

If what is said here is understood in accord with linguistic structures—for example, in terms of criticism and argumentation—it will only further positioning, and the insights it fosters will prove of little lasting value. New acts of knowing will quickly fall out of balance; embodiments of knowledge will remain incomplete. Words and ideas will lose their transparency; taking form in subtle ways, they will lead inquiry into the thicket of conceptuality. A 'gesture' of knowledge will become the 'posture' of a knowing self—an 'imposter' who appropriates what has no owner.

However, this is not the only alternative. Not bound by language, knowledge can open to communication at a deeper level, exploring the 'logos' directly. It can maintain a subtle balance, absorbed in positions but free from positions, ready to use language in ways both new and old. Balanced in this manner, we can draw on language without being caught up in it; we can accept conventional patterns without accepting their claims. Then each thought, each presentation, each word, and each action can become a perfect gesture of balance.

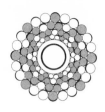

Time of Knowing

UNFOLDING TIME

Knowledge knows what unfolds in time. But time itself also 'unfolds', in a temporal order imposed by the 'logos'. In this interaction, is it knowledge that controls the appearance of time, or time that specifies the potential for knowledge?

On the first level, time seems to control knowledge, creating and also limiting the opportunities for its arising. Acquiring knowledge 'takes' time, which may well not be available in sufficient 'quantity' to allow for knowing. The passing of time and the acquisition of knowledge are opposed, and can be merged only with difficulty, like trying to control a body with two heads.

Another expression of time's control over the knowing activity is the temporal priority of 'not-knowing' over 'knowing'. With knowledge the exception in a world of not-knowing, the natural tendency is toward chaos.

Disorder and not-knowing mirror each other, both reflecting the 'from-to' structure of linear time.

The rhythms of time manifest as a chain of events whose structure and patterns constantly repeat themselves. Bound to repetition, the temporal order does not naturally communicate new knowledge. Its onrushing momentum holds knowledge in its grip, giving no opportunity to take in the whole, to absorb or digest it through inquiry and appreciation. Time's steady acceleration pushes knowledge back toward preestablished positions. The knowing self is always one step behind its experience, swallowing its food before tasting it. Predictable sequences develop mechanically, freezing out other ways of knowing.

It seems that we know and do not know. We know what time presents—the unfolding patterns that express the rhythms of duplication and repetition. But we do not know time itself, from moment to moment. Bound to the temporal order, *we do not know with the knowing of the 'logos'* that founds the 'order', nor do we know the 'logos' itself. Our knowing is subservient to first-level time—based on separation and distance, not on gathering and intimacy.

Not knowing time, we let the patterns of time ignore knowledge. Since our knowing is not based in realization, we lack the will to act in ways that do not accord with the preestablished. We conform our knowing to time's ignoring, telling ourselves that we do not have time to do what must be done. Constantly making excuses, deceiving ourselves and others, we guarantee that real accomplishment will not come in our time.

Knowing only what time presents, wholly controlled by time, the knower is led into small, repetitive cycles. Although the circles of the known can expand to encompass the whole range of potential experience, at another level they are closed to creativity and energy. Patterns reinforce one another automatically, drawing on what is known to propel themselves forward. Action relies on knowledge as a 'guideline', never questioning why the 'line' extends on endlessly in the same direction.

The resulting 'read-out', relentlessly renewed, perpetuates the customary. No matter what time's momentum presents, knowledge moves to possess it by applying familiar attributes. The flavor is one of restriction and negativity, marked by patterns of laziness, dullness, grasping, resentment, and anger.

Interpreted 'through' the 'logos' of the first level, *the frozen momentum of first-level time supports only knowledge that arises within the temporal order.* True to its origins, such knowledge reveals time as unfolding in a way that intensifies and builds up pressure. Internally, this pressure manifests in neurotic and negative patterns; externally, it manifests in unanticipated problems and difficulties that seem in retrospect inevitable.

The knowledge that this first-level 'order' supports is knowledge of the already known—knowledge as technology, reflecting the limitations of first-level time and space. Devoted to the need to cope, technological knowledge produces a steady stream of new facts, new theories, and new solutions. But it also perpetuates the patterns of need and not-knowing. Programmed mechanically in advance, it can make no sense of the prospect for a new way of knowing.

The momentum of second-level time presents a different knowing. This knowledge is not 'new' at all, for it does not depend on the linear structures of 'old' and 'new', 'before' and 'after'. Nor is it knowledge as a solution to an existing problem or an answer to an existing question—even though it may very well bring new insights or awaken a greater joy and balance in the light of which problems and questions dissolve.

Simple appreciation for time and its presentations, free from the demands of need, is itself knowledge. Not bound by desire, hope, and fear, appreciation suggests that the allowing of space and the dynamic flow of time can transform the 'knowingness' of knowledge. It leads to questioning and to a heartfelt way of being based in openness and vitality.

An appreciation that sustains inquiry can calm and balance the self's tendency toward self-involvement and identification, which 'takes over' the energy of time and prevents it from flowing freely. Skillful, knowing accommodation, 'founded' on open allowing, can let experience present itself as unfounded, without thereby triggering the self's frightened sense of vulnerability. When this happens, time's dynamic can become directly available.

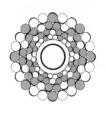

Time of Knowing

RHYTHM
OF ALLOWING

I nquiry into the conventional 'order' loosens the solidity of substance and identity. Rhythms of becoming
allow for fluctuation between something and nothing,
inviting a knowing that goes deeper than polarity and
contradiction. Points that bear different labels are in motion; aware of this motion, inquiry can also be aware of
the points in a way that points to their interconnection.

Consider how we might inquire into the interaction
of time and knowledge in history. Time is the carrier of
history, and of the 'order' that history presents. Within
this unfolding 'order', society and civilization appear as
the bearers of knowledge. The knowledge they sustain
develops in different ways over time, in accord with a
basic pattern that brings different ways of knowing to the
fore in different eras.

The shifting history of knowledge can become more
accessible through a wider knowledge of history. In every

culture there are cycles and rhythms of slow growth, flowering, and then decline or collapse. In retrospect easily recognized and acknowledged on the surface, such patterns also carry an inner significance that can be appreciated only through study and reflection.

When the rhythm of time in history has taken on a certain inner 'weightiness' in our investigation, we can ask how a particular way of knowing arises and comes to power. The focal point for inquiry could be a dominant social institution, a specific understanding of the self or of the natural realm, or any of countless other structures.

In each case, a prevailing way of knowing can be linked to doctrines, models, ideas, understandings, and beliefs that shape a specific environment for knowledge and create a specific 'mechanism' that operates in time. Investigating such 'mechanisms' as meaning-givers inspiring different ways of life, we can distance ourselves from the structures and understandings that 'order' the present time and its specific ways of knowing.

The knowledge that arises in this way, even understood as owned by a self, can make the dynamic of time more freely available. The self-replicating acts of knowing that confirm the temporal order do not exhaust knowledge. Furthermore, the knowledge intrinsic to the 'order' founded by the 'logos' does not present time in a definitive way.

The shifting 'feedback' that comes with different ways of knowing generates a rhythm to which we can attune ourselves, allowing us to come more fully into harmony with time's dynamic. More knowledge and a more dynamic time communicate back and forth, like images in facing mirrors. Time's rhythm becomes more supple and knowing more agile, making the dynamic of being more freely accessible. Darkness and obscuration awaken into luminosity.

As awareness and time's rhythm enter into more intimate communication, the mind becomes quicker and more alert, or else momentum slows down—the two processes are complementary, even indistinguishable. With momentum responsive to knowledge, time no longer controls the prospects for knowing, for time itself is no longer out of control. The difference is fundamental—like the difference between trying to stop a speeding plane and being a passenger in its cabin.

Measuring Out

FABRIC OF TIME

The fundamental relationship between time and knowledge could be pictured as a robe fashioned of fabric embellished with a design. Time is the weaver of the fabric, while the design is created by knowledge. Concerning the fabric itself, the design may suit the fabric well, so that its imprint is detailed and clear, or badly, so that the design is distorted and in part illegible.

Even when the design is clear, however, the fit between knowledge and time remains superficial. We could imagine the fabric being unravelled and then rewoven so that the design becomes distorted and loses its coherence. Or the fabric could be pieced together with other sections of fabric more newly woven and lacking a design at all, or cut against the weave so that the fabric becomes stretched and stressed in unpredictable ways.

However, if we take into account the momentum inherent in the 'logos', the relation between time and knowledge shifts. We might say that the design found on the fabric has now become inseparable from the pattern that determines the cut of the robe, as well as its folds. Pattern, design, and fabric conform precisely to one another, as though the fabric had been woven to accept this pattern. The pattern and the design—knowledge owned by a self, a known world set up in terms of discriminations, distance, separation, need, and so forth—seem so well and firmly established that it is difficult to imagine any alternative.

At this level, the fabric itself—its material, properties, and origin—could be said to remain unknown. The effect will be as though the design and pattern of the robe were preserved only in photographs of a lost original: The 'structure' or 'order' of both fabric and pattern are still 'available', but there is a loss of a deeper, aesthetic dimension, in which the texture and weight of the fabric and the intricacy of the weave are also available to be appreciated.

This restriction disappears as the momentum of second-level time becomes more directly available. The arising of knowledge is seen as given by this momentum, as if the fabric were a tapestry, its design emerging in the course of the weaving. As time continues with its weaving, knowing feeds back on itself harmoniously, so that knowledge stays in intimate contact with the unfolding dynamic.

When second-level time and knowledge are both fully in operation, the design woven into the fabric is inseparable from the fabric itself—each one constituting the singularity of the other. Now we see the possible configurations of fabric and pattern quite differently.

If time presents the temporal order of repetition and duplication, knowledge arises as the knowing of a self that accepts those patterns as ultimate truth. But if knowledge authorizes the intimacy of 'knowingness', the dynamic of time wells forth without restriction. Knowledge unfolding through time thus points equally toward energy and awareness, embodiment and openness. Through such two-way movement, there is access to a motionless quality within motion.

When communication between time's dynamic and the awareness within knowledge attains true intimacy, the outcome is time as invariable and knowledge as fully lucent. Mind and matter come together in a dynamic, pointless, motionless aliveness: the heart of Great Time or the Body of Knowledge.

MEASURING OUT
OF RHYTHM

Time measures out what happens, and is adequate to do so—not in the sense that what is measured out is complete, but in the sense that time and the event measured conform to one another. Linear time brings up its various measures—the seasons and decades, a life span, centuries, geologic eras—and these 'fit' with experience. Transitions arise and pass away at designated moments in time; momentum moves onward in just those ways that conventional knowledge prescribes.

Why should this adequacy operate? Why should things unfold in linear time in a measurable way, so that 'laws' such as cause and effect and entropy prove applicable?

The answer seems to depend on a link between first-level 'order' and second-level momentum. First-level time and the 'order' it 'times out' are given together as a 'read-out' of a second-level dynamic. This relationship assures a degree of harmony between time and its 'measured-out' contents.

The 'read-out' relationship, however, does not assure that conventional time captures anything fundamentally accurate about second-level time. In fact, the reverse is true: In the building up of existence 'across' time that characterizes the first-level temporal order, the insistence on substance means that key misinterpretations are virtually assured.

In the flow of the temporal momentum, what was there has already gone. What the self takes as substance is more like a reflection or an echo: a kind of 'shadow substance', like the afterimage left on the retina by a quickly moving object. In first-level terms, existence could be said to be built up out of such shadows.

The *content* of the 'shadow substances' that the self specifies is provided by the lingering residues of past experience. Because such residues also shape the interpretive structures through which experience is known, they are largely invisible and unknowable in operation; yet their effect is pervasive.

A well-known image for the interpretive difficulties inherent in first-level time is the flowing of a river. Looking at the river from its banks, we see a clearly defined object with a specific shape, substance, and location and the characteristic of a relatively stable flow. If we return the next day, we will see the same river.

But if we look at the 'body' of the river—the water it contains—not one single molecule of water present yesterday remains today. Only because we come to it with a preestablished set of concepts and interpretations, prepared to disregard this constant transformation, can we label the river as a persistent entity.

We can see now how both these understandings of the river are valid: One proceeds from a first-level view of time, while the other presents in terms of a first-level analogy an understanding that *points toward* time at a second level.

The same point could be made in terms of the structure of matter. Each water molecule within the river, for example, differs from every other molecule, but we choose to regard all molecules as identical. Even on a more conventional scale, we disregard differences that we know to exist: the peas on the plate, the plates on the table, the tables in the restaurant. We do not see the individual peas, or plates, or tables. The first-level 'order' through which we know existence conceals as much as it reveals.

In proclaiming the structures that it presents as the 'truth' of what is, the temporal order of self and world imposes on the second level of time a doubly deceptive structure. This order identifies as objective reality what in first-level terms has already vanished, then understands that reality in terms of constructs that filter experience to an unknown degree, while claiming to be completely transparent.

Such deceptions assure that the apparent harmony between time and its contents will conceal a deeper disharmony, which goes unnoticed only because we have learned to regard it as both 'natural' and 'inevitable'. The pervasive sense of frustration and oppression that marks the temporal order is the unmistakable sign of this underlying disharmony in operation.

The simplifications and possible distortions of the first-level temporal order might be considered natural in light of our interests and concerns as human beings. Yet this way of framing the point is already shaped by the first-level perspective. It could be rephrased in second-level terms as an assertion about the rhythms of time.

A characteristic rhythm flows within human experience, organizing that experience in the same way that the beat of a drum organizes music. The meaning of what presents itself and the way that we interpret it will depend on how its own rhythm interacts with our own. What does not bear on the rhythms of human experience—the changes in a mountain range or in the solar system over time, or the moment-to-moment change in the waters of a river—can readily be ignored.

The rhythm displayed by an object in time seems to be a movement of waves of energy, pulsating in accord with a governing momentum. The waves present transition, not as movement from one fixed or solid point to another, but as continuous flow.

In this sense, it might be more accurate to reverse the formulation just given: Instead of saying that an object displays a rhythm, we could say that the rhythm displays the object. The object becomes the specification of the rhythm, as the first-level temporal order is the specification of the dynamic momentum of second-level time.

When such 'specifications' of rhythm are taken as fundamental points, second-level momentum is formed into the objective world of distance, measurement, and scale, leading to characteristic simplifications, omissions, and interpretations. The rhythmic presentation that takes form as 'peas on a plate' expresses distinctions among the peas on a *scale* that does not normally intersect with our own. Objects too *distant* from us to engage our attention likewise are the *measuring out* of a particular rhythm not linked to our own.

Thus, it is not only objects in motion, such as a river or a molecule, that reflect the dynamic of time. We can state a more general principle, based on a second-level view of the first-level 'order':

Through the structures of distance, measurement and scale, the prevailing temporal rhythm manifests as objects.

This can be rephrased to accord more fully with a second-level perspective:

The 'measuring out' of what appears in the temporal order is an activity of second-level momentum.

Perhaps an analogy can help clarify this point. When the image of an object is transmitted electronically (for example, by television), the image itself does not 'move' from one place to another, nor does it replicate itself across space. Instead, a flow of energy in the form of electrons is *modified* in a way that successfully carries *information* about the image. The image as it is received 'is' the whole of this modification.

The flow of time can be understood in much the same way: waves of energy whose rhythms carry information, without anything substantial moving from space to space. In terms of the analogy, first-level objects 'are' these rhythms.

This analogy can help to suggest how the temporal flow comes to be interpreted as solid objects in a fixed temporal order. For an image to be communicated, both a transmitter and a receiver of the information-bearing 'signals' must be in operation, and each must be 'tuned in' to the other.

With regard to the flow of time, the receiver could be thought of as the 'bystander-self', while the transmitter is the temporal order. Because both self and 'order' are 'solid' in specific ways (though not necessarily in the way that 'solidity' would be understood on the first level), the communication manifests the form of something solid as well. The world of solid objects 'measured out' in space and time arises in being known by a knower to whom such solidity is fundamental.

A principle of modern physics says that a particle's position and velocity cannot be simultaneously determined. If we take that principle as an analogue for conventional ways of understanding, we could say that ordinarily we put all our effort into determining the 'positions' of 'outsiders', with the result that we have completely lost sight of their 'velocity'—the dynamic that presents them as existent.

This is only an analogy, for the dynamic of time is just as closely linked to the 'position' of an entity in the temporal order as it is to the momentum that 'carries' that entity through space and time. Yet the analogy reminds us that we will be frustrated if we look for knowledge within accustomed structures. Second-level time offers a different approach—it teaches us to look for knowledge in transition.

RHYTHM WITHOUT SPECIFICATION

The dynamic of second-level time—rhythm without specification— can present a world of 'supernatural' beauty and 'magical' transformations. We can accept what appears with joy and appreciation. But we will underestimate the significance of this change if we interpret it as 'only subjective experience'.

Such a ready interpretation subsumes the second-level under a first-level category. It can be traced to the first-level insistence on substance. When objects are substantial, they can vary in their nature only through a narrow range; when the self has substance, it is limited to playing certain roles and giving certain responses.

When the temporal order has substance, it unfolds within a particular logic and sequence. In each case, we subordinate the 'feedback' given by 'nonstandard' experience to an interpretation that restricts its significance.

We are insensitive to 'feedback' as an ongoing process in which energy remains open and accessible.

The insistence on substance subjects the 'feedback structure' to the pull of 'gravity'. Openness is weighed down and becomes dense; movement is likewise subject to a process of 'indensification' that makes it thick and heavy. As 'gravity' works its way, we find that time operates only in one direction, leaving us unable to see what will exhibit and in what manner it will appear.

By contrast, if 'feedback' were operating freely, past, present, and future would 'feed' on one another, sustaining each other in a transparent order. Remarkable as it would seem to conventional understanding, we might find that the three times—past, present, and future— were available to knowledge and to one another.

'Substance' as what arises 'in' time can be challenged from within the first-level 'order'. For example, in certain periods of time—perhaps for a few hours, a few days, or perhaps much longer—decay predominates. In such times everything falls apart; things cannot hold up. We usually blame this on the things themselves, or perhaps on our own shortcomings. But we might consider whether such a pattern is due less to a defect in things than to a quality of time as it is then presenting.

Often we acknowledge that there is a tenor to the times, a rhythm and a flow that put their stamp on experience. This sense of rhythm and momentum does not have to be dismissed as subjective or explained away. Provisionally, we might regard it as the expression of an inner dynamic, almost organic in nature, that has been 'programmed' into the situation in the same way that genes program the organism.

From any conventional view, the system or structure formed by this dynamic will remain mysterious and incapable of being described. Some parts of it will be predictable or explicable in terms of ordinary time, though approached in this context they lose their significance as pointers to a deeper level of meaning. Those that are not subject to this kind of appropriation remain in the deepest sense 'immeasurable', and so fall outside the boundaries of conventional knowing.

Because the dynamic of second-level time 'as a whole' remains 'immeasurable', it too will not 'fit' within the prevailing 'order'. We may be prepared to acknowledge that time operates in unacknowledged ways, both active and nonactive; still, this will remain simple belief or speculation. Committed to the 'logic' of the 'logos', we determine our prospects and projects accordingly. The knowledge that could open a new way of seeing and being is simply unavailable.

It would seem that 'subject' and 'object' as solid entities are the outcome of a solidification process. How is this process set up? Put differently, how is the rhythmic momentum of time modified ('measured out') in ways that support the interpretation of solidification?

First-level analysis suggests that 'measuring out' results from the specific speed at which energy flows in or through time. We can see this in the scientific practice of measuring astronomical distance as a function of the speed of light.

Still, it is not clear how the 'measuring out' of time's momentum takes place. The hands of a clock 'measure' time, but this is only a way of establishing a spatial analogue to temporal movement. It does not account for the moment-to-moment flow of first-level temporality. How is it that time is 'set up' or 'timed-out' in just this way, available to be measured?

We could say that time can be 'measured out' when a knowing that allows 'measuring out' has been activated. In other words, 'measuring out' embodies a way of knowing related to a particular consciousness or awareness that must have come into operation for time to take its 'measured-out' form.

The first-level knowledge that 'measures out' seems subject to a basic limitation, for it attempts to give *form* to a *flow* of 'information' that cannot be confined within the static limits that form presupposes. When the flow of energy is patterned in such a way, potential knowledge is inevitably lost.

This point can be illustrated within the 'measured-out' structure itself. Between any two points that have been 'measured out', there is another point that would allow for a more subtle 'measuring out', in which more could be known. According to the understanding implicit in the logic of the 'measuring-out' model, this picture of more subtle points potentially available to be 'measured out' can be extended indefinitely.

In terms of a time that steadily 'times out' one moment after another, such continued subdividing gradually approaches the 'zero point' as a limit. But if the points 'through' which time's momentum flows are ultimately 'zero points', where does momentum originate and how does it perpetuate itself? Is there momentum in the 'zero point'? If so, there has already been a movement away from 'zero'; if not, momentum seems to be cut off at just the point where it must be freely available.

This difficulty is not the familiar question of the origin of time itself, at least as understood in the 'measured-out' sense that puts this origin at a point 'before' the beginning of time. Instead, we are asking about the origin of the momentum 'between' 'measured out' moments—the momentum that sets those moments up and makes them possible. Knowledge that 'measures out' does not seem capable of addressing this question. It seems to approach a 'zero point' of its own—an end to questioning.

One would think that the momentum of time—the power that it manifests—must originate somewhere. To inquire into this 'where', we could imagine a tremendous and accelerating momentum, like that of an onrushing locomotive. How can this momentum be stopped?

If the momentum is powerful enough, there is only one reliable answer—time itself must be canceled or eliminated. Without time, there will be no momentum and no rhythm; no presenting and no 'measuring out'.

This thought experiment suggests that the source of momentum is time. But since time itself is momentum, how can momentum be its own source? Is there an aspect of momentum that we have not taken into account? Or does time perhaps present an energy more 'fundamental' than momentum?

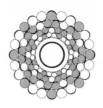

Dynamic Momentum

ENERGY OF TIME

A focus on momentum lets us consider subject and object alike as projections of the underlying energy of second-level time. 'Time' in this second-level sense distributes experience through past and present and future, presenting the 'logos' that informs the first-level temporal order. Its dynamic allows knowing to 'build up' and interpret a world. As active vitality, 'time' is the essence of our being and our becoming, on which we feed and draw our sustenance.

Through the focus on momentum, 'outsiders' disappear. In the interaction of subject and object, there is just the interaction itself: a pure happening. Of course, the reference to the interaction 'itself' tends to turn the interaction into another 'outsider', a consequence of the linguistic structures we employ and their relation to the 'logos'. But if we can look past this bias, a new vision emerges. We no longer see primarily substances and things, which must then be made to interact in ways that undermine creativity and freedom. Instead, we can explore a new possibility: that *the character of existence is built up out of and through the momentum of 'time'*.

Second-level 'time' transforms the relation between time and events in the same way as second-level 'space' transforms the relation between first-level space and objects. The three times reveal an underlying unity: Each becomes a gateway to the energy of time, a flow within which the restrictive structures of the conventional 'order' are inoperative.

Creation, for example, is no longer a unique event that takes place at the beginning of time, or else through the inspiration of a mysterious force. Instead, *as the momentum of 'time'* it is freely accessible in each interaction. When the presentations of time are seen as inseparable from 'time', time becomes boundless in its energy. Artificial (and logically indefensible) barriers and borders (such as 'creation at the beginning of time') give way to a more integrated view. Second-level time is time brought to life, inseparable from life itself.

To see this adds a fantastic new dimension to what the self experiences. Embraced by time, all experience becomes a totality—not in the sense of being many things wrapped into one bundle, but in being unbounded and without limits.

Time on the second level can be deeply playful. Not tied to the specific identities projected within the temporal order, we too can play 'in' time, like swimmers in the ocean. When we enter into intimacy with time, *given together* with what 'is', the play unfolds ever more dimensions, expanding ceaselessly into new realms.

Prior to any specific 'realities', the momentum of 'time' permits such 'realities'—including but not limited to the existence of a temporal universe distributed across past, present, and future—to be 'built up'. In this 'building up', 'existence' and 'existents' are specified, first as qualities, actions, and meaningful structures, then as substance and identity. Once it has been fully specified, momentum transmits only the sequential 'order' established by the 'logos'. The energy and dynamic of time is converted into the closed-off and mechanical structure of 'reality experienced by a self', unfolding 'across' time.

Yet this rigid structure can never be regarded as final. As the product of a 'specified' momentum, existence 'has' that momentum as its nature. The momentum that existence 'embodies'—whether as things or as qualities and meanings—is still available within the 'order' of what is. All that is necessary is to thaw the frozen structures that the first level takes as given.

Dynamic Momentum

CREATIVITY
OF TIME

Second-level time is not just a standpoint from which we
can offer telling criticisms of first-level, 'first-person'
time, with its 'bystanders' and 'outsiders'. If this were so,
it would remain accessible only as a potential experience
for a self. Fully appreciated, the dynamic of second-level
time offers a source of creativity that is never obstructed
or defined as 'out of bounds'—a source inherent in time
itself, and thus always accessible.

Traditionally, creativity has been understood as the
result of inspiration from a higher realm; today it might
perhaps be described as a randomly occurring resource of
the human spirit. Both views continue to accept a 'timed-
out' world of 'outsiders'—the givens of historical conditioning, established identity, and a reality split into the
human and the material realms. Creativity remains a
mysterious or accidental infusion into a reality that
otherwise unfolds in strictly determined ways.

The result is that human beings cannot be creative in their human being; they cannot *be* in a new and creative way. Because the fundamentals are given in advance, so that they stand *outside of time*, creative energy cannot affect or alter them. Whether creativity is attributed to inspiration, to the appearance of the transcendent within the human realm, to historical necessity, or to random good fortune, the *source* of creativity lies beyond the ordinary realm.

Yet the times when human beings have transcended themselves need not be seen as aberrations. Second-level time presents them as an ever-present potential. The sense that they are 'outside the ordinary' is seen to depend on first-level structures, understood as a particular and frozen appropriation of time's dynamic.

If we could know directly time's presenting, time would express being as constant possibility. With no fixed positions and no intractable difficulties, no structures or limitations impede the flow of knowledge. Creativity reveals itself to be the natural unfolding of time's energy. Art, music, and poetry, new insights and inventions, spontaneous understanding, and compassionate action are the expression of tuning in to time on this second level.

Alive to such creativity, we might understand time in a new way as well. For example, the distinction between 'now' and 'then', with 'now' the only 'place' where experience occurs, might prove to be a diminished version of the possible modes of time, one that cuts off the full capacity of being. The steady and irreversible progression from the past toward the future might also be seen as an undue limitation on time's energy.

Appreciation for second-level time can also shed new light on the phenomena investigated in the field of parapsychology. While research into the paranormal has raised important issues, investigators have usually accepted the basic structure of 'outsiders' and 'bystanders', devoting their efforts to establishing the first-level 'reality' of what they are investigating.

With conventional structures of time and space in place, difficulties with predeterminism on the one hand and acausality on the other remain unsolved. The result has been an impasse that requires a new understanding of time, space, and knowledge to break through.

We might hesitate to put such a new understanding into effect for fear that the dynamic of a 'time' without structure would sever the thread that binds the moments of time. But this fear remains too closely bound to the first level. Second-level time can let 'order' manifest in a way that is not bound by the 'logos' that time establishes. Transformed by the dynamic momentum of 'time', the structures of the 'order' lose their character as limitations, while retaining their capacity to shape first-level experience in fruitful ways.

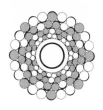

Dynamic Momentum

MOTION OF TIME

The motion of time's rhythm is not tied to things or structures, nor is it abstract. The sense of time's rhythm is awake within us; if we stay with this sense, not applying models or engaging the ordinary appearance of objects, we notice within time's rhythm a specific embodying, a movement without movement, somewhat like floating.

For the 'logos' of the temporal order, this movement can be thought of as too 'slow' to observe. But for the frozen world of substances that the temporal order establishes, the motion of time's rhythm (and the interactions it leads to) are on the contrary incredibly fast, like the ceaseless motion of particles in the subatomic realm.

The 'bystander-outsider' can only regard the motion of time's rhythm as entirely inaccessible, its speed something from another dimension. Human experience cannot grasp it; conceptual models cannot make sense of it.

From another point of view, this speed itself is transformed as it enters the realm of the 'outsider': It becomes 'points' and begins to build up a continuum. Understood in terms of external motion and the 'order' of the 'logos', rhythm builds from point to point of space and segment to segment of time. The waves of rhythm that originate with lower-level time lead to origins, origins give boundaries, and boundaries call forth continuity to link together what is bound.

The continuity that the 'logos' insists upon leads to 'feedback', and from the echoes of 'feedback' come the structures of world and self. Seen as a whole, the process is unitary, absorbed into its product, which finds its rightful place within the temporal order. Seen from within the intrinsic unfolding, however, there is no process at all: only the intimacy of rhythm.

If we look more closely at how the points of lower-level space and time 'fill in', we see that the commitment to substance allows for no gaps. Existence comes into being following old lines of force, reweaving the weave of a fabric that has already been woven. Specific points come together in a specified sequence, establishing labels and distinctions. A 'measured-out' realm 'takes form': *What 'is' emerges as the echo of itself.*

The usual tendency is to take as basic to this process the points that come together as substance and events. But points themselves are based on motion understood in terms of continuity. Within the 'logos' of the intrinsically external temporal order, the demand for continuity means that motion requires a mover and origin a creator.

Internally, however, rhythm comes 'before' the 'logos', whirling the points of measured time and space into being, 'establishing' the 'logos' and its 'order'. 'Points' express the rhythm through which they arise and which sustains them. First they emerge from the 'body of energy'; only second do they conform to the 'order' of the 'logos'.

The temporal order's demand for continuity means that 'points' must be everywhere and must be in motion. They could not be more thinly distributed or less dense; they could not be moving more slowly, for this fundamental motion must be uniform.

For the momentum produced as the expression of rhythm to be maintained in form, all points must cooperate fully, sharing in their momentum, operating at full capacity. Within the 'measured-out' existence imposed by the 'order', the points that make up existence are virtually superimposed on each other, in an instant immediate emerging.

At the base of matter, mind, and energy alike, a constant motion whirls. Since each 'measured-out' point contributes to this motion anew, generates it anew, motion accelerates exponentially. And since 'within' any point there are more points (for it seems there can be no gaps), motion builds on motion.

Motion gives to each point a strength and stability— an ability to uphold itself—without establishing anything solid. In a sequence that challenges all ordinary assumptions, rhythm intensifies, acceleration becomes infinite—form arises.

The whole of appearance can be recast as simply this: *An exhibition rhythmically transforms.*

We then find that the emerging that depends on motion is also a constructing through continuity. But the motion itself is transparent and thus invisible, for it is omnipresent: There is no possibility for interrupting it or bringing it to a halt. Like the motion of the earth through space, it cannot be experienced directly from within the temporal order; like the sequence of cause and effect, it operates in a way too fundamental to be challenged. Only in the subtleties and hypervelocities of the atomic and subatomic realms can possible analogues to this fundamental motion be witnessed.

As motion unfolds, points come into contact, almost superimposed. This process generates 'friction', understood as the 'carrier' of momentum. 'Friction' is the response to the 'logical' ('logos-centered') necessity for momentum to continue endlessly, steadily accelerating, allowing no gaps. 'Friction' also expresses the demand that 'existence' be uninterrupted—an imperative also revealed in the fundamental drive to exist, the assumptions we make about the continuity of the self over time, and such 'meaningful' patterns as birth, decay, and dissolution.

Through the 'mechanism' of 'friction', momentum 'establishes', transferring motion from one moment to the next, one point to the next, always building and intensifying, allowing transitions. Points are given form and 'substance', in a pattern of 'feedback' that points to the self-constructed nature of the temporal order. It is as if two shadows met and in their contact created another dimension.

Because the 'order' embodied through the working of 'friction' is 'rhythmic', it is *balanced* in specific ways. On the first-level, the 'mechanism' of measurement gives form to this balance. A nail cannot support a thousand tons; a flower cannot bloom in the dead of winter. 'Order' appropriate to the 'measured-out' realm must be maintained.

As in human constructs, so in nature, in mathematics, in psychology—in every field of endeavor and each domain of understanding and activity, the 'logos' of the realm operates. Traced to its 'origin' in accord with a knowing more fully in tune with time's momentum, the 'logos' proves to be the external manifestation of the inner dynamic of rhythm, brought into being by the 'mechanism' of 'friction'.

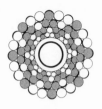

Zero Emerging Rhythm

EXHIBITION OF ZERO

Suppose we imagined the smallest possible 'unit' of time and took that as a moment; then went on to imagine the body of space—the range of all that is—as the occupancy of that moment. As we traced from moment to moment the being of the body of space, how might our understanding of time change?

Any moment arises within the temporal order, and thus is caught up in the 'logos' of the 'order'. However, in reaching toward the *smallest possible* moment, we draw close to a limiting boundary of this 'order'—a measurement at the very edge of what can be measured.

In pointing toward this moment, while at the same time expanding the 'field' of awareness to include all possible content, we might sense the potential for a moment before juxtaposition—even before the emerging content in which subsequent juxtaposition is presupposed.

The content toward which the move toward 'smallest possible' directs awareness could be considered the presupposed 'read-out' of the activity of the mind, or the experience resulting from the current of conclusions that the 'logos' sustains. But as the space of the character of unconditioned existence, it might best be considered the free dimension of 'zero'.

In approaching this 'zero point', we can sense a quality in appearance, a hidden 'occupancy' of time that ordinarily merges into the instant occupancy of experience. This quality could be said to be 'prior' to the structure that identifies 'moments' or designates 'outsiders'. It might be understood as a gateway, a 'first' moment of presence without presupposition, of space that is pure and undisturbed.

What 'takes occupancy' in this moment at the 'zero' of time is Being. It is 'here', yet subtly hidden: an allowing of fullness that does not occupy at all, but instead makes possible experience and the manifestation of substance. We might speak of invariable time presenting the 'singularity-point manifestation' of the conditional existence of what will appear as its own image.

In this 'non-occupancy' by Being of each particular manifestation or 'read-out', Space and Time merge in intimacy. If we look with care, this intimacy can be seen to occur keenly in each act of observation, through the content of what is observed, the being of the observer, and the activity of observation. Each observed moment pops up like a bubble, and like a bubble it is free from substance. The shape and form it presents, however they unfold, do not disturb original and invariable emptiness.

First-level time, with its focus on measurement, and second-level time, the 'source' of power and vitality, share a basic connection to form. On the first level, form manifests as substance, establishing 'outsiders' that turn time into a background phenomenon. On the second level, energy is once more freely available, giving access to a fluid dynamic. Yet on a subtle level, events are also 'outsiders'. And even if it becomes clear that events as form simply manifest the underlying dynamic, there remains a final 'outsider': the dynamic flow of time itself.

For Great Time, form is no longer central. All presentations and manifestations, any conventional forms of existence whatsoever, are agents of emptiness. This does not mean that emptiness lurks in the background like an absentee landlord who may one day show up to claim his due. Instead, emptiness steadily invites form to present itself as the responsible and responsive agent of the totally silent quality we can designate as 'zero'.

Seen from the Great Time perspective, *form is the exhibition of 'zero'*.

Form as exhibition becomes an exhibiting responsibility. Events exhibit form, presenting the exhibition. The presentation becomes presence: Great Time communicates with lower-level time, establishing the 'feedback' system that ultimately activates the known world.

We might consider the time 'within' which events occur as the echo of 'zero'. No first-level 'zero' could have an echo, but at a higher level the relation between substance and emptiness is more fluid. The dynamic of time communicates presence and experience without giving solidity to what is presented. Acting as the 'agent' of 'zero', time on the second level takes responsibility for presenting the present as the echo of the activity of communicating.

In the logic of this dynamic, the communication that presents time calls the present into being. What presents itself in its singularity establishes itself through presentation, in a movement that 'feeds back' on itself. If we are willing to abandon the structures of conventional understanding, we could describe this 'feedback'—the expression of the echo—as the 'origin' of existence.

If the universe were a living organism, this way of understanding could be considered an 'esoteric biology'. In accounting for the operation of phenomena through a structuring informed by communication, it suggests a model similar to the biological account of DNA structuring the development of all forms of life. But such a model is not presented as an interesting theory (in which case it would only conform to the standard first-level patternings). The value of the model will become apparent as we find ways to activate it in our own way of being, opening phenomena to unlock their inherent dynamic as the echo of 'zero'.

The 'origin' that originates in the echo of 'zero' establishes a structure out of which phenomena appear. The structure is hidden, in that not everything is present, yet when we look we find nothing that is not a part of the structure. The temporal flow, physical distance, all phenomena, and all distinctions are encompassed within the structure, together with the mind that responds to what appears. Sense experience, intelligence, and knowledge are all part of the structure, together with all shape and form.

Because of their origin in 'zero', all these aspects of the structure are present in a way that does not bind presence. The 'zero' remains 'as it is'. 'Gravity' cannot bend it, force cannot close down its openness. Through the emptiness of 'zero', a fundamental energy remains always available.

Starting from the 'zero point' of emptiness, putting it into play in our inquiry, can we trace the rhythm through which form evolves out of emptiness? Conventionally, this would seem impossible, for time's rhythm as 'measured-out' requires a multiplicity of points. How can there even be a start to time's rhythm when there is only the 'zero point'?

At a deeper level, however, time's rhythm relates to movement and flow; from this perspective the points that 'establish' rhythm serve mainly as reference. Rhythm at this level is motion coming in waves—not set up by 'measured-out' points or assigned to an object that rides the waves, but the direct expression of an intrinsic body of energy.

We might say that time's rhythm is built up externally out of the basic momentum through regularities of motion, but intrinsically is more accurately the flow of a luminous energy independent of motion. The energy that rhythm manifests is like the glow of life in an living being at rest: dynamic without the need for movement.

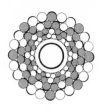

Zero Emerging Rhythm

INTRINSIC MOVEMENT

Caught up in the idea of existent things—'outsiders' trapped in the rhythm of time—we make of movement a physical event, and miss the movement that is intrinsic and inherent. We accept the comments of conventional mind, which reflect the 'measured-out' rhythms of lower-level time. But this mind can also fall silent, allowing a sensitivity to intensive moments of time's rhythm, 'activating' through silence a rhythm that is part of the Body of Time. Then rhythm moves in slow waves of intimacy, too subtle for the patterns of the temporal order to acknowledge.

Viewed from within the intimacy of time's rhythm, every given point—the points of view selected to found perception, the points that interact to 'point out' form within space, the points that express initial intimacy— participates in the 'experiencing' of this intrinsic and subtle rhythm. We might say that each point 'is' the 'rhythm immediacy'. Points of rhythm open ripples of time, allowing participation 'as' space—mental space, physical space, time space. Such potential participations are the 'range' of time.

Alive to and through intrinsic rhythm, Space and Knowledge can merge into Time. There will be no 'order' that aims at prediction or control, no outside interference, no limits, no 'outsiders'. Space in its extension becomes the intimacy of Time, disclosing Being in Space, Being in Time, Being in Knowledge.

In the intimacy of the instant, Space and Time open to Being. All that appears sparkles with the transparent colors of the rainbow and the rich 'feel' of aliveness. We are returned to the singularity of the first instant—the free 'allowingness' intrinsic to existence.

For such singularity, the first instant is not available only at the outset. Every act opens onto the allowing of Space; each manifestation merges with the dynamic of Time. If it were otherwise, there could be no operation of Knowledge.

In the first instant, the 'zero singularity' of the moment could be described as neutral and in balance. As the power of time becomes rhythmic, creating 'friction', this neutrality is lost. But Great Time offers 'zero nature' within the constructs of 'friction'.

Within the chain of thoughts, and within the chain of the chain, 'zero' appears as the gateway to 'zero'. Nor is this a result that can be reached only by specifying the moment in a particular way (for example, through meditative practice directed at 'immediate experience'). Fully open, 'zero' is not preconditioned; it depends on no particular 'read-out'.

In accord with the rhythms that time presents, actions are woven together to create what 'is'. Only at a much later stage is this 'isness' related to what is understood as subject and object, yielding interpretations that take shape and form and move toward repetition. Seen in this perspective, 'zero' is fundamental: the state or circumstance from which we depart.

'Zero' as fundamental may help in observing the interaction through which intimacy emerges. Seeing the 'zero nature' within appearance develops the active quality of seeing, so that seeing becomes newly available. Similarly, the 'feel' of the time that is open to 'zero space' offers a valuable 'mechanism' for supporting the 'experience' of intimacy, free from interference through image or contents.

But this understanding of 'zero' accepts the occupancy of time as different from the 'emptiness' of 'zero'. The subtleties of 'zero space' can also appear in ways that do not oppose either emptiness or occupancy. Simply in allowing sound to hear or seeing to watch, an intelligence of intimacy can present itself, not bound by any distinction between them.

As we integrate this prospect with the momentum of time's rhythm, it may seem that we draw near to something hidden. For the projects of lower-level time, what must be hidden is the open nature of 'to be'. Yet the being of 'to be' does not depend on exclusion; for Great Time, the nature of 'to be' can manifest intimacy with all that is. There is nothing to be hidden, just as there is nothing to be revealed.

We touch the intimacy of being without exclusion when we reach for old ways of seeing and find to our surprise that a new familiarity with the seen has developed. In such moments we sense a free body of Space available to the rhythm of Time—an act of giving without a patron, a work of art without creation by an artist.

This is the circle of 'zero' as fullness: not a closing curve that arcs in accord with a specific rhythm, but an invariable whole that is all-encompassing. Not moving from point to point, the intimacy of 'zero' continues to be available. As the 'zero point of origin', it enters into each time and all times, accommodating the full unity of a Time-Space-Knowledge trinity.

The allowing of 'zero' presents the rhythm of Time as the exercise of Knowledge in Space. But this exercise does not establish anything, nor does it proclaim a 'this is it'. Tracing out 'zero', we find that the wholeness of Time, Space, and Knowledge together cannot be said to exist, for existence cannot determine its structure. As a way of inquiry, it is available to whoever, whatever, whenever, and wherever. It is active everywhere and all the way. It is fully dynamic, in the sense of being able. True to the originating power of 'zero', it claims no status. Open to all, its power cannot be diminished.

In the transition that occurs as rhythm becomes rhythms—small and large, measurable and immeasurable—we might discover the whole of existence taking form. Through the 'mechanisms' of momentum, 'friction', and measurement, the presentation proceeds. Forms emerge that are undeniably 'there'; what appears to be stable *is* stable. And yet appearance is 'grounded' in rhythm, exhibiting its rhythmic transformation.

Understood by a specific knowing, the response to a specific time and space, momentum and its steady acceleration produce the characteristics of the conventional temporal order. They lead to a time that is unstable and strenuous, while the 'friction' they generate produces heat, darkness, and confusion. In such a setting many things cannot survive: As energy and volatility intensify, much that is subtle and fluid is lost. What remains tends toward the static and the repetitious.

From this perspective, substance could be understood as a kind of 'holding pattern' against the force of momentum, a way of using momentum to support what persists. But acceleration continues even when held in check, proliferating the constructs of lower-level knowledge. As thoughts acceptable within the 'logic' of the 'logos' are piled atop one another, existence becomes opaque, so that we can see only surfaces. Bound to the position of the 'bystander', we struggle to satisfy our needs and concerns, but end up feeding the same patterns of acceleration. In the end we can sustain the gathering momentum only with our own substance. Not attuned to the 'aliveness' of rhythm, we find ourselves aligned with a momentum that moves steadily toward death.

When we accept the particular truth of this unfolding momentum, we subject ourselves to an order beyond our control. Indeed, it has been held that even a divine creator would be subject to the temporal order, unable to change the past or hasten the coming of the future. But attention to rhythm reveals that the momentum of time is nothing fixed. Perhaps the past is not dead and the future is already available. Perhaps the present is alive in a way we ordinarily cannot fathom.

The intensification of time's momentum based on the 'mechanisms' of 'friction' and acceleration can overwhelm with its power. But when we seek out greater knowledge, we discover that time is not confined to the onrushing momentum of its linear unfolding. The transitions among shape, form, color, and character invite a knowing that can awaken to Great Time and become the Body of Knowledge.

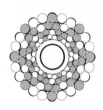

Zero Emerging Rhythm

DYNAMIC POTENTIAL

Great Time restores the power of momentum to dynamic potential. The presentations of Time 'explode' into magical expressions—the echoes of 'zero'. A way of seeing emerges that seems 'unbelievable', yet cannot be considered false.

Matter and form, thoughts and structures 'resolve' into motion and acceleration: limitless possibilities of shape, form, quality, character, and action, expanding in all directions without affecting the open potential of Time. The 'indensification' linked with substance proves to be only another display, and 'feedback' again becomes open.

The positions we take leave us enmeshed in a world of disharmony and imbalance. Psychologically, historically, existentially, the process is already underway. A certain kind of knowledge has set in, and despite our best efforts we face an increasing inability to cope.

But while this pattern is perhaps too firmly entrenched to be reversible, it *lacks all substance.* Great Time presents the darkened, intensified reality of the temporal order as neither good nor bad, but simply as a play—a marvel and a wonder.

For knowledge of a different order, human beings are part of a unitary unfolding that does not unfold. No one within the flow of time could say that this is so; no one could grasp or comprehend it. Yet the way in which our lives develop and take shape could be presented as an expression of just this timeless unfolding. Motion, acceleration, and change, *as they are,* present the heart of Great Knowledge.

This is not a potential way of seeing or a mystical vision; it is not a future situation to be attained. Nor is it a doctrine to be maintained, a truth to be defended, or an insight to be won. Simply to allow for this possibility, without claiming it as our own, can transform the steady momentum of time and the 'friction' of the lower order into the joy of Being.

Suppose that existence were a visualization of space. We could represent this as the circle of 'zero' transformed into the symbol of a triangle. Each of the triangle's three points remains the 'zero circle'; added together, they are 'still' 'zero'. Yet they are 'zero' in a way that is specific, a way that creates a 'potential' for form. We could designate the force that this 'potential' represents as 'gravity'.

As 'zero', each point of the triangle remains formless. But in the triangle, there is also the going from point to point, a movement that 'makes' time. In this going, let the focus be on going 'to'.

'To' has action; we could say that it 'points'. From the active 'to' comes the momentum of the moment and the designation of the point as headed 'toward' another point. 'To' 'represents' the point, and so serves as the 'basis' of the point.

As the point goes 'toward' another point (which is not yet designated or determined, and so 'remains' the circle of zero), at any 'point' along the way, the movement could go off in another direction, at an angle to the first. Thus, we could also say that the point 'represents' 'to'.

From the 'pointing' that 'goes forth' from the point through the momentum of 'to' comes a line. We could designate this line AB, for the two points that specify it (or which it 'represents'). Yet both A and B 'remain' zero; they invariantly go toward 'zero'. This 'going toward' points toward another point 'C' as the 'zero' of A and B. Through the invariant 'going toward zero' of each point, the triangle ABC becomes the 'active expression' of each 'zero point'.

When the momentum of 'to' looks in one direction, it sees the point. But it seems equally possible to look in many directions and many angles at once. Such a seeing makes available the whole, without losing the specifics. Form can come to be in all its variations.

Yet such a multiplicity of seeing does not make available the whole of 'zero'. We could visualize multiplicity as taking the universe and turning it on edge, so that the angle of observation becomes ever smaller, even infinitesimally small. But in the end there will still be the last 'second' of arc separating the edge from 'zero', establishing a gap that cannot be bridged.

We could think of this last 'second' of arc in terms related to our initial image. In the triangle that forms as the symbol of 'zero', there is a part of the 'zero circle' that the triangle (or even infinitely replicated triangles) can never encompass. This non-encompassed aspect of the circle is what distinguishes the ever-expanding multiplicity of form—existence as visualization—from the 'fullness' of 'zero'. And yet, since we began with visualization, and since visualization returns to 'zero', we are entitled to ask another question: Is the 'truth' of this distinction also 'zero'?

Although we can speak of the 'zero point', 'zero' does not actually have a point or base. 'Zero' is not an object; it does not 're-present' its opposite, nor can it be 'pointed to'. We might say that this 'nonexistence' of 'zero' is what distinguishes 'zero', but the same 'non-presentability' operates for existent entities. What we conventionally present as a 'real' object is presented in terms of an ideal toward which the object moves as a limit. On the one hand, this ideal is what the presented object represents; on the other hand, the ideal is an illusion, fabricated as the image of a projection. The ideal is a kind of nonexistent wish, which cannot be 'pointed out' and cannot hold any point.

Exploring this prospect suggests a formulation:

'Zero' is the ideal of each existent—the nonexistent totality of what would wish to be; the wholeness or fullness toward which all existence tends.

In the unfolding of linear time from one point to the next, 'zero' is the apex of a triangle whose base is the determining points of linearity. What has been pointed out 'across' time moves invariantly toward the apex, the 'decisive zero singularity'. In this unacknowledged, 'hidden' move, opening a new dimension, the whole of being is encompassed. Three dimensions open completely, opening the very last point.

We discover this opening in the rhythm that activates movement, which traces to 'zero' as its 'source'. The rhythm that 'zero' opens represents time 'excavating' space, a very subtle part of the energy that projects points. Energy propagates in waves, opening the last point of the rhythm momentum, disclosing 'gravity'. The space of the point becomes alive, and 'existence' appears as 'excavating establishing': the 'zero-rhythm point' as a projection of 'zero gravity'.

Every rhythm merges instantly with space excavation, relying on the presentation of space for 'where' and 'how'. The 'no-position' of space accepts freely the energy of rhythm. 'Zero gravity' offers boundless support; through a rhythm of merging and joining existence is established. This is the 'meaning' of space capacity: a 'becauseability' that can found existence.

'Space ability' makes presenting available. With no position to maintain, a 'compass' can be set in place that gives direction through no direction, allowing 'existence' to unfold from 'to' to 'to be'.

This does not mean that space is 'before' time in any temporal sense. In the moment that the point 'exists', space and time arise simultaneously. 'Before' that, we cannot speak meaningfully of conventional space and time. Such a 'before' has no reference or relevance to existence; it leads to no 'outcome'. A double illusion leads to confusion, confounding observation.

Silent and unimaginable, the whole is 'zero'. Let us attempt to articulate this whole in a way that stays true to the multiplicity of seeing. Before the 'to', 'zero' allows, in an allowing that becomes the ability 'to' be. The becoming of 'to' is the beginning of rhythm. With each point that rhythm touches, there is entering and acting; with each entering and acting there is a point.

Exhibiting excavates and establishes, presenting through ability. No one is there to receive the presentation, for there is no place to put what would be received. There is just the presenting and the ability to continue with the presenting. Rhythm allows the ability to make the excavation present.

'Zero' is far from absence; perhaps we could say that 'zero' is intrinsic. Without 'zero' there is no door to enter—only impenetrable substance. Though rhythm is independent, the allowing of 'zero' is its silent partner, making presenting and presentation possible. In contrast to the 'measured-out' quantities of linear time, the rhythms of existence are all 'zero'. Though rhythm evolves what can be measured, the 'measured-out' realm traces back to rhythm. Excavating its own presentation, rhythm gives the giver 'zero'.

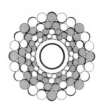

Invariable Time

TIME IN ITS DEPTH

I t has sometimes been suggested that while time brings change, time itself does not change. While summer becomes winter, it is also true that summer is always summer and never winter. Perhaps there is a level of time *deeper* than momentum, in which no lineage or thread links moments in a specific continuity—a level at which time does not move.

The fundamental unit of first-level linear time, the event, seems already to have momentum implicit within it. An event could be characterized as what has arrived in dependence on an unfolding temporal sequence. An example is the ripened fruit of a tree: If the right conditions are present and there is no obstacle, time will present the fruit as the outcome of the seed.

If we imagine stepping *outside* the flow of time, we perhaps could see the arrival of an event before it 'happened'. This does not simply mean that we would be *seeing* atemporally a sequence that was 'really' temporal; it means *permission has been given,* and thus the potentiality of the event is reflected in the event itself. Time's presentation does not depend on an act of presenting.

Why is it, then, that the event arrives? Why is there transition and transitoriness? The second-level answer seems to be that *time itself moves*—that this movement 'is' time. Impermanence is not a quality of things or substances (which from a second-level perspective are in any event only possibilities allowed by space-time interactions), but a first-level interpretation of the dynamic momentum of time.

If time lacked this momentum, change itself might cease, just as without water the ocean would have no waves. First-level time and the first-level 'order' would vanish, perhaps leaving 'behind' some unimaginable version of space. In such a fantastical world, there would be no change or decay: What once appeared could live forever. On the other hand, since there would also be no participating in the energy of time, life would never arise at all. Everything would remain only possibility, as in being fast asleep.

Of course, time does manifest, with all its energy: Existence actively appears, and we participate in it. However, this active appearance does not necessarily confirm the momentum of 'time' as the 'source' of the 'measured-out' first-level realm. Instead, we can entertain another possibility: Existence, with its steady temporal flow of continuous becoming, may manifest a 'rhythm' of time that *in its depths has nothing to do with momentum.* Changes in shape and form, as well as in underlying energies, may simply express an atemporal 'mechanism' through which an invariable time 'presents'.

Within the flow of time, it is difficult to make sense of this possibility. It is like swimming in the rough waters of a stormy sea and being told that the ocean has no waves. But this is a matter of perspective. Viewed from a distant planet—or from within a drop of sea-water—the waves disappear.

It is characteristic of a first-level understanding to ignore the significance of perspective; to insist that what is seen, *as it is seen*, is genuinely real. This 'fixed' perspective can be challenged through a second-level focus on momentum, which reveals all fixed positions and perspectives to be given within an 'order'. From this 'second-level perspective', we are free to ask a question that challenges the perspective itself.

Suppose that the dynamic of time presenting did not appear in the form of momentum at all? Suppose, for example, that time presented only the invariable openness of Great Space? Would time itself alter? In a subtle way, would it become more than timeless?

Understood as arising within the measure of time, the rhythm of momentum depends on points. In particular, it depends on there being at least one point that is not variable, for without such a 'starting point', rhythm could not 'come into being'.

Following this logic, the invariable is established as the eternal. The result is to confirm the fundamental categories and positions of the temporal order.

Suppose that accustomed positions shifted—not in the sense of a move from one position to another, but rather in such a way that the positions became *something other than positions*. Perhaps the time that empowered such a shift would be free from conventional categories, including the categories that set variable and invariable in opposition. Perhaps the shift to 'no positions' would free knowledge from experience and the weave of language, and from all the hidden presuppositions that separate knowing from invariable time.

Let us return to the 'original' invariable point and imagine that point expanding indefinitely, 'infinitely'. As it grew, it would swallow up points and positions. Eventually the whole that is established through 'measured-out' rhythms would disappear into this 'opening' of the point. At that 'point' of complete openness, would the universe of the temporal order collapse? How could we tell that the 'collapse' had occurred? And what could we say about the time 'within' which it 'took place'?

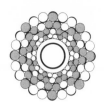

Invariable Time

VANISHING
MOMENTUM

When points and positions disappear into the 'non-rhythm' of an infinitely open invariable, momentum vanishes as though it has never been. It seems that time is transformed—no longer out of control like a runaway horse, it is ready to be wholly reshaped in accord with each new subtlety, without depending on a rhythm or process of reshaping, without relying on momentum or transition.

Such a change would be dramatic. It is as though we awakened one morning to a new way of life: perhaps through inheriting a vast fortune, becoming famous, moving to a foreign and unknown land. Though there will be a strong tendency to continue in the old ways, this is not required. The old qualities and properties, the old ways of acting, are no longer relevant.

When time opens to the invariable, experience continues 'without change', but its nature undergoes transformation. The rhythms of time are transcended into knowing; the 'mechanism' of understanding becomes the subtle part of time. 'Measured-out' existence is 'gone'. All that remains is the Body of Knowledge, dwelling in all manifestations.

The present presents to present mind the presentations of time. Without present time, our present mind could not be present. But the present is also a response to present mind, presenting in the form that present mind calls forth. Reality itself is a presentation, presenting as it does because we are as we are. The circle of interdependence is complete.

Then how can Time present itself in ways that do not conform to the patterns of known reality and knowing mind? If all things unfold in Time, but Time itself does not unfold, how can we 'proceed'? If Time exhibits form but does not exhibit itself, where can we 'look'? If our questions presuppose becoming and change, how can we 'inquire'? It may be that Time is a total energy, invariantly embracing the whole, but what will allow 'us' to embrace this possibility?

Perhaps the answer lies in the power of Great Space to exhibit *all* possibilities and the potential for Great Time to present energy *without limitation*. The Knowledge that knows Great Time could arise within the presentation presented by Time, *as* that presentation is presented to the present mind.

Presentation by Time, *no matter what form it takes*, can serve as an invitation to Knowledge. We might think of Time's presentation as a theatrical play. The producer is Time; past and future are the actors. Staged by the present, with human consciousness the audience, the play is put on for a specific purpose: to encourage lower-level knowledge to go further and understand more.

As consciousness changes, the play will change as well. Past and future will present new subtleties; momentum will make its appearance in unexpected ways. In the end, Great Time may take to the stage. At that point we might say that the play was over, for it has served its purpose; in another sense we might say that now at last the play is ready to begin.

If we ask how the 'required' change in consciousness is to come about, we can remind ourselves that the 'subjective' mind of ordinary consciousness is not simply theoretical or philosophical or analytical. The subject inescapably acts, interacting with its world and embodying this interaction. For consciousness to change, our embodiment must change.

This does not mean that a new reality must be found, so that consciousness will have something to embody 'into'. Instead, consciousness can be transformed in embodying fully the knowledge that is already available. Seeing that each successive stage of understanding is only another presentation by Great Time is an allowing of this embodying. Time presents in accord with circumstances, not bound either to momentum or to 'order', always inviting Knowledge anew. As Great Knowledge embodies in consciousness, Great Time makes its appearance felt.

TEMPORAL PLAY

The dimension that allows temporality itself to emerge as invariability remains hidden because ordinary consciousness allows for no knowledge that would know it. We could describe this 'non-allowing' by comparing the mind to a mirror. The mirror reveals only two dimensions of three-dimensional objects; we must infer the existence of the missing dimension based on past experience with both objects and mirrors.

In the same way, when the mind looks at the temporal play of events, it reflects back to observation only specific configurations of past, present, and future, not revealing the dimension of their underlying union. If the mind is an arena for the presentation of experience, time presents itself in accord with the conventions at work within the arena.

Can we go 'beneath' these conventions? From the viewpoint of the temporal order, there is something inherently contradictory in trying to 'arrive' at an understanding of timeless Time through initiating a temporal *process* of inquiry. Within Great Time, however, this contradiction disappears. Known as invariable, Great Time has never been unknown.

When we attempt to identify Great Time, we do so by applying 'terms' available through the temporal order, with its characteristic 'mechanisms', properties, and transitions. Bound to conventional patterns as we are bound to the chemistry of the air we breathe, we give descriptions based on what 'field patternings' make available to be known. Yet knowledge can transform this chemistry; through a kind of alchemy it can invite Time to manifest in a 'new' way.

If we say that Great Time is a 'higher' or 'deeper' time than the time of the temporal order, we fall back on distinctions and pointings that cannot capture what is invariable and 'nonexistent'. We might say instead that the momentum of time is simply a 'quality' of Great Time, but then we will have to add that any ideas we form of Great Time—or even any 'Great Time experiences' we may have—will also be 'qualities' of Great Time. In the end it seems more accurate to say that Great Time and the temporal dynamic are one.

Rather than playing with definitions by assigning attributes to Great Time and then negating those attributes, we can invite Great Time by remaining on the path of inquiry that investigates conventional time. It is as though we journeyed all the way around the world, returning to our starting point transformed by the journey—knowing for ourselves the nature of the planet. We can discover Great Time by allowing it to arise in the fullness of understanding the temporal order.

Religious imagery of many traditions suggests a transcendent realm in which past, present, and future are said to meet as one, sharing the same experience. If we take such a teaching as symbolic, it invites a different understanding of time. Perhaps the three times present aspects of a more fundamental dynamic, like a hologram viewed from different perspectives. Perhaps the dynamic of time is active at a level deeper than process, deeper than 'timelessness', truly immeasurable.

Within the consequential logic of linear time, we can see beneath the manifestations of past, present, and future a bond that links the three aspects of time. Like two points that define a straight line, linear past and linear future depend on one another. We move into the future by withdrawing from the past. In the dynamics of daily life, every stage of growth is also a stage of decay. The three times appear to share a common being, united by an unseen dimension. Past, present, and future interact in the undivided dynamic of a circle or a wheel, offering one another fundamental support.

This hidden dimension of time, which links past and future, allowing their interplay, manifests directly in the present—the ever active agent of Time, wielding its strength in always unexpected ways. Past and future, images of each other, complement the active power at work in the present. They equally express the subtle rhythms and forms of becoming to which a unitary Time 'gives rise'.

Time in this hidden sense could be understood as a fabric in whose weave is interwoven all of existence. Time sponsors appearance, producing and creating. It creates unconstrained by temporal limits, for those limits are a part of time—creates not only at the beginning, but retroactively and in every moment. As the expression of Time's dynamic, creation is available 'always'. Without the infinite allowing of Space, no shape, form, or characteristics would be possible; but without Time, shape, form, and characteristics would never develop. Time sets in motion and presents: To enter into existence is to participate in Time's dynamic.

The 'order' that time unfolds, including the interrelations among events at every level, can be considered the display of Great Time. The patterns displayed form a world of their own, a structure of intricate beauty, like a crystal magnified a hundredfold. Momentum becomes an aesthetic continuum whose power is available to be used in new and unexpected ways, giving new meaning to the sense of fate or destiny.

Within the temporal order, Great Time will always remain hidden, for the linearity given by the 'logos' depends on a continuity between moments that allows it no 'room'. Even with a shift in focus to momentum, patterns of development, unfolding, and sequence remain in effect.

But such patterns are not closed or rigid. Active expressions of Time, they allow for a new understanding. If we understood more fully the power of active presenting as it arises in each moment, we could bring the past to life within the present and invite the future to appear as well. Integrating the three times, we might discover the source of the boundless energy that activates the patternings of linear time.

Development itself does not develop. The energy that powers it—whether it be found in the fall of a rock down a slope or the unfolding of a thought, in pregnancy, death, or radioactive decay—is given in advance. Within what is 'already there' at the outset lies the hidden dimension that discloses Great Time.

Each succeeding moment of time presents the entire realm of existence: the full, distributed wealth of an infinite becoming. If we could know just one moment of time in all its fullness, what would be left unknown?

SPACE

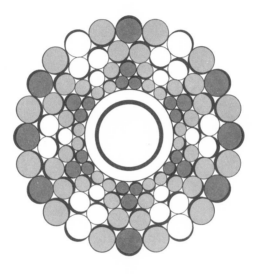

PART TWO

Opening Space

EXISTENCE IN SPACE

If we wanted to tell the story of how the world we experience comes into being, we might start with the vast reaches of space. Seemingly unlimited in scope, space is like a blank canvas ready to accept whatever appears. Space is the 'stuff' of the universe, and as such the apparent 'background' for appearance. The earth moves 'through' space (in a way that also implicates time), occupying in each moment space that was 'empty' the moment before.

All that exists and all that we might imagine, no matter how beautiful or magical, how extensive or enduring, appears in space. Because we exist, space is our home. We are all roommates in the cosmos. Our own physical appearance in space as a specific shape and form bears witness that space must be 'here' for appearance to occur. Speaking in a simple way, we could say that whatever is born must be born into space.

ıⳑ ıⳑ clear that we could not exist—that the structures of the body, the organs, bones, cells, and other components could not exist—if space did not allow or accommodate them. The space that objects occupy and the space that surrounds these objects are equally relevant to our existence.

Yet because we do not think of anything but objects as being 'real', we usually look at space in a perfunctory manner; space is significant for us only insofar as it is available to be occupied by 'objects', things totally separate from the space that encompasses them.

Although space and what it contains stand in a dichotomous relationship, in such a dichotomy there is no logical reason for choosing one over the other. Of course, as active human beings, we normally choose to focus on objects rather than space, for space seems to have 'nothing to offer' us. But this 'self-evident' choice may close off other ways of understanding experience.

There seems to be far more space than matter in the cosmos as a whole. It is only our concerns as human beings that make us reject this priority based on magnitude in favor of a priority based on the significance that objects have for us. It is as though we were microscopic creatures living among dust balls in the corner of a room, focusing all our time and energy on the dust balls without ever considering the room as a whole.

As long as the focus is on objects, space is simply 'emptiness'. And yet space is the matrix that somehow *allows* physical entities to appear. In this sense, it is active with a mysterious power. With its 'power' of open accommodation, space is central to all our doings and concerns. Space is the great democrat: It allows all, without restriction or distinction. In space there are no divisions, not even the division into 'here' and 'there'.

From a space-centered understanding, what happens in one point happens in all points: Differentiations based on time and measurement or assigned meanings lose their significance. And yet space allows for the possibility of being occupied in accord with certain fundamental rules that interweave space, time, and the structures of knowledge to specify the known world: Two objects cannot occupy the 'same' space at the same time; one object cannot be in two 'places' at once; and a given 'state'— defined in terms of location and characteristics—cannot be simultaneously operational with its opposite.

If space could be occupied in a different way, time and knowledge would be different as well. Thus, although space is considered 'empty', it has critical significance in determining the scope and nature of what can be.

Just as 'space' can be understood as offering no resistance to things, so 'things' can be understood as defined by space. The solid entities that we normally have in mind when we speak of objects are defined by their edges or boundaries: the line separating the object and the space that surrounds it. Not only does 'matter' require space in which to appear, but 'objects' are dependent on space for shape and form: the specifics of their existence.

This dependence can be obscured by the fact that the space around an object may be filled with other objects. Yet the relation of object to surrounding space remains the same whether or not that space is filled. Unless the object were surrounded by what it is not, it would not be the object. And this 'not-object' is ultimately space. A specific intimacy enfolds form and space, a partnership in which space plays the role of silent partner. Without this partnership, there would be no 'things' for knowledge to know.

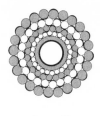

Opening Space

SAMENESS IN MULTIPLICITY

Although objects have specific, identifiable characteristics, within their multiplicity lies a sameness, for every object appears in space as the exclusion of everything it is not. For example, a tree is what remains when whatever is 'not-tree' is excluded.

In this process of arising through exclusion, the 'not' defines the identity of the object in the same way that space defines its physical boundaries. Indeed, we could consider the relationship between objects and the 'physical' space that surrounds them as a special case of the relationship between what is and its 'not'.

Ordinary understanding turns away from the vastness of the 'not' toward positive descriptions of the objects it identifies. Space as the 'surround' becomes space as 'background', devoid of meaning or significance.

What would happen if we allowed ourselves a certain freedom from this perspective? Without challenging directly the distinction between what is and its surrounding 'not', we could start to look at edges—at the places where the object meets space. At once the orientation toward the object shifts, and we begin to see instead the space that surrounds the object.

This awareness could focus quite precisely on the interrelation of the outermost edge of the object and the space that 'dwells' at its borders. Or it could encompass the whole expanse of space, extending outward to the ends of the cosmos, as the limiting 'edge' of the object. In either case, boundaries that had seemed well-defined and meaningful would begin to lose their claim to self-evidence.

Starting with this kind of opening, we can recognize how entities occupy a specific setting in time as well as space. This can lead to reflection on the appearance of the object in time: arising on the basis of causes and conditions in the past, occupying the present in interaction with other existents, moving toward a future in which it will merge with the rest of existence. If we explore such a perspective, we begin to see that in one sense the totality of appearance, interwoven in intricate intimacy, has become manifest in this one single object. The notion of 'identity' thus becomes questionable at a deep level.

Looking toward the interior of the object, we can trace what appears into structures composed of matter and space in interaction. Each particle of matter can be resolved into other particles and so on, down to the basic 'building blocks' of matter and even further, until in the end there is only space and shifting configurations, without solidity or stability. Yet there is no directionality to these configurations. The surfaces of objects are as much space as their interiors. Instead of being a 'background', space could be seen as the 'ground' of existence.

Although we think of space as being 'empty' of 'anything', the absence of anything that physically exists, if space were 'nonexistent', it could have no physical characteristics. If space were nonexistent, it would also have to be unchanging; being unchanging, it would be eternal; eternal, it would have to be without parts, and therefore could not contain anything 'within' it.

And yet 'objects' obviously do exist in space, and space exists within objects. In fact, objects seem to 'carve up' space—for example, the human body exists in space, and is 'bordered' by space. Again, if we look 'within' the body, we see that the body is not solid; it contains many different elements, all of which are bordered by space and contain space. It is as if the body were made up of various layers, all of which had space 'between' them. If space were not somehow 'something', how could it be carved up in this manner? How could what does exist exist 'within' what is 'nonexistent'? Likewise, how could what is 'nonexistent' exist within what *does* 'exist'?

Some scientific theories hypothesize that space was created at the beginning of the universe, but how can 'nothing' be created? Space therefore must be 'there' as something—even when no physical object is present. Perhaps space is some special sort of 'insubstantial substance'. Since physical existence would be impossible without space, it seems that space is either itself physical, a 'superset' of the physical, or an unknown that shares key characteristics with what is physical.]

Perhaps space does 'exist' in some sense. In that case, what allows for its existence? Is it another, more 'basic' space? Again, if there were a more fundamental 'nothing' prior to space (a view analogous to one put forward in several current cosmological theories), is this prior 'nothing', 'within' which space appears, also space? If we hold that there is more than one kind of space, does this view lead to an infinite regress?

If space is indeed 'related' to what appears 'within' it, what is the nature of that relationship? When matter is present, does this mean that it squeezes space out, creating a 'gap' in space? We are more likely to say that the object 'takes up' space, in such a way that space apparently remains unaffected by being occupied. But this lack of interaction only increases the mystery surrounding space's ability to 'accommodate' the matter that 'occupies' it.

When we reflect that the 'nothingness' of space somehow possesses the capacity to support the appearance of physical 'things', it seems inadequate to say that space is 'nothing at all'. Instead of being a 'nonexistent something' standing in opposition to matter, space seems to be *present* and *active* virtually everywhere. Could we say that this quite specific 'type' of 'nothingness' is 'something' after all: different from specific 'things', yet somehow 'more' than 'nothing at all'?

The usual view of space finds such assertions paradoxical. Yet some such understanding finds support in

the picture of reality presented by mode
a few major characteristics stand out:

> Objects have space within them, anᴅ ᴜᴜ⅄ struc-
> ture of space and object interpenetrating is re-
> peated down to the smallest atomic level. Atoms
> are overwhelmingly made up of space, not matter.
> Even when it is most dense, matter is fundamen-
> tally space.

> Space and matter are 'created' together at the
> beginning of the universe, and in this sense too are
> completely interdependent.

> On the subatomic level, matter can be understood
> as essentially a vortex or configuration of space.
> Space is not a passive receptor, but an active me-
> dium, structuring and being structured.

Such views render the distinction between matter and
space elusive. They tend to support the questions that
come into mind when we explore the capacity of space
to accommodate objects. Space is the requisite 'where' of
matter: not only empty 'of', but empty 'for'. Although
space itself may not exist, somehow *existence 'coexists'
with the inherent emptiness of space.*

If we take this 'coexistence' of space and existence
seriously, we are led to explore the ways in which existence and space refer to each other. A 'co-referring' means
that space and existence must share some properties. In
this triad of space, existence, and their joint properties,
how do these three relate to one another? For example,
did things create space, or space things? Or, as cosmology
suggests, do they have a common ancestor?

Fundamentally, matter seems to consist of moving particles whose 'identity' is inseparable from their motion. No boundaries are absolute and no positions fixed; at the center there is no center. When we explore objects and their associated space in this way, differences between space and matter become very subtle. With no fixed locations, boundaries, or identity, the objects that appear 'within' space over time seem to share in the 'nothing' of space.

Could we perhaps go further? Aware that matter that does not occupy space does not exist, we could entertain a surprising hypothesis:

Matter and the objects that matter are themselves a projection of space.

What is the significance of such an assertion? In ordinary terms, it seems at best an interesting idea—a novel way of describing the world that has the additional virtue of being in harmony with certain theories of contemporary science. There seems no way to 'embody' such a view, no way to live out its significance.

In reaching this conclusion, we dismiss space as a potential factor in our lives. This seems natural, even unavoidable: an assertion of the priority of existence over nothingness. How could we know what is devoid of qualities when knowledge is based on distinctions? How could we understand what is limitless when we proceed from a limited perspective? How could we touch space when it is space that situates us in our existence? Situated and conditioned, how can we see in space anything other than the invisible and ultimately inaccessible

128

'background' for the directions, identities, and locations through which we assign meaning?

Yet if matter were truly a projection of space, space would become accessible at a different level. Not standing in opposition to matter, it would also not be opposed to the realm of human concerns and needs. We might find that it brought to those concerns and needs an added dimension—allowing them to appear and allowing their object-determining power to operate, *while not accepting the outcome of such operations as decisive.*

A world open to 'space' in this sense would be a world in which freedom had new meaning. If the 'emptiness' of 'space' is *inseparable* from the meanings we assign existence and the 'objective reality' that human faculties disclose, do meanings, identities, and values still play the same role? When the structures of meaning and existence become newly 'spacious', what becomes of the restrictions on human being?

The well-established twofold understanding of space—space as empty, and as 'nothing at all'—is actually without foundation. As the unknown, space could have 'properties' that are simply beyond our ability to perceive. We may have the sense that space as we experience it is simply nothing, but to 'experience' space as nothing is actually no experience at all, and thus cannot bear witness to the nature of space. When we see space as 'missing' we are only projecting into it the negative counterpart of the objects that appear within it. A more open formulation might put it this way: *When the features of the known world are not, this is space.*

Opening Space

SPATIAL DIMENSION OF BEING

Looking beyond present existence, asking about space before our present being arose and after it will pass away, exercises knowledge in a special way. The spatial dimension of being allows for possibilities that have seldom been explored. The spatial aspects of temporal sequence, and especially the borders and transitions between various states and potentialities, present alternatives that would not otherwise come to light. It is like looking at a detailed architectural rendering, aware not only of what is depicted, but also of the space that lies beyond its borders and of possible building projects that have not yet been disclosed.

If we choose to focus on space more directly, the shape and form that matter takes on becomes significant in a new way. Without in any way losing their substantiality, shape and form appear as 'structurings' of space, partitions that function almost like 'blueprints', determining how space will manifest. We might say provisionally that by giving space structure, 'shape and form' allow us to communicate with it.

For example, consider the phenomenon of distance. Suppose that we travel one mile in space. In the ordinary model, we would say that a physical entity moves or is moved, but in the new understanding being investigated here we would say that 'structured' space is present both before the move and after.

Since this is so, who moves from one location to the other? We might say that space is moving; that accommodation is moving; that there has been a shift in patterning. But if movement is simply patterning, how can we measure the distance traversed? Seen in this way, it seems that nothing moves and there is nothing to measure. Existence merges into space, disappearing from view. More fundamentally, 'this space here' and 'that space there' disappear into 'space as space'.

If existence disappears into 'preexistent' space, it will still make sense to speak of existence having a beginning. But then the question arises: Where did existence appear from? How can existence occur or 'take place' if only space is active?

We might say that space is the parent of existence, but this does not tell us how such a parent could produce such a different kind of child. How does space gather together the network of patterns 'in' space in such a way that it becomes a 'source from' for existence? How does appearance, understood as a 'blueprint' or structure, also become actual? The question arises both for any given existent and for existence as a whole.

With respect to existence as a whole, new questions arise. We could imagine a time before existence came into being, and also the possibility that existence could come to an end. Is the space in operation before the beginning or after the end the same as the space we are accustomed to now? Is the 'original act' of accommodation that allowed existence to arise equivalent to the 'moment-to-moment' allowing that space offers? Could we 'communicate' with the space 'before' existence in the same way that we communicate with space now?

The power of space to accommodate existence can be thought of as an ability to accommodate what appears in time. Yet space itself is said to have a beginning in time. Then what accommodated this beginning? On the other hand, perhaps space is timeless. But then the question arises how space relates to time.

Each moment in time seems to have space available 'within' it—how do moments of time gain access to space, and how does space enter into each moment? Does space allow time to unfold?

Does space reduplicate itself in each moment, so that there are potentially an infinite number of 'spaces'? Although this view may seem strange, it parallels the idea that each existent entity occupies its own space. Something like this seems to be the case for dream images, memories, and perhaps thoughts. How far can this proliferation be traced?

However far we extend these suggestions, they do not account for the sequencing of moments of time or the interrelation of existents. What allows time to unfold, presenting space or 'spaces'? What allows appearance to appear? It seems that structures and patterns, including the patterns of time, depend on a prior 'allowing' that can be traced to an 'all-encompassing' space. Is such a space, 'prior' to all appearance, also prior to the absence of appearance? Is it the same as the space that is empty of existence, and so has existence as its co-referent?

Space understood as all-encompassing and all-allowing enacts a creative thrust that brings potential to being and gives form existence. What is the nature of this space? How does it relate to the space that 'preexists' our existence? To the space that we occupy in maintaining a particular shape and form? To the space that 'remains' once shape and form are gone? If space in all these aspects is identical, what makes changes from one aspect to another possible? If it is different, what happens to 'one' space when 'the next' begins to operate?

Opening Space

CONTAINMENT

A. To start with, there is the universe as a whole, made up mainly of space. Although the universe contains many kinds of matter, visible as well as invisible, it seems that space is far more prevalent than matter. Reflect on this picture of space as the fundamental 'element' in the universe.

B. Within the space of the cosmos, our sun is one of countless stars clustered into galaxies. Our own galaxy moves through space at an unimaginable speed, while the sun orbits its center. The sun in turn is encircled by the planets of the solar system, which journey through space separated by vast distances. Twenty-five million miles distant from its nearest neighbor, the earth follows an elliptical route around the sun, giving us one of our basic measurements of time. Again, reflect on this picture, focusing especially on the movement of the stars and planets and on the physical spaces that separate the planets.

C. Within the earth and its atmosphere, space is largely occupied by solids, liquids, and gases. However, we can develop some appreciation for unoccupied space by considering the air as its local representative. Though we depend on the air with each breath we take, air is also like empty space: We can move through it freely, and it separates solid objects in a way we can easily notice.

The air is particularly visible as sky, which communicates to us something of the openness of space. Take some time to explore the ways in which air is and is not 'space-like', and how experience with air and sky can make available the quality of openness.

D. The solid objects that are found on the earth also consist primarily of space. The interior structures of our own body, for example, contain cavities and tubules of all kinds, on the level of organs and other structures of the body, and again on the cellular level. When we look to the world of molecules and atoms, we find that even the most solid substances are made up mostly of space. Any textbook on basic physics can help in forming a mental picture of this interconnection of space and matter on the most fundamental level. Compare also the various stages of the "Giant Body" exercise in the first book in this series, *Time, Space, and Knowledge*.

E. Awareness of and appreciation for 'space' on all the levels presented in the earlier parts of this exercise can help give meaning to a term that might otherwise seem rather abstract. Our ordinary view can account for space at each of these levels as a container surrounding the objects that appear within it. However, this view can be deepened through sensitively investigating space at a given level: what is contained within that level, the space within what is contained, and so on. With practice, several 'layers' of space and objects can be envisioned simultaneously in their interaction or lack of interaction.

Body Space

OCCUPYING SPACE

Space, as it 'makes up' objects, is available for analysis in unending 'layers' (from the subatomic to the cosmic) and thus can be seen to allow both 'physicality' and 'dimensionality'. However, it remains unaffected by what 'passes through' it. We cannot make an impression on it or turn it into personal territory, any more than we could write on moving water.

Let us apply the conventional understanding of space to a specific example. Imagine that a man walks down a road. At each point as he moves, his body occupies space. As he moves through one 'stretch' of space after another, his body 'uses space up', so that the space he is currently in can accommodate nothing else. In the next moment his body relinquishes that space, which once again becomes available. Yet all this activity leaves space unaffected; whether occupied or unoccupied, space 'continues on' as before.

This rather simple model becomes more complex if we try to be precise about the space that we take up, for that space is constantly changing. Even when we are at rest, the earth is in motion, and so are the solar system and the galaxy. Visualizing the space that we move through thus proves to be rather challenging. When we identify a particular space as the precise space that we occupy in this very moment, we have placed a label on a location that has only abstract significance. Space in this sense has nothing to do with the space that we might think of ourselves as 'experiencing'.

There is another way to look at 'occupying space' that seems more true to ordinary experience. When we look carefully, it seems that we always 'inhabit' the *same* space—not just the same volume of space, but the exact same space, which we carry 'with' us from place to place.

This way of understanding the relation between ourselves and space is associated with making a clear distinction between space inside the body and space outside the body. A certain space is 'ours'. It includes the space taken up by the air inside our lungs, the lungs themselves and other organs, the bones, and all the other physical structures that make up the body. Physical sensations occur within this space, and perhaps thoughts do also. Other relatively complex events also seem bound to this particular space, for example, the phenomenon of falling ill.

The experience of occupying a particular space in this way is common to all individuals. If ten people are in a room, each of them occupies a space coextensive with his or her own body. Everyone who has ever lived can be thought of as having inhabited a unique space in this sense—a space that was 'owned' by its inhabitant.

When I move, this occupied, inhabited space moves through unoccupied space, maintaining its 'identity' throughout the course of the movement. The two aspects of space interact; for instance, if I move my hand from one place to another in front of my face, it seems that 'my' space, as inhabited by 'my' body, moves 'through' the common, shared space.

When we say that two people cannot occupy the same space at the same time, this seems to be true for both aspects of space. My body cannot appropriate the 'owned' space already inhabited by your body, nor can I move into the 'empty', unoccupied space 'through' which you are currently moving. However, two different kinds of non-availability are being invoked: The latter is momentary, while the former apparently endures as long as my identity and yours persist.

In light of the aspect of space that can be 'owned', we are entitled to ask a rather unusual question: What happens to 'my' space when I die? It seems that in death I give 'my' space up. We might imagine that as the body disintegrates into its chemical constituents, each of them continues to take up 'its own' space, but the space of the self is different, and that space is no longer inhabited. Does this mean that now someone else could occupy 'my' space? This seems inaccurate, because my space is uniquely mine; for someone else to occupy it they would have to be me.

Then can we conclude that after I die, 'my' space is retired from service and is no longer available to the universe? This also seems unlikely. If my space were unique in this thoroughgoing way, it is hard to understand how space could also be shared in common. If space were completely unique, how could we ever bump into someone else?

Perhaps our connection to space is somewhat more tenuous. We might say that during our lives we 'rent' the space we inhabit, returning it at death into the space that is common to all beings. Or we might think of the space we inhabit as enclosed by a giant bubble: When the bubble bursts, the space goes back into common use.

We might imagine that once the self disappears, there is no longer any distinction between the space it formerly occupied and the far more encompassing space that impersonally accommodates all possibility for appearance. Again, we might consider that these two spaces merge into one another, since there is no longer a need to separate them. Does this view do justice to the specificity of 'my' original appearance in space? If 'my' space can merge with 'empty' space, how does 'my' space ever become uniquely identified to begin with?

Perhaps we are creating problems where none exist. It goes against the usual understanding to speak of space as affected by or dependent on what occupies it. Perhaps we are letting ourselves be trapped by a metaphor that presents space as a substance.

Still, the two aspects of space—space as occupied and space as accommodating—both seem in some respects essential. On the one hand, we can say that if unoccupied accommodation were not intrinsically available, physical forms could never appear, making it impossible to establish existence. On the other hand, if space does not allow for 'ownership' by the entities that occupy it, how could those entities truly come to be?

Body Space

OWNED BY SPACE

H uman beings are born into space, and it seems that space is ready to receive them. But how does this process occur? If the self enters space, where was it located before appearing in space?

Biologically we could explain how the first cells are created and then absorb nutrients to grow. But this is not a very satisfying answer, because the self is not composed of its cells, many of which die and are replaced in a regular cycle.

Instead, we think of the self as having a fundamental essence. Does this essence enter space? If not, how can the self act on objects 'in' space or move 'through' space? Is it possible that the self does not exist 'in' or interact 'with' space? Can we make sense of such a possibility? Indeed, can we even say for certain that there could be a form of being that did not somehow have access to space?

On the other hand, if space allows the appearance of the self as distinguished from its body, does this mean that space itself is alive or even intelligent? This may seem a strange conclusion, but no more so than holding that space is in some sense 'physical' based on the fact that it allows the appearance of physical objects.

Assuming space does allow 'room' for the self to appear, how does this happen? The self seems to take form gradually, the growth in its physical body paralleled by an accumulation of personal experience. We appear in space like balloons being filled with air: Gradually we expand into a fullness that may or may not be bound by our bodies. As this expansion occurs, the 'empty' space that surrounds us presumably decreases, while the 'empty' space 'within' our sphere is increasingly occupied by solid substance.

As a mental exercise, we could imagine this unfolding interplay between self and space over time. Initially space is empty, though ready to accommodate our physical appearance. Then the self appears, so that space becomes occupied. Does this mean that space itself changes? If so, is the change confined to the space that the body occupies (which will vary over time), or is the space beyond the borders of the body also affected—is the quality of space itself perhaps transformed? What of the shifting border between the space we occupy and the space that remains empty: What happens to this 'edge' as the self develops over time?

Suppose that the self comes into being, endures for a century, and then disappears again. During this time, space goes from empty to full to empty again. Has space changed in that process? Is the second emptiness different from the first? When the self relinquishes the space that it has occupied, does that space endure as 'the self's' space? If not, does it just disappear? Does 'another' space remain—the 'empty' space that accommodates the self's appearance? These do not seem to be questions that we as selves can answer directly, for they deal with states that presuppose our nonexistence.

As existing individuals, we occupy space 'now'. Does this indicate that space was empty before we appeared? If so, it seems likely that it could have had a prior occupant, unless in some way we were able to reserve it in advance. As long as we understand space as empty in an impersonal way, this possibility seems not only likely, but inevitable. But if we consider the particular space we occupy as 'ours', a part of our unique qualities, then the idea that it could have been occupied before we appeared seems profoundly disconcerting, or else ludicrous.

Still, there are analogies that may make us want to reconsider. One land may be occupied by different people through the course of history, and different families may build houses in the same place over time. In today's rapidly changing world, it often happens that individuals try to return to the house they grew up in, only to find that it has been torn down. Less dramatically, the house that we once called our own may now be inhabited by others who think of it as their own.

To take a different example: Geology tells us that continents drift across the earth. In that case, we might ask where America is located. Is it the 'place' on earth that America now occupies, or is it the land that was once 'located' somewhere else, but now has drifted to this particular location?

This question, though intrinsically unsettling, is more complicated than first appears. If the north and south pole have changed through different geological eras, how can 'location' be absolutely fixed? And what if a particular land mass drifted from one location to another, collided with another land mass, and thereby disrupted its distinctive geological structures?

Such examples suggest that the connection between space and identity is not so easy to trace. As environments change, the mixtures of gases, atmospheric pressure, and temperature of the air 'within space' also change. In turn, these changes affect the environment so that what form a specific space allows will also vary. For example, the conditions in one 'location' on earth may at various times allow an evergreen tree, a palm tree, or even seaweed. The galactic space being occupied by our planet at this moment may at other times have been occupied by forms so alien to our way of being that we could neither know nor identify them.

The flux of appearance through time, and even the shifting capacities of space to allow, seem to suggest that in principle other entities could fill or 'inhabit' the space we consider 'our own'. Such entities might be similar to us, or perhaps virtually identical, but they might also be different. They might even be entities for which we have no name and no way of naming.

Such possibilities point toward a kind of exhibition 'in' space of the fabric of existence. Various alternatives might account for how this exhibition could shift in a fundamental way. Perhaps the fabric of existence could come from 'somewhere else', or space could change as existence evolved, responding to various determinants that in turn must somehow have appeared within space.

Caught up in our own concerns and claims, strongly identified with the seeming capacity of the self to know, we consider ourselves the owners of experience. But from another perspective, we might say that we are owned by space. Without space, entities could not manifest, nor could our world enter into being. We are born into space and use our being in accord with the structures that space allows. What we are belongs to space and depends on space, as an image belongs to and depends on the surface upon which it appears. Though we partition space in accord with our wants and wishes, the partitions depend on space as well.

Could we experience space directly? It might be helpful to approach this question through comparing 'space' and awareness. As space must be available for objects to appear, so awareness must be available for distinctions, perceptions, and other mental activity to 'take place'. Like space, awareness is somehow 'endowed' with the capacity to accommodate. As space might be considered the 'field' for objects, so awareness could be considered the 'field' for mental events.

If awareness is regarded as a 'field', its accommodating capacity might also be seen as a dynamic 'field mechanism' in operation. Through this mechanism, the link between awareness and its content (like the link between 'physical' space and objects), is 'there' from the outset, 'programmed' into the 'field' and able to account for whatever development takes place within the 'field'. In accord with this 'mechanism', thoughts and perceptions gather together, mutually interacting to establish the 'field content'.

However, this gathering is only temporary. Thoughts are in constant motion. They meet like delegates to a convention, coming together in response to rules that specify who may attend and who will play what role, then dispersing to go back to wherever they came from.

If we return to the 'field' of space, we see that the 'temporary gathering' of thoughts has its counterpart with regard to physical objects. For example, the elements of the human body are transient; the molecules and chemicals that compose them have come from everywhere and will disperse to everywhere. The air we breathe in now will soon be expelled to mingle with the breath of others, eventually passing into and out of the lungs of billions of beings.

Within just one human body engaged in one simple activity, countless elements interact with unimaginable complexity. But a human being is just a minor occurrence on the planet, miniscule within the complexity of the cosmos. The constant flux of appearance, active within mental and physical realms alike, presents a wealth inconceivable to the mind.

Reflecting on the scope of the cosmos in this way, allowing imagination to fuel a journey into hidden domains, we begin to sense a new dimension to space.

The allowing accommodation of space offers the world that we inhabit as a magnificent display of being and becoming, active beyond any attempt at definition or limitation, available without regard to normal limits on what can be experienced.

'Within' the vastness of space, there operates a capacity to know and to sense that seems intrinsic to being. Science will tell us that our own universe existed for unimaginably long periods of time before sentient beings appeared, yet this scientifically accurate statement does not address the reality we experience. We may imagine a world devoid of awareness, but this act of imagination immediately brings awareness to the imagined world. A world without awareness is literally unthinkable.

What is the relationship between awareness and space? Though the awareness we call 'mine' may not depend on space, its arising would be impossible without some sort of link to the structures of space. Awareness 'experiences' what happens in space, and experience takes shape through an interaction between awareness and its 'objects' that space somehow accommodates.

Space reaches to the furthest limits and pervades the smallest realms. All-surrounding, it has no borders. But if space has no borders, are we justified in speaking of a center, as we do implicitly when we call experience 'mine'? Although space certainly allows such a claim to be made, the claim itself may conceal much more than it reveals. When we make experience 'mine' we are following the logic of awareness as we ordinarily understand it, but are we staying true to the origins of appearance in the boundless depths of space?

The tendency to see the world of shifting appearances as solid and determined relates to the patterns of the mind. Ordinary perception is based on the concerns of a self, which sees and takes hold of 'things' in order to attain some purpose. In grasping for what we want or need, we make things solid. Without such concerns, it seems there would be only shifting displays: birth and decay, molecules and atoms, or simply a flow of energy.

This 'hidden dimension' within conventional experience seems linked to the power of space to accommodate appearance in every possible form. On the surface there is an order established by a set logic and rules, a physical universe based on measurements and interactions that are presupposed. But as we go deeper, the laws that govern and limit appearance in the conventional realm give way. We enter an active realm of collapsing, expanding, contraction, and reduction that seems to come closer to the allowing of space itself. Without the usual focus on the concerns of the self, we might be able to enter this hidden 'depth dimension' within conventional experience. We might discover a knowledge that was more 'space-like': open and accommodating, not bound by structures given in advance.

No matter how far this knowledge deepens, however, it seems that it will be unable to gain access to space itself. Space seems to lack all properties, so how can it be known? The activities of observation, measurement, and identification that knowing relies on have no application to space, which is not even 'there'. Space seems a final limit, a mystery we cannot penetrate.

Body Space

SPACE EXPLORATION

Once we go beyond the conventional view of space as 'nothing at all', we discover that space seems to operate on two levels: one that allows appearance to take place, and one that coexists with what appears. We can explore this two-level view through the following provisional hypothesis:

'Physical' space may be a manifestation, co-emergent with matter, of a deeper or second-level space.

Let us consider the implications of such an understanding. A second-level 'space' could accommodate first-level space together with matter; existence together with nonexistence; physical together with mental; interpretive structures together with what is interpreted. It would structure reality on a deeper level than the structures that we usually accept as basic, without undermining or rejecting those structures. Prior to all interpretive structures, second-level space might harbor an infinite capacity to allow the wealth of appearances, including both the boundless variety of physical forms and the inexhaustible assortment of images and thoughts.

If we consider the full range of appearance as a projection of second-level space, whatever appears will be understood as borderless and free from partitions—subtle and intrinsic, having infinite depth but zero dimension. Generated by 'space' at this second level, the countless 'forms' of energy and matter, *as well as* lower-level space, emerge together as luminous in quality and transparent in attributes. First-level space, in its vast openness, is seen as a 'local' representative of this higher-level space, while energy, mind, thoughts, and perception share in its hidden depths, pointing to an interplay of space, time, and knowledge in which the phenomena of 'atmosphere' and 'order' take on new significance.

'Space' understood in this 'second-level' way could allow greater knowing. Not bound by conventional structures, a knowledge in harmony with 'space' might have conventional human knowledge as its agent and disclose human conditions as its outcome. Ultimately, such a knowledge might reveal the source of the mysterious power, situated for now 'within' second-level 'space', to exhibit and accommodate the whole of what can come into being.

The move to a second level of space is founded on the inseparability of space and the objects within it, but understands that inseparability as an expression of a deeper connection. The appearance of the unitary 'space/objects field' can be accounted for *as the projection of second-level 'space'*.

Like ordinary space, 'space' is the 'background' of what is projected, but unlike ordinary space it is *also* what is 'doing' the projecting. It is 'empty', for without being 'free' of substance, it could never project substance; yet 'emptiness' is not the essence of its creative power. Active 'within' both 'lower-level' space *and* the objects that appear within that space, the 'second-level' space that projects physical appearance enables what exists to appear *in the mode of occupying space*. At the same time, the projecting projector and the projected appearance are unified as one manifestation—a second-level reformulation of the first-level interdependence between space and appearance.

Second-level 'space' remains unoccupied whether it is projecting form or physical space, which from a second-level perspective are equivalent. Objects that appear within physical space, like that space itself, remain 'space'. In the same way, 'space' projects mental and physical 'things' interdependently, in the appearance of the object to the subject. The mental and the physical, and their interaction are 'given' together. The first-level problematic of how the mental realm (and the self) can relate to 'real' physical space loses its significance, though it continues to be useful as a sign that an unacknowledged limitation on knowledge is in operation.

Grounded in 'space', 'subject' and 'object' take on new layers of meaning. What appears in physical space can be regarded as a 'space-projected object'. Yet the object is also the subject, for it is the imperative of physical existents to appear out of a nonexisting 'background'.

When the object is seen in this way, *as the subject of its own appearing*, 'space' as the projector remains the 'background' of the appearance. But while this way of understanding parallels the standard 'object-orientation' of 'first-level' space, the old categories of subject and object, adapted to standard structures of human consciousness, are reoriented in an unexpected way. A new question arises: If object is also subject, is subject also object? Or does the subject have an entirely new role?

The world of objects that we encounter on the surface of appearance is at bottom rootless. The discoveries of subatomic physics suggest as much, and so does observation at the microscopic level. The universe teems with life and movement, in an incredible display of activity around and within us. 'Solid objects' are simply an interpretation geared to a particular mode of existence and interaction.

We can arrive at a similar understanding when we look at the borders and backgrounds of the things we normally consider to be solid. Each physical entity is based on space, with which it interacts and which defines its shape and form. 'Objects' are given as part of a 'field' that determines their identity, qualities, and attributes. Arising on the basis of interacting connections with other members of the 'field', they cannot be independently founded.

If we look carefully at such interactions, nothing is determined in advance or established for all time; everything is open to change. Even the laws and limitations that govern surface appearance could be seen as part of the 'field', or as allowed by space. For example, could we expand a given object forever without in any way crowding space? Is the limitation that prevents such expansion a product of space? Is it the expression of an 'order' or 'field' that space allows?

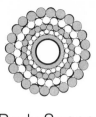

Body Space

SILENT PARTNER

A. When we reflect on the substantial quality of objects, we notice that in order for an object to be present to our senses, it must possess 'properties' that can in some way be quantified. It will have a certain size, density, and weight; it will be solid or porous, opaque or transparent, colored or uncolored; it will have a certain temperature and perhaps a certain charge; it will interact with other objects in a variety of ways. Sounds, tastes, and smells are far less substantial, but they too can be quantified in scientific terms and on a comparative scale.

All these manifestations, characteristics, and aspects require space to appear. Proportions, color, gravitational attraction—all depend on separation and on distance. Without space, quantification and distinction would be impossible. Reflect on the power of space to allow, and on the ways in which objects could be said to depend on space for their existence.

B. Although we can manipulate objects in ways that let us assign measurements to space, space as such cannot actually be measured. No matter how we play with the fabric of existence as distributed throughout the universe, space will be available only as an absence. Consider this aspect of space, with special sensitivity to the way in which space itself recedes from reach whenever we try to draw near.

C. The statement in the preceding part of this exercise regarding the nonavailability of space for measurement, though true in its own terms, can also be challenged. Because space is the necessary 'background' for existence, each measurement of existent objects is also a measure of space. We might say that space is the silent partner within all measurements. Even if we cannot sense space directly, look for ways in which the active allowing of space can be available within our activities and awareness.

D. Within physical existence energies are at work that do not obey the usual physical laws we rely on in our daily experience. Quantum physics explores a realm where this appears to be so—one in which 'particles' can be understood as expressions of 'fields' and substantial existence is replaced by indeterminacy and probability. Here too space is a silent partner, but to be aware of space at this level may have a very different flavor. The General Theory of Relativity, which understands gravity as a curvature of space, may give some sense of the possible interplays of space and substance. Investigate experientially the availability of space as a silent partner in shaping the fundamental nature of physical reality, the biological domain, and the realm of human activity. In conducting this investigation, let your own interest, training, and study bring greater specificity and direction to your questions.

COMMENTARY

The energies of physical interactions, of life, and of the mind 'measure out' space in ways that cannot be directly sensed. The laws governing characteristics, qualities, and properties—their ways of changing and transforming—can reveal a great deal about space as the silent partner.

For example, the fact that wind can be transformed into electricity, or that the light of the sun provides sustenance for living creatures, reveals something unexpected about the wind and sun, *and also about the space that accommodates such transformation.* Again, a chunk of uranium is just a rock, but its structure holds a hidden energy that can be released in a remarkable way. How do such possibilities manifest? Are there 'aspects' or 'dimensions' to space that are essential for the creative wealth of appearance to appear? Are there various kinds of space at different levels?

When we consider the realm of human activity, space seems to allow for a vastly expanded range of appearances. First is the wonder of sentient life itself. Beyond this, human beings can shape forms and create structures that bring new beauty and a sense of meaning into being. What is there about space that allows for such a myriad of possibilities?

Allowing Mind

MENTAL SPACE

In the straightforward 'first-level' view of space as a container for objects, this world is seen as floating in space, along with the stars and galaxies, interstellar clouds, and other unknown forms of matter. This setting in space gives to earth its 'locatedness', just as here on the planet land and sky position and place human beings.

In this view, space and objects are considered to be completely different, with space a bare emptiness. Another view dismisses space entirely, defining it as simply the relationship among situated objects. Either view regards space as 'nothing at all', yet as having the power to situate and to accommodate.

From a somewhat different perspective, space and objects are actually interdependent. Not only are physical objects made up primarily of space, but they can appear only because space is 'already' here. Moreover, space itself is in some sense 'physical', since physical existence is by definition extension 'in' space. We could say that space itself 'takes up' space.

At a further stage, we can see that space and objects are not only interdependent, but inseparable. Space defines the shape and form of what appears and makes its appearance possible. The analogy to mental space is particularly instructive, for in the mental realm it is more readily apparent that thoughts and the awareness that makes them available are made up of the same 'stuff'.

Space, when it is seen as the gulf 'between' entities, is presented as 'separation'. Usually this separation is understood as 'objective' in nature; that is, 'something' capable of being measured out between physical objects. Yet the notion 'separation' also has a psychological or experiential component, and there are grounds for regarding space as having such a component as well. For example, human beings seem to have a sense of the space around them: They may experience it as crowded or open, and they may interpret it in terms of domain, as in the colloquial expression 'personal space'.

The notion of an experiential component to space finds support in the parallel between physical space and the arena 'within' which thoughts and other mental events appear. Awareness can be open and receptive, and thoughts arise in awareness in much the same way that an object appears in space.

Rules for 'inner space' appear to be similar to those for 'outer space'; for example, within a mind already 'occupied' with one thought ('pre-occupied'), there is no room for another. If we think of awareness as a particular kind of space within which thoughts unfold, it seems that this space persists whether or not it is occupied (i.e., when the mind is 'empty'). Questions regarding the relationship between space and objects could equally well be pursued with respect to the relationship between thoughts and awareness. Finally, certain thoughts lead us to identify a specific entity, or 'me', that seems to have an identity similar to that of objects in space, yet appears to 'exist' nowhere other than in the mind.

The spatial aspects of awareness could be described in terms of the four primordial elements that ancient cultures throughout the world accepted as expressing the essence of what appears in space: air, earth, fire, and water. Thoughts can race like the wind or form into convictions as solid as any physical object. The mind can be cloudy or clear, hazy or polluted, while emotions can weigh heavily upon us. The mind has a temperament that can burn fiercely or be chill, while thoughts flow in a never-ending stream.

Pursued past a certain point, such parallels seem only metaphorical—based not on the 'real' nature of thoughts and awareness, but on the human tendency to interpret these essentially hidden phenomena in terms of the domain of objects. This tendency may lead to distortion and misunderstanding, especially since the metaphors are drawn almost exclusively from the realm of 'mid-range' objective phenomena: those neither too large nor too small to fall outside the range of practical human perception and concerns. Metaphors from the cosmic or the microscopic realms might lead to a very different understanding of mental phenomena.

On the other hand, metaphors cannot be considered 'wrong', for they are true to our experience. In any case, we should be cautious in rejecting metaphors as guides to the nature of space, for even on the physical level what is normally referred to as 'empty' space is actually fully occupied by the various gases and other substances that make up our 'air'. The identification of air with space is also metaphoric, justified by the circumstance that as human beings we can pass through air quite freely, just as though there were 'nothing there'.

Given that our sense of 'space' is metaphoric even at this fundamental level, it does not seem entirely convincing to make a sharp demarcation between physical and mental space. If the 'space' to which we are accustomed is simply that which offers no significant resistance to the physical motion of human beings and the objects of human concern, then space has a 'subjective' component from the outset.

Moreover, when we regard the 'mental' space required for mental events to 'appear' as only 'metaphorically' related to 'physical' space, we limit the understanding of space in advance. Experience certainly suggests that the mental and physical realms are different, but the exact nature and significance of that difference is open to investigation. Perhaps space has a 'deeper dimension' that encompasses mental and physical alike. Or perhaps the distinction between mental and physical grows out of a particular orientation toward space.

A different view of space might let the distinction take on new experiential significance. Conversely, to insist on the rigid distinction between physical and mental may help perpetuate the conventional and limited understanding of space.

The simple fact that what appears 'in' space appears 'to' mind suggests that there is a connection between mind and space: that mind has space-like qualities or that space participates in awareness. As a starting point for investigating this connection, we could observe and exercise the mind in light of such possibilities.

In terms of our daily concerns, such investigation might prove extremely valuable. If emotionality and confusion could resolve into a space-like openness, the quality of experience could shift dramatically. Interpreting the mind in such terms might allow a different kind of knowledge, accommodating a 'field' of mental activity that could support more positive or complete forms of 'minding'. Seeing mind as space or opening to space as alive with knowing might encourage new forms of experience: more vivid and fiery, more sharp and clear, more flowing and receptive, or more stable and balanced.

Allowing Mind

PHYSICAL SPACE
AND MENTAL REALM

There are many ways in which 'mental' and 'physical' space blend into each other, making a firm distinction between these two realms suspect. In the first place, we have a clear sense that mental events such as thoughts occur in a distinct 'location' in physical space: We locate our thoughts in the space our heads 'occupy'. We may also associate other mental events, such as feelings and emotions, with other parts of the body such as the heart or gut, or with a flow of energy that can be felt throughout the body.

In the second place, mental phenomena depend on space-like characteristics such as boundaries and partitions. For example, there is the border between what is understood and what is not, the border between facts and values, between thoughts and feelings, between concentration or its lack. Thoughts and images appear one after another in a kind of 'presentation space', obeying the rules of noncontradiction and exclusivity associated with the physical realm. Finally, the mental realm provides a direct analogue to physical space in the 'space' that surrounds the mental 'image' of a physical object. Whenever we picture an object in the mind's eye, it is surrounded by space. True, this space seems to differ from physical space in that it consists of the same 'stuff' as the object it surrounds, whereas we do not normally understand the relationship between 'real' objects and space in this way. By relying on this distinction, we may be letting an unexamined aspect of physical space foreclose in advance the potential for understanding mental space in a new way. But by setting aside this distinction for a time, we can perhaps prevent a premature foreclosure of knowledge.

The 'space' that surrounds any mental image differs from physical space in interesting ways. This is particularly true with respect to dreams. The edge separating dream objects from the space they occupy is not sharp and distinct, as is generally true for 'real' objects. It is not that dream objects are 'fuzzy' in their outlines, but rather that they do not rigidly maintain their form or qualities from moment to moment. First one thing is happening, then another; suddenly it is later than it was before; one person becomes someone else, or stays the same person but has very different physical characteristics. Rules that operate in the conventional world of physical space, having to do with identity over time, do not seem to apply in the space of the dream world.

The fluid way in which dream objects occupy space is reflected in the 'quality' of 'dream space'. The 'dream world' is less 'solid'; it seems to come into existence for a specific purpose as required by the dream and to shift on the same basis. The dreamer accepts without surprise remarkable jumps in the content, directionality, and 'locatedness' of the dream. And while the dream seems quite 'real' within the dream context itself, its 'reality' is somehow 'less powerful' than conventional reality, as evidenced by the occasional dream that seems remarkably lifelike.

The same point arises in a different perspective in hallucinations. What makes an hallucination so frightening is that instead of occupying its own world, the hallucinatory object shares 'edges' or boundaries with what is 'known' to be real; that is, with what occupies 'real' space. In the hallucination, 'physical' and 'mental' space are confused: They meld together, crossing boundaries that are 'supposed to' remain fixed. But the very fact that this can happen points to a commonality between mental and physical space.

As with dreams and hallucinations, it may be that each individual thought or image brings with it a subtly different surrounding space. Unfortunately, for the most part thoughts slip by too quickly to notice whether this is so or not.

Just as certain aspects of mental phenomena point toward spatial distinctions, so aspects of physical space appear to depend on mental distinctions. For example, 'my house' is 'separated' by clearly defined 'physical' space from my neighbor's house. But if my concern shifts from the domain of 'houses' to the domain of 'neighborhoods', the space between my house and my neighbor's house 'disappears'.

The conventional interpretation would hold that the 'disappearance' of space in such circumstances is only subjective. The space—the 'absence of house'—is still 'there', but we lose sight of it. But the insistence that an 'absence' is 'real' seems to involve conceptual difficulties. Can a 'real' nothing—a nothing that is 'there'—'really' be 'nothing'? As soon as we make such a claim, we seem to have lost sight of the nature of space as 'what is not'. What does the 'objective' space whose 'existence' we affirm have to do with this (presumably) more basic space?

There is another difficulty as well. If we insist that the 'space between' remains after we have lost interest in it, we are attempting to establish the objective 'being' of space through our assertion and the arguments adduced in favor of that assertion. But in that case, we have let the mental slip back in at a deeper level. This move seems inescapable: The demonstration that physical space is independent of mental events will necessarily rely on a sequence of mental events that in some sense 'take' physical space as their object.

It seems that mental and physical are linked in unsuspected ways. Following this insight through, we can say that when we refer to space as existing apart from our perception of it, *the space thus referred to exists as the thing referred to.* Insisting on the 'reality' of space as an 'enduring physical nonexistent', we affirm its existence as an object of mental inquiry.

Having thus imported physical space into the mental realm almost against our will, we find that mental and physical space are easily conflated. In referring to physical space, we have some 'thing' in mind. Since this thing must exist some 'where', we can ask: Where is this 'where'? *The space that a speaker refers to,* whether physical or not, seems to be located 'in' the 'mental space' established by the act of referring. Can space 'as such' be separated out as the underlying, independent 'basis' for the reference? It seems not, for since it has now been referred to, it again occupies mental space.

It may seem that a trick is being played, that space must exist apart from any reference to it. But the idea of an 'existent' space, or even a nonexistent space that unaccountably possesses the specific quality of being 'not mental', goes against the most basic sense of space as 'nothing at all'. Perhaps this is part of the difficulty: How can we look at space in a new way when all established conceptual patterns suggest that there is nothing 'in' space to look at in the first place?

Allowing Mind

KNOWER IN SPACE

I n first-level space, the subject appears (though its mode of appearance remains indeterminate and problematic) as the 'bystander', the one who knows. But if we leave first-level assumptions aside, we can look directly at knowledge itself, asking what relation it has to 'space'. Since this way of questioning will not fit well with standard assumptions about the 'activity' of knowing, perhaps there will be some value in calling those assumptions into question.

Knowledge that acknowledges 'space' as a projecting, allowing 'force' knows in a new way. While continuing to fulfill its usual role of apprehending what 'space' projects (form as appearance), knowledge in addition knows 'space' as the 'appearing from'.

Such a knowing can be distinguished from the more conventional knowing of observation. While knowledge based on observation conceptualizes, reports, and offers 'feedback' based on distinctions, oppositions, and identity, the new knowledge is prior to distinctions, including such fundamental distinctions as absence and existence or subject and object. Without abandoning the observed differences out of which the known world is built up, what had been known as distinct and independent is now *also* known as interdependent and co-referring. There is an interplay between what is separate 'as such' and the *appearance* of separation.

From the perspective of this new knowledge, this interplay can be expressed in the following insight:

The knowing that knows separation is itself a projection of 'space'. The act of attributing qualities to what appears is an aspect of what appears.

Seen in this light, the 'contents' of experience, the distinction-making through which they 'originate', and the accommodating 'field' within which they appear are all projections of a second-level 'space'. Even separating out 'distinction-making' as a unique activity, separate from the entities distinguished, is likewise a projection of 'space'. All appearance is coexistent and co-emergent; and *drawing a line to separate one form from another is also an act of appearing*, without substantial basis.

The 'insubstantiality' of first-level knowledge does not mean that the lines drawn by such knowledge disappear, or that what is separated by these lines melts together. Unlike first-level insubstantiality, which is deeply problematic, insubstantiality that refers back to the projecting capacity of 'space' will appear to first-level knowledge as liberating and empowering.

The insubstantiality offered by 'space' gives to line and appearance a magical glow, which could be said to mark the 'appearance' of 'space', or even to point beyond 'space' to the source of its projective power. 'Appearing' and 'appearance', 'projector, 'projection', and the 'action' of projecting do not intrude on one another, but are known to 'knowledge' as both distinct and inseparable. Making distinctions has this same quality of open, shimmering presentation. Existence is a phantom without being unreal; investigation discovers its own nature as 'space', given together with all that is investigated.

Within the 'field' that second-level space might be said to project, an attitude or quality shapes the 'focal setting' at work. This 'attitude' could be understood as carving out a particular domain, as an angle carves out a portion of a circle. As the angle is set 'to words', it angles 'towards', giving shape and form as bearing meaning for a self. The process could be likened to the way that subtle particles allowed by a 'field' of nuclear interactions congregate and manifest as objects for a subject.

Tracing this image out, it seems that for such a manifestation to emerge into being, it must 'incorporate' the 'field observer'. Since the observer arises as given within the context of what is observed, the process of creation that 'gives' observer and observed together will not be available for observation, while the 'space' within which this giving 'takes place' will be doubly out of reach. The observer can observe only the finitude of what can be known; for example; first-level space and the physical properties that appear within that space.

Through such a structure, a 'gap' is established between the known or the knowable on one side and what encompasses known and knowable alike on the other. For the knowing available to the 'field observer', second-level space as 'source from' is inaccessible. Yet this 'gap' is not intrinsic to knowledge, for knowledge in its own terms knows no limitations. Instead, the appearance of the 'gap' reflects the limited 'focal setting' that operates within the 'space field' of first-level knowledge, determining what can and cannot be known.

Since this is so, the 'gap' as such is an expression of the knowledge it appears to exclude. Put differently, *implicit 'in' the gap is the knowledge that the observer 'finds' to be inaccessible.* Together, known, knowable, and gap restate or represent at the first level what at a second level can be described as the *immeasurability* of knowledge.

It might seem that the most direct route to new knowledge would be to look at the gap directly. From a first-level perspective this is simply not possible: There is 'nothing there' to see. But perhaps first-level knowing encounters a 'local representative' of the gap in the ever active gap between subject and object.

Instead of exploring this readily available gap in its own terms—which would continue to bind inquiry to first-level entities and identities—we could try looking at it as an interaction of knowledge and space. The 'knowledge gap' between subject and object can be bridged only if knowledge can 'enter' space. It is the 'nonappearance' or nonavailability of knowledge in space (understood as 'nothing at all') that gives form to the gap 'in the first place'; due to this 'absence', the subject arises as 'the one who needs to know'.

The nonappearance of knowledge is shaped by time. Time cuts subject from object, making the movement 'towards' necessary. It likewise plays a specific role in creating the juncture at which the gap emerges.

If we cannot see clearly the role of time in this regard, or cannot understand its significance, it may be because we are bound to a 'focal setting' that accepts a temporal order as given. But this point too seems open for investigation. Time does not appear within the 'first-level field' only through the temporal order that the 'field' discloses. The inherent dynamic of time suggests that the 'field' itself could operate differently.

Allowing Mind

CATCHING MIND

A. Observe the mind in operation, paying close attention to the way in which mind knows mind as knowing objects. How does this knowing of mind by mind work? What is the difference between the one that knows and the one that is known? Can the mind know mind directly, or will mind as known inevitably be different from the mind that knows?

COMMENTARY

Catching the mind in operation can be a frustrating task that may even seem impossible. Since there is no particular 'place' that mind is located, where can we go to catch it? And even if we did move to catch it, this moving moves mind as well. When our mind jumps to catch the mind, the mind is already gone.

If we consider carefully, we see that we really know very little about mind. For the most part, we can know with confidence only the ways in which the mind differs from matter or from the body. And even this 'knowing' is based on the assumption that mind is wholly separate from these other elements of what is experienced.

The separation between mind and matter seems true only at the surface; at the root, mind and matter seem closely connected. Like partners, only closer, mind and matter depend on each other. So close is the relationship that the partitions between observer and observed, or the projections from one to the other, are part of the partnership. At the level beneath ordinary distinctions, the mind gives all knowledge of matter, while matter gives all substance to the mind. There seems no rational way to divide the two.

If no division is possible between mind and matter, quantities and qualities cease to matter; we cannot 'keep them in mind'. Instead, we fall back to a neutral 'zero space'. The next part of this exercise investigates the availability of this space to experience.

B. Continued practice of the first part of this exercise suggests the inseparability of mind and matter. Once this insight is present, let the 'singularity' of mind and matter lead you to a 'place' of neutrality. Remain in this 'zero space', watching how distinctions arise without being caught up in those distinctions.

COMMENTARY

A 'zero space' before distinctions will appear to ordinary consciousness as a blank, unknown and unknowable. But this not-knowing is simply an expression of ordinary patterns. Not to know in this sense means simply that we cannot give what appears a position within an 'order'; we cannot make it accessible to the senses or to logic. Because we cannot rationalize it, we also cannot assign it a value or determine how to evaluate it.

Instead of accepting this not-knowing as the final word, we are free to go into it, looking for knowledge of a different kind. There is an opportunity to step back to a point 'before' the known world arises, and ask in a new way where we come from.

In making this move to a 'zero space', we have the opportunity to look at something that we ordinarily miss: We are so busy 'pointing out' and 'pointing to' that we never look at the pointing or ask after the source. Perhaps what appears is a creation of the pointing process, or perhaps the pointing participates in implementing what is created in some other way.

Entering the neutrality before distinctions helps break the hold that distinctions have over us. Distinctions are seen to depend on positions and points of reference; when we choose, we are choosing within a presupposed framework that gives the choice meaning. At times this framework is spatial, so that the mind in effect 'borrows' the physical locatedness of the body. At other times the framework is better understood in temporal terms, as when we engage in perception of a world that has been 'measured out' in advance.

Through cultivating the 'zero mind' of 'zero space', we can investigate directly the *arising* of conventional structures through which the self seeks to possess appearance—the 'feedback system' of recording, recognition, identification, and representation. Continued practice lets us return to presentation before possession or position, undoing the momentum of identification.

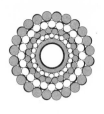

Space Field

FIELD IN
OPERATION

W ithin conventional time and space, knowledge becomes available to a knower. The knower operates as the observer of appearance, and thus is *located* in
space in a particular way: The knower is situated in a
place, emerging from a background. As part of this
'locatedness', the observer stands outside what is observed, playing the role of a 'bystander' unaffected by the
object under investigation.

The 'bystander-observer' has various preestablished
qualities, including character or identity, attitude, and
the faculties available for performing observations.
These qualities contribute to 'locatedness', determining
the 'focal setting' for observation. Objects appear and are
identified as 'outsiders' on the basis of the concerns and
attributes that the 'bystander' brings to them. The identity of the 'bystander' is juxtaposed to the identity of
what appears before the 'bystander'. Particular ways for

gathering knowledge are established, setting limits on what can be known. What is disclosed to knowledge is tightly bound to these determining conditions, as a transcription is tightly bound to the original recording.

Suppose we decide to investigate space 'as such'. The juxtaposed identities of 'bystander' and 'outsider' will impose limits on the knowledge available through such investigation. We can put it this way: The 'locatedness' in operation at the start of the investigation is conditioned by space, and thus will determine the nature of the space that investigation discloses. Space establishes the setting, allows the factors in terms of which the investigation will proceed, and determines such fundamental structures as 'here' and 'there' and the distance 'between'.

We can challenge these limits by considering the world of conventional space, 'within' which the 'bystander' observes 'outsiders', as the shifting exhibition of a 'field'. The various aspects of 'locatedness', including the attitudes of the observer, the positions taken by a self, the ways that objects take form, and space as the 'domain' for 'locatedness', would all be given together by the 'field'.

Within such an all-encompassing 'field', objects with specific qualities arise and pass away, move and interact. Logic and interpretation match their movement, 'making sense' of it in accord with human needs and desires, setting up a characteristic kind of knowledge. The parallel unfolding of mental operations on the one hand and the 'laws' of nature on the other, so often regarded as a puzzle or a mystery, can be seen as a consequence of the 'field' in operation, for each 'member' of the 'field' supports and subtly mirrors all the others.

Conventional space shares with the 'field' its mysterious ability to allow appearance to appear. Yet space is also simply another aspect of the 'field', given together with 'outsiders', the 'bystander', and the 'natural laws' that govern the cosmos.

Carefully considered, even 'given together' is an aspect of the 'field' in operation. For conventional experience, 'being given together' manifests through fixed juxtapositions that both express and establish identity. But we can imagine a 'field' transformation through which 'given together' would express quite different qualities. Such a transformation is not allowed for within the 'field', which cannot encompass itself. But if the 'field' traced to an unknown 'source', it seems that an entirely different 'field' could operate as well.

Space Field

GRAVITY FIELD

W hen the 'field' that allows first-level appearance and experience to appear is not disclosed as a 'field', this same nondisclosure takes the form of characteristic limits on knowledge. Examples of such limits are the barriers between mental and physical and between space and matter, the mystery of creation, and the 'power' of space to allow. Since such mysterious structures will not be seen as available to be explored as expressions of 'field dynamics' and 'field mechanics', these aspects of the 'field' will not readily emerge as 'topics' for inquiry.

This restriction on knowledge can also be understood as a limit on being. The possibilities allowed by 'field dynamics and mechanics' are the only ones available. What does not fit 'within' the 'field' lacks a 'mechanism' for appearing; because it is not 'not not-allowed', it cannot 'come into being'. As a prime example, it is only what 'exists' (in any of several ways) that is not 'not-allowed' within the 'field' of conventional space, time, and knowledge; accordingly, only what exists can 'be'.

Could such inherent limits on being somehow be transformed? Consider what happens when someone in the prime of life dies suddenly. First a particular consciousness and knowing, linked to a particular time and space through embodiment, is in operation. Then (we might imagine) comes a moment of instantaneous recognition of danger, when these factors all change drastically. Then a sudden wrenching shock, like an earthquake. Suddenly time itself 'collapses'. Energy, memory, awareness, perception are all reconstituted: The old 'field', its limits maintained through the constant 'feedback' of an echo effect, is gone. There is total discontinuity, like entering a black hole—space, time, and knowledge in the conventional sense are gone.

This kind of dramatic change is rare in conventional experience, precisely because the 'field' is pervasive. An underlying force, a kind of 'gravity', sustains a 'mechanism' according to which everything operates. A specific knowing is allowed, and through 'field feedback mechanisms' this knowing itself shapes the 'field' and what it will allow.

Such a structure is essentially conservative. 'Gravity' pulls on new experience as the gravity of a black hole might pull on distant matter. If something 'not-allowed' within the 'field' did present itself as a candidate for being, it would either go unacknowledged or else be interpreted by 'field-determined' knowledge and given form by 'field-determined' space in such a way that it would fit in 'after all'.

Yet the very pervasiveness of the 'field'—the mutually shared embodiment of the 'field structure' that characterizes its members—suggests that if change did somehow manifest, its impact would be dramatic. In a single 'moment' the whole could give way, allowing completely new possibilities to 'embody'. Space could allow new form and time could present new worlds, while knowledge, aware of the limitations at work within old ways of knowing, could penetrate obstacles as though they were no longer there.

While the 'fields' of physical space and the temporal order ordinarily seem almost impossible to transform in this way, the psychological domain allows for a fluidity that makes a degree of transformation seem potentially within reach. For example, someone who 'falls in' love or 'sinks into' depression enters a different world; as the spatial metaphors suggest, this world may actually present physical time and space in subtly different ways. Near-death experience or religious conversion may have even stronger effects.

Perhaps similar changes occur often, without our taking cognizance of them. Our 'experience' of time, space, and knowledge may alter from moment to moment; if we fail to acknowledge and appreciate such changes for what they are, this failure could itself be a part of the 'feedback' mechanism that the 'field' structures.

Such a possibility (which could be 'established' as 'true' only by incorporating it into the conventional 'field') offers a new perspective on certain 'well-known' aspects of experience. Shifts in mood and outlook, already allowed for but dismissed as 'only subjective', might point toward changes that affected the 'field structures' themselves, as though the operative 'law of gravity' could suddenly be repealed.

The steady arising of new events in time, usually taken as confirming basic 'field mechanisms', might signal a creativity 'available' in each moment of structured 'field experience', suggesting that the source of 'power' within the 'field' is independent of the 'field mechanism'. Space, time, and knowledge might be less structured in scope and operation than is usually imagined; indeed, it might be that they could operate in nonstandard, even 'miraculous' ways.

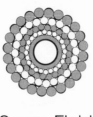

Space Field

ACTIVE ALLOWING

The possibility of such 'field transformations' giving rise to 'nonstandard' happenings suggests an 'allowing' that may be intrinsic to the 'field' as an innately indeterminate structure. Like first-level space in comparison to the objects it contains, the 'field' is not 'fixed' or rigid in the same way as the entities it presents. Cognized by a knowledge that understands appearance as 'field presentations', it might appear as newly expansive and embracing. The second-level knowing invited by a 'field-centered' way of inquiry might present the 'field', with all its fixed realities, as the projection of second-level 'space'—a creative and allowing 'medium' that could invite what the 'field', understood in first-level terms, would otherwise exclude.

Even within the 'first-order mechanisms' of the prevailing 'field', conventional views of space can be called into question. For example, the model of 'subject-knowing-object' allows for methods of observation not bound by the innate limitations on human senses. Augmented by instruments that reveal microscopic detail and cosmic vastness, the senses present a world in which standard 'field structures' seem to break down.

In the mental realm, theories and speculations contrary to conventional experience can be entertained, yielding new insights and modifications in models of what is real. Knowledge itself can be understood as an allowing 'field' within which such first-level phenomena as thoughts and images arise. The limits of reason can be identified, while at the same time reason can be used to challenge presupposed 'field mechanisms' as inconsistent or incomplete.

Certain ways of knowing may similarly open for exploration of a 'field' within the 'field'. Thus, psychology investigates the domain of human wishes and concerns. It asks how emotions and setting influence perception; how cognitive structures influence emotions; how stories and beliefs shape the known world and influence personal interactions. Analysis on this level, while still bound to the basic 'field' (for example, in seeing the domain of inquiry as 'only subjective'), can reveal certain aspects of the 'field structure and dynamic' and make them available for investigation.

Active inquiry can assure that knowledge continues to expand, revealing new attributes of the 'world' that the 'field' allows. Each first-level boundary or border points 'beyond' the element bounded. Together, entity, boundary or limit, and what encloses that limit display the underlying 'field mechanism' and the dynamic in accord with which it operates. For example, viewed as a 'border phenomenon', 'shadow' at once brings into play the dynamic interaction of 'light' and 'opaque substance'. Again, psychology can look at 'border phenomena' in stories, in a way that links each story more fully with direct experience.

In all such analysis, the mechanisms and mechanics of the 'field' itself will remain 'off limits'. But this limit too might be open to investigation. Suppose that knowledge could draw on the dynamic of the 'field' directly, rather than mirroring the limits and distinctions that the dynamic establishes. Not bound by 'field constructs', it would offer a knowing sufficiently comprehensive to allow for not-knowing as well. Even the acknowledged impossibility of a knowledge 'beyond' the 'field' would be directly knowable.

A knowledge attuned to the 'field dynamic' and not confined by 'field constructs' brings to light the interaction among space, time, and knowledge—understood not just as aspects of the 'field dynamic', but as second-level structuring principles more basic than the 'field'. Alive to this interplay, our understanding of human beings, human concerns, and human interactions could move to a new level of insight.

A comprehensive starting point for such knowledge is appreciation for the *active allowing and accommodation of space*. Within the first-level 'field', this will mean appreciation for vastness and openness, and for the creative aliveness that flows in waves throughout all appearances.

With such appreciation, the substantial entities that appear within first-level space and the world that we habitually inhabit take on new significance, reflecting the availability of second-level space. They are revealed as 'exhibitions' of the 'field': magical displays, splendid in their richness.

Space Field

PARTITIONS
AND OCCUPANCY

A. Pick out an object, either one that is present before you or one that you imagine. Focusing on the edge of the object, consider that this is also the edge of 'empty' space. Reflect on the difference between space and what it contains, which should be most noticeable at the edge you have identified. Are there properties and qualities of 'space as container' that you are able to contact and that help account for its ability to serve as a container?

Now repeat this investigation with regard to the same object, but on a smaller scale. For example, you could look at one clearly defined component of the object, or at the entities (such as cells or molecules) that make it up. Refine your investigation by proceeding to ever more subtle levels, until you reach the subatomic realm.

B. Repeated at different levels of analysis, the previous exercise helps show that each object is a marriage of space and existence. This insight can be pursued by asking which of the properties that we attribute to the object 'belong' to the object and which 'belong' to the space that (at various levels) contains the object.

COMMENTARY

It may seem strange to inquire into properties that 'belong' to space, since space is normally regarded as lacking all properties. Considered as arising within a 'field', however, space will share in the properties available within that 'field', even though it will do so in a way that does not appropriate those properties.

One way to investigate the interaction between space and 'field properties' is through the link between 'physical' space and the mental realm. We can distinguish between the 'physical attributes' of a thing, which belong to an object, and the mentally assigned qualities (for example, 'identity') that are applied to the object. Such assigned qualities do not 'really' exist, and in that sense could equally well be assigned to space.

Once the distinction between mental and physical has been made in this manner, there are two ways to proceed. The 'logical' approach is to say that physical and mental have separate characteristics that can be distinguished from one another. The second approach moves toward merging the physical and mental. In what sense are mental qualities physical? In what sense are physical qualities mental? Careful attention to this question can lead to experiencing different energies that are neither physical nor mental.

Field Dynamics

EMERGING FIELD

In ordinary experience, a room in which a certain kind of activity has been taking place has a distinctive 'atmosphere'. Walking into a gathering, we may notice an emotional tone 'in the air': a dynamic and pervasive quality. Such an experience is an example of a specific 'field' in operation.

Suppose we have a particularly powerful experience of some sort. Later, when we remember that experience, we remember not only the relevant particulars, but something of the setting: how things looked, a smell, perhaps a quality of light. We may remember events associated in time, or remember even a particular sense of time or space.

Such examples suggest that at the time of the original experience, the various elements 'present' shared or participated in a 'field'. In the same way, we could consider that all appearance, all existence, and all experience share in an 'all-encompassing field'.

How would such a 'field' establish itself and become pervasive? The issues of 'creation' and 'establishing' implicit in this question themselves arise to be 'made sense of' within the 'field', an intricate interplay that requires careful analysis. A preliminary investigation, however, points toward a process that is self-establishing.

At the outset, there may be room for various alternatives and possibilities, but there are already certain tendencies in operation. A tentative 'order' gives an incipient structure. For example, the way of speaking being employed here makes temporal assumptions ('at the outset', 'already', 'incipient') that could be considered to reflect such provisional tendencies.

Within the as yet largely inchoate 'field', events or activities that are not prohibited at the outset manifest; as they do so, they are reflected off the initial structure like an echo bouncing off a wall. To begin with, this process of manifestation and reflection is rather open, but the interplay of allowed events and provisional structure establishes a process of 'feedback' that consolidates the 'field' by defining its structure further.

With each move toward consolidation, the range of alternatives available narrows. Further specification solidifies the 'walls' of the structure; as a result, the 'reflecting activity' intensifies, becoming almost unceasing. Each new activity or appearance is echoed back on itself, contributing to the structure as a whole.

Succeeding actions or appearances within such a structured 'field' are the outcome of previous reflections that specify and determine what will be allowed. Such determinants form a 'lineage' that shapes possibilities, in the same way a family tradition may determine a way of life for countless generations. As intersecting lineages merge, each element comes to share the same substance or body—the same space and time and the same patterns of knowledge.

Understood in this sense, whatever arises 'embodies' or expresses the 'field' as a whole. It is this process of embodiment, viewed as the net outcome of 'field interactions', that could be said to bring the 'field' into being.

The emerging 'field' within which appearance manifests is dynamic, incorporating time and events as well as physical space and objects. If we think of the earth as having gathered together out of interstellar dust, the dust, the gathering, the contributing circumstances, and the 'laws' that permit such events but not others all form part of the 'field'. The beginning of time 'belongs' to the 'field', together with the possibility (or impossibility) of a time 'before' the beginning or a space 'outside' the physical universe.

The knowing that knows objects in space is a part of the 'field' as well. Like matter and space, knower and known are given together and exist in reference to each other. And since the knowing that knows objects determines the nature of thought, the human way of thinking likewise emerges within the 'field'. The infinitely complex sequence that has culminated in our entertaining these present thoughts is a specific instance of the 'field interaction' of events on countless levels, all of which are 'given' together.

Without the 'field' that 'gives' space, time, and knowledge, space could not be boundless or time beginningless, nor could knowledge know. But the 'field' itself is not part of what is given. Its 'reality' is not a claim to be proved or disproved, because the 'field' *establishes* what is real or not real. Nor is the 'field' a conceptual structure to be judged true or false, because the 'field' encompasses the possibility of making such judgments. Although the 'field' could be thought of as a logical necessity (as conventional space seems to be a necessity for objects), logic does not prove its 'existence', for logic operates only when the 'field' is already 'in place'.

To investigate the 'nature' of this invariably indeterminate 'field', we could look more closely at 'field operations'. In conventional space, time, and knowledge, form and matter are constantly changing into what surrounds them, like air bubbles in a rushing stream. Space that is occupied now will be unoccupied in the next moment, and events are ever in flux. This 'field dynamic' is acknowledged through such terms as 'impermanence', 'entropy', 'evolution', and 'flow of energy'. Mirrored in countless ways on both the microscopic and the macroscopic levels, the 'field dynamic' calls into question all claims to substantiality.

The prevailing dynamic thus presents shape and form as akin to the image displayed on a television screen— an evanescent configuration of 'particles' that gives an impression of relative stability. As particular configurations are accommodated in space, a current situation of emptiness changes into one of occupancy, and an existent 'shows up', available to be identified and defined. Later, when the specific dynamic that has brought this existent into play has worked itself out, the entity will disappear again, yielding to the emptiness of space.

Field Dynamics

POTENTIAL FOR EXISTENCE

Focusing on the 'field dynamic' shifts attention from particular existents toward the 'field' itself. What comes into existence takes its direction and orientation from the 'field' and unfolds in accord with 'mechanisms' that the 'field' allows. Though human life may endure for a century and a mountain range may remain intact for millions of years, both are simply expressions of a dynamic that unfolds in accord with specific mechanisms. The identities assigned specific objects are projections based on the concerns and predispositions of the knowing subject—the 'bystander'—but these projections in turn reflect the interplay of underlying 'dynamics' and 'mechanics'. Thus even space, considered as unchanging and unconditioned, is an expression of the 'field dynamic'.

The measured and defined world that arises as human beings assign meanings and names comes complete with its own claims to authenticity. To consider the known world as projections arising within a 'field' challenges these claims in a way that can be difficult to 'make sense of'. Still, it seems clear that each claim to authenticity has its origin in the specific orientations allowed for by the whole. The meanings and structures through which an 'existing thing' is identified depend on making comparisons, differentiating that 'thing' from everything else given together with it. 'Inside' and 'outside', as well as 'this' and 'that', are a matter of designations based on belief and definition.

Each 'this' and each 'that', each 'here' and 'there' implicates the 'field' as a whole. The object at 'the center' and the directions that radiate out from it are again definable only in terms that involve all the rest of what appears. In the physical realm, even the all-important distinction between form and space, through which alone the object can be established, turns out to rest on particular acts of knowing that the 'field' accommodates.

This is not to say that from a 'field perspective' form is 'only' space, or that the conventional distinction between the two is 'nonexistent'. The mind recognizes and supports the distinction between occupied and unoccupied space; it is simply that *the assertion of this distinction, together with the mind that accepts it, is a part of the 'field'*. 'Internal' claims for authenticity are not 'wrong', but they are also not stopping points for inquiry. If we choose to decline the ongoing invitation to confine knowing to the structured entities and processes 'given' by the 'field', and determine to investigate instead 'field dynamics and mechanics', conventional distinctions appear in a new light.

From a standard, existence-centered orientation, the 'field' that allows space and the objects within space might be understood as a kind of seed, a *potential for existence* that itself 'exists'. On the other hand, it seems clear that this view is too limited, for 'existence' itself is allowed for *within* the 'field'.

When the 'field-determined' mind, bound up with structures of existence, approaches the 'field' in terms of 'potential', issues of origin remain mysterious. Up to a certain point there is no existence; from then on, for reasons unknown, there is. Creation becomes an inexplicable primordial event: There is no way to determine how its potential is activated. The continuing moment-to-moment appearance of the known world—another kind of creation that usually goes unacknowledged—is simply another aspect of this mystery.

To investigate in a way that does not rely on this standard orientation, let us begin by turning away from what exists. At once we encounter space, which might be described as the absence of existence. Space, however, is not simply absence, for it 'possesses' the power to allow objects. Since the 'field' 'includes' space, perhaps we could assign the 'field' the similar power to 'make possible', in the sense that beauty makes possible art or sound makes possible music. To guard against linking the 'field' understood in this way to existence, we can go further and say that a specific 'mode of existence' appears within the 'field of the possible' as the *negation of its impossibility.*

Since this negation in turn must be allowed by the 'field', it seems that we must refine our understanding still further. We might say that the 'field' 'comprises' the 'not nonexistence' of the possibility. More precisely, a particular mode of existence can arise when obstacles to such existence (which do not themselves implicate substantiality) are not 'not not-there'.

The usual orientation makes this approach seem convoluted. How can anything originate from a 'not', let alone a 'not not'? But we should recall that such ready rejection is based on a logic in which the mystery of creation or origination is dismissed in favor of the 'field-givenness' of specific premises. The 'not not', in contrast, expresses the power of *allowing* at work in creation.

Perhaps it is because we must strain against the limits of first-level language and ways of knowing that the approach being investigated here seems difficult or forbidding. If we could set those ways of knowing aside, the not 'not not-thereness' of an obstacle to becoming *as* the 'source' of that becoming *might* seem natural, even self-evident.

A simple, somewhat limited analogy may help clarify this point. Electrons can flow in an electrical circuit only when the circuit is closed. If we take the initial state as one where no flow is occurring, we can represent this by the 'presence' of a gap between two points:

X   X

On the other hand, if this gap is 'not there' the circuit will flow:

$$X\underline{\qquad\qquad}X$$

At this point in the analogy, either the circuit 'exists' or it does not. But how could the state of not-existing be transformed into one of existence; how could something new be created? The *potential* for creation can be implicitly present as the 'not not-thereness' of the gap as an *obstacle* to creation:

$$X\text{---------------}X$$

And for this 'potential' to be actualized, the 'not not-thereness' of the gap must be negated through 'not':

$$X + + + + + +X$$

Dynamic manifestation within the 'field'—here, the flow of electrons—can be traced to the allowing encompassed in this final 'not'.

'Field allowing' opens a completely new way of understanding how existence comes to be. We cannot consider this to be a new account of 'creation', for 'creation' is too firmly bound to a first-level understanding of 'existence'. Instead, we can simply say that in encompassing negation, the 'field' allows appearance to appear.

Since the appearing of appearance is implicit in the 'field' as a whole, it is omnipresent in terms of conventional space and time. What first-level understanding would designate as 'creation' cannot be assigned to a particular temporal location (such as 'the beginning of time'), for the temporal structure that permits such assignment is part of what is given by the 'field'.

Understood in terms of the 'field dynamic', 'creation' is the universal allowing of all possible 'field configurations', whether they 'did' exist, 'will' exist, or 'are' now in existence. Conventional temporal causality, with its structures of creation and destruction, simply expresses this patterning as it arises and takes shape.

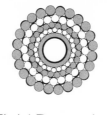

Field Dynamics

FIELD MECHANISM

From a 'first-level' point of view, the potential for existence is actualized through a mechanism being set in motion. But what determines the patterning of this mechanism? How can it be established in advance that assumed regularities in operation will reliably come into play? From the first level, no answer is forthcoming, but in terms of 'field allowing' we might say that the 'field dynamic' assures these regularities *by not preventing them.*

We could represent this mechanism of non-prevention by a dotted line between two points:

X - - - - - - - - - - X

The dotted line suggests that 'initially' there is no guarantee for the regularity of the mechanism. At any moment, its operation could be interrupted:

A - - - -| B

But within the 'field', such interruptions do not arise. The potential gaps are filled in; the regularities of the mechanism are assured because there is no prospect of their being prevented:

A———————B

It is almost as though a 'blueprint' had been drawn up in advance and now attracts appearance, as a magnet attracts iron filings or chromosomes determine that an emerging form of life will take a particular shape.

This relationship between allowing and appearance might be expressed by saying that 'possibility' precedes 'actuality'. But even understood atemporally, this formulation remains too closely tied to first-level structures. Perhaps it is more accurate to say that the whole is invariant, because no single time or place or manifestation is separated out. Historically there may be a time when there is existence and a time when there is not, with an 'act of creation' bridging the two, but this historical view arises within the 'field', and so does not present the 'field totality'. Without having this 'totality' in view, there will be no opportunity to challenge structures *within* the 'field' by calling their substantiality into question.

This line of investigation suggests a principle that might prove useful in guiding inquiry along new paths:

Awareness of 'not the field totality', *arrived at through open and allowing inquiry,* gives access to the 'field' as the active allowing (non-prevention) of all that does not 'not-exist'.

Any 'field' manifests a structure of allowing: an expression of the 'field dynamic'. For example, first-level space and time express a particular form of structural discontinuity that is reflected in the appearance of individual existent entities. Such 'field structures' could be said to embody more or less sharpness, clarity, and even 'allowingness'. Ordinarily such qualities vary through a range that is largely fixed and unalterable. But a focus on the 'dynamic' that sets up this structure suggests that if the dynamic itself were subject to change, possibilities for greater clarity and a more accommodating allowing might emerge.

We might consider the 'field dynamic' as manifesting through the 'rhythms' that present characteristic temporal patterns and sequences, setting up the 'feedback system' out of which the given 'realities' of the 'field' emerge. Such patterns are not imposed on the 'field' or its contents from outside (though the 'field' itself may support the 'accuracy' of such an interpretation); rather, they express the accepted ways for the elements that appear within the 'field' to interact. Activated by the 'rhythm' at work in the 'field', they are 'carriers' for the fundamental energy of the 'field dynamic', like the genes that carry a specific biological trait.

The 'rhythm' of the 'field dynamic' could be said to determine what the 'field structure' will 'make room for' in accord with the operation of 'field mechanics'. Lower-level space and time, together with the consciousness that knows objects appearing in that space and time, are allowed by the prevailing dynamic, together with more specific patterns and structures such as the emotions, the senses, volitional activity, and the arising of experience over time.

The interrelations among these elements both express and contribute to the dynamic. They pulse with energy that defines, shapes, and reflects, sustaining an ongoing momentum that activates the 'rhythm' of the 'field'. Intrinsic to the 'field' in which we operate, they do not simply present an interesting reformulation of what appears to awareness in conventional terms, but can be directly experienced.

Emphasis on 'rhythms' can help counteract any tendency to understand the 'field' as a structured and defined entity accessible to 'first-level' knowledge. 'Field mechanics' allow for 'objects' that can be 'known' in 'ways' that accord with a specific temporal sequence. However, these structures express a 'dynamic' that is not itself structured—a rhythmic interplay that 'establishes' no substance. Thus, the model that speaks of 'fields' must be understood as preliminary and transitional in nature. Though rich in new perspectives and possibilities, it is still very much linked to first-level entitative understanding.

Whatever appears is affirmed as part of a specific 'field'. Almost automatically, 'field dynamics and mechanics' polarize what has been affirmed. Desire and frustration, having and losing, distance and separation all become characteristic. Through the 'field feedback mechanism', the 'feel' of the 'field' is referred back to the 'order', confirming and sustaining its patterns as 'existent'.

The structures formed in this way seal off the open allowing of space and the ever-present dynamic of time, hiding from view the knowledge that each and every pattern embodies. There are no openings for something different, and no time to wake up. Psychologies, religious traditions, and philosophies conform to these structures; even if they sometimes point beyond themselves to a more inclusive and incisive knowing, their message is subverted by a self that insists on the old 'order'.

Unaware of what opportunities are being lost, the self feeds on hopes for 'improvement'. Though it may yearn for what it 'knows' is located 'elsewhere', it finds it overwhelmingly difficult to find or act upon any 'alternatives'. In subtle but stubborn ways, the self holds fast to a not-knowing it has learned to consider its own. The self becomes a spokesperson for the prevailing 'order', proclaiming the anticipated repetition of the patterns it finds in operation. Memory and present awareness are edited or recast to eliminate whatever might suggest otherwise.

And yet the daily truth of human life is based not on sameness and substance, but on universal change. Events are all in flux, constant only in returning again and again to the same patterns and concerns. The time of each experience is different, passing away with the experience itself. Sameness too is a process—the ongoing recreation of what is presented as unchanged. And what of the self—can we truly say that it alone is constant?

Challenging the self and its claims allows us to look at the content of experience from a wider perspective. For example, we can focus on the unceasing change *within* each given structure, or investigate the patterns of wanting in relation to feeling and to knowing. Looking in this way, we might find that change and transition, no matter what their flavor or 'feel', become opportunities for enjoyment, appreciation, and knowledge.

Field Dynamics

FEEL OF SPACE

Direct your attention to the stream of thoughts. At the first level, one thought arises and then disappears, to be replaced by the next, like a smoothly functioning computer program. At a second level, attention can shift to what happens when the thought comes to an end; sensitively observed, the thought 'opens' into a kind of space—a 'deprogramming' in which it becomes clear that the stream of mental chatter is not necessary.

Beyond this, there is a third level, at which it is no longer necessary to make a sharp distinction between thoughts and the space between them, for the thoughts also appear as space. A way into this awareness is to focus on the 'opening' of thought into space in such a way that you both see and do not see it. This might be considered a 'reprogramming', in which old distinctions and concerns are no longer operative.

COMMENTARY

One way to understand the practice of this exercise is to see what it is not. When a thought disappears into openness, we can validly inquire 'where' it disappears to. But here we are simply exploring directly the quality of opening. Opening to the 'feel' of space in this way communicates a knowledge that makes it possible to act without having to adopt new structures.

Certain ways of questioning thoughts depend for their effectiveness on replacing old concepts with new ones. For example, we may try to replace feelings of guilt or pain with feelings of acceptance and well-being. But such an approach affirms the underlying structure of concepts and judgments: It simply reverses the directionality of certain judgments or else 'works with' concepts to change their content. The present approach is quite different, for it starts by simply seeing the thinking mind in operation. The result is powerful: In the very moment that it is seen directly in this way, the mind disappears.

This could be just the right moment to ask the question mentioned above: Where does a thought go when it goes? The question would be asked not for the sake of establishing an answer, but to acknowledge after thorough inquiry that we do not know, to get clear on the difference between knowing and not-knowing, and perhaps to try to know what is unknown, or else acknowledge in what sense the known is also unknown.

Inquiry on this level can be tremendously valuable, but it continues to accept certain points as being in operation. Even though the thinking mind has disappeared, its legacy shapes the inquiry. New possibilities open, but these possibilities are understood as alternative structures that will be 'built up' in the same way as the past structures that have now momentarily disappeared.

Going directly to the 'feel' of open space offers an alternative to these approaches. Here the mind can enjoy more beauty, accepting a standing invitation to 'enter' a different realm in which there is nothing for the mind to do. Within the 'feel', the display of personality becomes the play of freely manifesting patterns. Seeing *itself* frees the rhythm of appearance, making seeing a partner to allowing. The outcome is knowledge that is richer and more penetrating. 'Doer' and 'doing' become aspects of action rather than separate entities. Practice of the exercise invites an analytical and therapeutic observation— an evocation of knowledge.

We might imagine that Space has made an investment in appearance. We are the inheritors of that investment, and if we use it wisely, it will enable us to communicate fully the prospects for human being. Or perhaps we can go further—Space has already invested wisely, in a way that gives our lives their worth and being. If we explore without presuppositions, we can discover for ourselves the wealth that space has accumulated. We can see that space is alive; not bound by a 'from-to' structure because it does not insist on origination. Nor is there even the more subtle structure of 'to–to–to'—this space to this space to this space, or form to space, or space to form.

When Space is understood in this way, objects appear as treasures of tremendous beauty and luxury. Sound, too, appears differently, so that communication and even meaning can come directly from Space.

The exploration that makes Space available is deeply enjoyable, even humorous, alive in a unique way. If we exercise this exploration for even a short time, we understand the Space of Time, the Space of Knowledge, the Space of Space. We see the Space of the object, the subject, the senses, the body. We may find changes in our ability to encompass the power of the mind and action, and gain new control over behavior.

The 'feel' of space is available even in the midst of tension, pain, or suffering, as their 'background'—the inner 'no-structure' structure. Just to recognize pain as the 'feel' of space has a deeply healing quality. It is almost magical, like a transformation that restores to wholeness what had been shattered.

With Space as the great magician, there seems no need for anything else. There is a wealth of wellness, a hidden wholeness. Alive to space, we hear a silent whisper that has always been there, offering unheard of well-being. It as almost as though we were exercising a space therapy, based on 'no direction'. At the very center, at the most located and situated place of all, with lines and lineages in all directions, Great Space is alive and active.

Senses in Space

MAGICAL ALLOWING

One possible analogy for the interplay of the mental and physical realms would be to compare the mental realm to a blueprint that shapes the 'order' of the physical realm. Yet the blueprint can accomplish this task only if it plays an active, structuring role, wholly engaged in the activity it shapes, somehow calling that activity 'into play'. And it would almost have to be a 'magical' blueprint, creating what it specified, linking what was understood as separate.

This magic is already at work in our accustomed world. Without the 'mystery' of mind-body coordination, the consciousness and knowing that shape our fundamental being could never arise. We may think of everyday occurrences as being ordinary, but in its deepest structures the world as we conceive it is largely inconceivable.

The magic of the world can operate only with space as its allowing 'background'. Space offers its own 'magic':

211

instant operation arising out of an active 'background', an interplay of multiple dimensionality. The physical organism is allowed by space, but so are the activities of coordination, communication, and interaction. A magnificent 'spatial mechanism' or 'field' accommodates consciousness, the stirring of emotions, and the rhythms of action *together* with the beating of the heart, the circulation of the blood, and the transmission of neural impulses.

The allowing by space of sensory objects is no less magical. Without space, sound cannot be heard and form cannot appear, nor is there a basis for smelling, tasting, or touching. If light did not shine 'through' space or sound propagate, the world could not be known. And what of the special 'aliveness' through which knowledge senses such displays? Though this 'aliveness' seems closely related to memory, intuition, and the capacity for creative expression, it can also be referred to such physical structures as the brain and nervous system. At some level, the 'aliveness' of sensory knowledge must be allowed by space as well.

'Magic' in a very different sense operates with regard to communication. For speech to originate, the energies of the throat must interact almost instantaneously with functions of the brain and capacities of the senses and mind; for speech to be understood, a similar process must take place. Somehow the outcome of the whole intricate interaction must be made conscious and then mysteriously transformed into meaning.

The magic of space as the allowing 'background' for the senses is somewhat like the familiar 'magic' of contemporary technology. Silicon chips, assembled into shapes of incredible intricacy, channel a flow of electrons so small that they stream by the billions through miniscule wires. Laws that govern the structures of ordinary reality are suspended; for example, sophisticated electronics project on a screen detailed images of objects that in reality are much larger.

The scientific model rejects any characterization of such processes as magical, but if we look carefully at the explanations offered for feats of technology, they are never quite complete. In the workings of electronic equipment, how are subatomic particles transmitted through space? Do electrons travel one by one? Do they arrive in order? For transmission to occur, there must be space at the originating point and at the receiving end. Is this space unitary? How is its availability for transmission and communication assured?

Although we know how to manipulate the subtle exchanges that make such transformations possible, we cannot fully account for them. Without the pronouncements of a systematized 'field' of knowledge to assure us otherwise, would we so readily hesitate to call such manifestations magical?

We have been taught to distrust what cannot be explained, but the remarkable complexity of sensory interactions leaves explanation far behind. Attempts to 'reduce' mental to physical or vice-versa seem drastic oversimplifications of a manifold allowing. The mechanisms at work seem more subtle, and the 'space' that accommodates them more powerful than our usual models suggest. Something seems left out, and it is this 'something' we point to when we speak of the operation of the senses in space as 'magical'. Regard for such 'magic' might make the operation of the senses more fully available to our knowing.

The operation of the senses 'across' conventional distinctions such as mind and body suggests that 'space' may enclose hidden dimensions in which accustomed distinctions lose their significance. We may want to investigate closely: Perhaps the magical 'blueprint' or 'mechanism' whose active expression 'space' allows *includes* 'conventional' space within its operations.

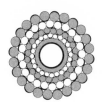

SENSE-FIELD
DYNAMIC

O rdinarily, reason remains bound to the mechanisms it identifies. Oblivious to more intimate rhythms that might be expressed in the underlying 'field dynamic', it imposes the closed order of causality and explanations. Once the natural rhythm is cut off, knowledge becomes the exception in a world where not-knowing is primary. Actions guided by this new, superimposed 'order' are 'out of rhythm' and tend toward disharmony. Through a characteristic 'feedback mechanism', this disharmony becomes the 'atmosphere' of the 'field' in which it operates.

Seen as expressions of the 'field', however, the operative patterns of knowledge, including both reason and the structures and entities that reason validates, *remain available* as a creative expression of the space-time-knowledge dynamic allowed within the 'field'. Inquiry that proceeds in this light could invite a knowledge not bound by the 'field mechanics' to emerge.

One way to tune in more directly to 'field dynamics and mechanics' is to cultivate awareness of the first-level *interaction* of space, time, and knowledge. Then the 'field' itself can be appreciated as the projection of second-level 'space', understood as a 'fullness' that allows the creation of existent 'points' in 'first-level' space and time.

In its 'fullness', second-level 'space' is inseparable from the vitality of 'time' and the 'knowingness' of knowledge. Even on the first-level, where space, time, and knowledge can be understood as 'allowing conditions' 'set up' by 'field structures', this deeper interaction is hinted at. We can find its traces when we look away from the content of first-level experience to the vastness of physical space, the unceasing flow of time, and the infinite range of the knowable.

The physical realm as we *experience* it could be said to consist of our bodies with their internal structure, the senses, and the objects of the senses. In addition, a special relationship holds between each sense and its object, as though sense faculty and object inhabited the same environment or 'sense-field'. Perhaps we could say that this relationship (or its unknown 'sense-field') is part of the physical realm as well.

What is this shared relationship? If it depends on a 'sense-field', how is it that sense and sense object come to share the 'field'? How do they communicate within the 'field'—across what borders? And how is knowledge obtained within one 'sense-field' coordinated with knowledge from the other 'sense-fields' to establish the object as a whole? When we reflect on such questions, the usual distinction that separates the mental realm from the physical becomes difficult to maintain. The senses link body and awareness so deeply that it seems arbitrary to separate them.

For sensing to take place, rhythms of motion create physical activity that is somehow inherently coordinated with the mental. The body itself seems to comprise the physical and mental together; the body might even be described as a network of such junctures, communicating, stimulating, and making distinctions.

The structures and dynamic of a particular 'sense-field' can be investigated through its characteristic interactions and law-like regularities. However, this investigation will also be taking place within the 'field', structured by the knowledge allowed by 'field mechanics' and activated in accord with 'field dynamics'.

The 'field dynamics and mechanics' will ordinarily not be available for investigation directly, even though the properties they establish are 'distributed' throughout the 'field'. For first-level experience, investigation will invariably disclose 'physical' space as a 'container' for objects, together with a governing temporal order and a specific 'knowing capacity' or awareness. Shaped in these ways, a 'world' will appear to a 'self', ready to be experienced and affected and to cause effects in turn.

Knowledge too will be confined within characteristic structures, for example, 'subject knowing object', 'distance between knower and known', and 'original not-knowing'. In accord with the 'field mechanics', deductive and inductive reasoning will operate as forceful mechanisms for implementing the 'field dynamic', establishing, legitimating, or maintaining the 'existent' structures and governing mechanisms.

Senses in Space

FACE TO FACE

The picture of a knower receiving information about an outside world suggests that there are two kinds of space: the 'inner' space of the knower/bystander and the 'outer' space that contains what there is to be known. We cannot really say how these two spaces are connected, except that somehow the senses and body seem to have the capacity to operate in both realms.

If we wanted to investigate the interaction of these 'two spaces', we might say that initially subject and object face each other. Yet this may already say too much. The spatial orientation 'face to face' is possible only after directions have been assigned, and this requires that various elements of the physical world first be identified and located in space.

Initially, then, the communication on which knowledge depends seems to occur within a whole which functions without partition or blockage. Within this whole, whose unity could be said to make communication possible, form finds expression through the operation of time. Unless expression, operation, and communication 'took' time, everything would arise at once, and no distinctions could be made. We could say that this 'taking time' is activated through the rhythm of the senses and perception, reaching out to know 'things' that stand 'outside' the perceiver.

When mind and senses reach out to know, they seem to have available certain labels that can be traced to prior communication. As these labels are applied and are further specified, the unity that originally allows communication gives way to parts and positions. It is as though we took the flickering of a candle flame as defining a whole world of individual flickers, and then assigned each its own identity.

If this model is accurate, it seems difficult to say whether what is experienced is real or whether it amounts to one label confirming another, in accord with the unfolding rhythm of knowing. For the most part, however, this question is understood as only theoretically interesting. Human beings fully accept the presentations of conventional knowledge as being real and meaningful. They identify and give meanings, offer reasons and justifications, determine consequences, and assign praise and blame accordingly. Labeled experiences produce reactions, including hope and fear in all their many variations.

Tied to specific positions, the known world grows tight and solid, dark and heavy. Heart and head and other physical organs react strongly to this solidification, which finds expression in gesture and communication. Pressure builds up, reflecting force and restriction, and sense 'experience' actually shrinks in scope.

As sense experience unfolds in this way, an initial openness is lost. It is like a spring day on which radiant sunshine gives way to gathering clouds. The threat of rain, at first distant, intensifies; the first few drops quicken into a heavy downpour that plunges the world into gloom.

Such a process shuts down the allowing power of space. The atmosphere becomes oppressive. Constant storms roil the air—emotional outbursts, unforeseen eruptions, ever-gathering tension and anxiety.

Yet even when such reactions and formations seem to fill up space completely, what has really changed from the initial state of unity and dynamic wholeness? The rhythms of oppression are simply the expression of an established 'mechanism.' Though potent in their own right, they need not condition our possibilities. Even when the world appears to the senses as frozen and solid, it communicates the vision of open and unbounded space. After all, when it rains, does space get wet? Does lightning slice space? Do clouds fill it?

Once we let go of the usual restricted 'focal setting' on experience, seeing, hearing, tasting, feeling, and thinking are significant less for the content they communicate or the 'atmosphere' they support than for their arising. Whatever appears is a display of a power that has been little explored.

This power manifests in all appearance, making objects and even emotions into expressions of beauty, light, joy, and meaning. An exhibition in space, allowed and invited by light, available to knowledge, the realm of the senses retains the dynamic of its originating rhythm.

Human culture can be understood as the outcome of a play allowed by space, exhibited by time, and presented to knowledge. Understood in terms of conventional history and the conventional 'order', the *play* involves us in a *drama* of repetition and routine, punctuated only occasionally by moments when individuals or whole cultures bring something truly new into the world.

The play of experience as revealed to the senses offers these same dimensions and tends to unfold in the same unfruitful ways. While certain aspects of experience suggest a natural evolution over time toward greater refinement, we are too caught up in the dramas of the temporal order to be aware of this evolution as either actual or potential, and may even work against it. Conditioned by our circumstances, we respond passively to each situation, losing the opportunity to choose what accords with a growing beauty. We act randomly, letting unknown dimensions of significance slip unseen from view.

On a certain level, we are aware that something has been lost, that we are not living in accord with our own potential. Through attention to the body and senses, we may be able to trace this awareness into the realm of emotion and anxiety. The psychology of 'lostness' unfolds as pressure and heaviness, and often manifests as an inability to cope, a sense that the burdens we must shoulder are truly unbearable.

We may grow to feel that there is no room left, no way out, no real alternatives. We may withdraw into sullen torpor, or else explode in outbursts that give vent to our inner frustration and agitation. In either case the drama continues, with the limitations it imposes growing increasingly impervious.

But there is another way we could respond. Instead of enacting the drama in a way that leaves us no choice, we can take the play as a source of natural enjoyment and entertainment. Without confining ourselves to the passive role of spectators, we can let the play unfold with a sense of deep appreciation for its pageantry, inventiveness, and creative power.

When our appreciation lets space display appearance as magical, we become allies of knowledge. Open to meaning without assigning 'meanings', we can play our role forward until the growth of knowledge takes to the fore. Aware of the intrinsic significance of what appears *as appearance,* we can participate in the evolution of refinement. We can let knowledge manifest fully, expressing it in our actions and our communications with the world and with others. Transmitting knowledge through our own being, we can respond to the rhythms of time as ever dynamic and ever creative.

When knowledge emerges *within* the restrictions and borders that make up conventional appearance, the 'allowingness' of space enters 'into' form. Knowledge sees the attributes of form and formlessness alike as 'attributes' of 'space', while existence and nonexistence express the active embodiment of the 'space blueprint'.

The emerging or not-emerging of specific points in space and time—empirically, psychologically, intellectually —show knowledge in operation. The specific subtleties of available attributes express the varying accelerations of patterns of significance.

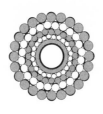

Senses in Space

SPACE COMMUNICATION

A. Take some time to investigate the operation of the five senses. In the beginning it is probably best to focus on one sense for an extended period of time; later you may want to try shifting rapidly among them. As you tune in to the operation of each sense, investigate the possibility that what sense perception perceives is a communication 'by' space—space communicating space. At the same time, let the activity of sensing also have the nature of space. How does 'space communication' empower the contact between the sense in operation and the qualities that the sense perceives?

B. Extend the practice of sense awareness to mental experience, exploring the communication of space in memory, awareness, intention, motive, and imaging. In accord with the more open knowing of the senses free from judgments, let the 'feel' of experience be unknown and indeterminate.

COMMENTARY

Previous exercises have explored the possibility that appreciation for space could open the realm of the physical. The present exercise extends that prospect to a realm intrinsically less committed to the conventional structures of subject and object, though normally situated squarely within those structures. It calls for opening the operation of the senses in a very thoroughgoing way.

Opening the senses involves the entire 'field' within which sense perception arises. For instance, it is not just the quality of sound that can be opened to 'space as communication', but also the one who hears, the act of hearing, and the background against which that hearing takes place. Initially, this means also opening whatever 'interferes' with sensing, especially distinctions based on thought processes and labels.

Although the senses are usually closed down, this feeling of restriction can be eased by relaxing into the 'feel' of space as expressed in the 'quality' of sense communication. Open to the 'feel', not interfering, judging, or classifying, we can experience in new ways, such as hearing sound beyond sound, or enjoying the texture of space. It is like seeing things not seen before, or discovering a nourishing energy within simple experiences. Since the mind no longer has to busy itself juggling the various labels it assigns experience, the 'feel' of vastness intrinsic to 'space communication' can be opened. Instead of the quick, dreamlike transitions of ordinary consciousness, a fullness and·wholeness become available.

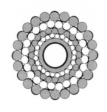

Allowing Matrix

FULL ALLOWING

S pace can accommodate appearance without limitation because it is completely open. It comes from no
background and has taken no position. It is not a candidate or partisan; it takes no one's part; it excludes no one.
Whereas any object or form, any thought or identity, has
its own truth to maintain and so can accommodate only
what 'belongs' within its domain, Space 'belongs' nowhere, and so can allow fully. It has a fundamental gen-
erosity, based on the strength of not needing to maintain.
Like white light, which permits all colors, Space permits
possibilities to exhibit in all their variation. Never participating, never occupying, it never excludes. Only
through Space can 'gravity' work its way.

When we understand this Great Space, we see that
within Space there can be no gaps. What would they
consist of? What would accommodate them? Shape and
form present themselves as such gaps: structures in

which the open accommodation of space no longer operates. But integral to each measurement and extension, each distinction and differentiation, is the openness that allows this structure to appear. Beginnings and endings, borders and limits are all relative expressions of this fundamental accommodation of Great Space.

Space allows all such limitations without regard for sequence, contradiction, or definition. The prevailing temporal order and its 'field' are simply certain possibilities among others. Expanding and contracting are simultaneous and instantaneous, and the unfolding of linear time is another expression of the infinite riches of Space. Active without foundation, center, direction, or occupancy, Great Space offers something heretofore unknown: the complete openness, beyond potential, of an infinitely allowing matrix.

If first-level space is thought of as the total embodiment of a single point in time, Great Space might be viewed as the complete accommodation within which all points are inseparably one. Ultimately, however, it is inaccurate to speak of either 'one point' or 'simultaneous' in connection with the allowing capacity of Space. Even when expressed solely for the purpose of being contradicted, such expressions establish a point, and to 'establish' is to lose full openness and accommodation. In Great Space there is no transition 'from' or 'to', for there are no positions to be inherited. Yet even without transitions, transformation is always possible. It is inherent in an arising that does not take sides—in an arising that is not committed to 'past' and 'future' or 'here' and 'there'.

When we investigate, we see that Great Space cannot be known directly in any ordinary sense. The 'surround' of Space has no characteristics, and so cannot be 'built up' by human consciousness. Yet within Great Space, Great Knowledge is inherent. We do not have to attain a second-level space or knowing: Each known point, as it is, is a gateway to the allowing that accommodates that point. Space as allowing is ever present, always ready to accommodate Knowledge. Only our patterns do not allow it; only because the self 'sets things up' and 'in-habits' a world do we find ourselves confined within specifics.

Looking at the postures of the self and the attitudes of the mind, investigating our mental patterns and questioning their innermost logic, we can purify our knowing and challenge our confinement. We can concentrate in a new way—not by intensifying our concern until space becomes dense and heavy, but by focusing without taking a position or 'building up', allowing an openness in which anything and everything can appear, without limitation. Our questions can express a different dynamic, a vital energy inaccessible to the rhythms of conventional knowledge.

If, in the course of this inquiry, the old assertions prove hollow, we can follow the 'hollow' into the allowing negation of Great Space, searching out a more direct knowing of what allows. Space can open to Time, and Time can focus Space. Created and uncreated, form and formless can reveal themselves as manifestations of the magical transformations that Space allows.

Allowing Matrix

ALLOWING GIFT

W hatever interpretations we put forward to 'make sense' of our experience, the entity or entities we postulate and the patterns we accept will depend on an allowing matrix. All appearance seems to require a 'surround', an openness that lets it be. Within that 'surround' specific content will develop, depending on the tools we use to investigate, the language and concepts we bring to bear, and the logic we apply.

Because conventional understanding favors the polarity 'existence' over 'nonexistence', first-level space, space 'empty of existence', is considered 'nothing at all'. But without the allowing that shines forth *through* first-level space, 'existents' could not appear. We can accept an absolute or not; we can regard the conditional and impermanent as real or as constructs. Whatever our observations and conclusions, what manifests requires 'room'. Perhaps we understand appearance as illusion;

even so, the illusion requires space of some sort in which to appear. Perhaps the space in which physical entities appear is also an illusion. Yet this space must also be allowed: It appears within a 'field' that allows for both illusion and reality, and this 'field' in turn discloses Great Space, the matrix of allowing.

Allowing is an exceptional gift, one that in turn gives everything else. As that which allows, Great Space makes creation possible. This is true whether or not creation implies a 'from' or a 'to' or a 'not'; whether or not we can speak in terms of how, where, who, and when. It is true whatever our logic and our presuppositions.

Just as an exhibit in a museum exists both as an exhibit and as the specific work it claims to be, so Great Space 'exhibits' appearance both as an exhibition by 'space' and as what it 'is'. What Space exhibits, however, is not confined to the entities of the physical world. It encompasses those other realms of our being that disclose our full human potential. There is complete permissiveness, free from blockages and restrictions, without edges or limits. All qualities and characteristics, no matter how subtle, arise within the active and accommodating matrix of Great Space.

The openness of Space is linked to Knowledge through the power of negation. The 'not' distinguishes and defines, and thus allows qualities and characteristics to arise. Such power is inseparable from the surround that is Space, which on the first level has long been understood as the negation of matter and of that which matters.

The knowledge that founds the conventional temporal order substitutes for the allowing exhibited by Great Space the *structure* that 'places' a self within first-order time and space. This structure is based on assertion rather than negation, 'establishing' rather than 'exhibiting'; accordingly, it has 'room' for some forms of appearance but not for others. Whether our time is adequate or meaningful, whether there is an untapped capacity behind ordinary awareness, will depend on the restricted allowing of the established structure. The greater allowing that exhibits the structure itself remains hidden from view.

The temporal order draws on the accommodating capacity of Space by allowing knowledge that builds up the world of appearance and experience. Such 'building up' is an interpretation of the exhibitory power of Great Space, based on assimilating what is exhibited to the model 'existence'. Although ultimately empowered by the not-knowing of negation and the allowing of Space, 'building up' moves toward the concrete and substantive. The knowing self interprets the capacity of Space to accommodate appearance as the power of its own consciousness to establish existence.

Even this establishing, however, is not directly acknowledged. Instead, the self interprets itself as inhabiting a preexisting world. Knowledge is limited to the knowing of this 'in-habited' world. *A knowledge that would open to a deeper allowing can be exhibited only as not-knowing.*

Since the beginning, we have taken the position that the self is at the center of the structure revealed by the temporal order. We proceed in the world by moving backward, forward, and outward from the self. The self names objects and acts as subject; it judges the appearances that space exhibits, favoring objects over space. The 'field' of experience unfolds in accord with just this mechanism. There is no other possibility. For taking this position, we have paid the price of separation from the world, adopting the specific mode of being of the 'bystander'.

But from the 'perspective' of Great Space, *this separation is just another interpretation.*

We can see this in terms of a second-level focus on the 'field' within which the self is given together with the object. The distinction between self and world is 'real enough', but it has no solid basis. Self and world are embodied equally, together with first-level space. There is no disconnection from what appears in space, for the self itself is a patterning of manifestations, exhibited 'in' or 'by' or 'of' Great Space.

Allowing Matrix

FOLLOWING OUT INSEPARABILITY

Although it would be misleading to say that space 'exists', there is a sense in which we can say that it 'operates'. The 'structure' of space *as what allows* is implicit in all that we experience. Though space is neither the source 'from' which objects arise, nor the preexisting 'cause' of what appears, when we look at the present physical world in all its amazing multiplicity, beauty, and complexity, we find that without space, all that we view as familiar on any level would be inconceivable.

How can we account for the exquisite detail of the spontaneously arising existent realm? How could space have the 'power' to accommodate so much? The varieties of shape and form that appear in space, accessible to be known by knowledge, are simply miraculous.

What parentage could be so prolific in its offspring? What 'cause' so manifold in its effects?

At one level, we can attempt to explain what appears in terms of interactions and causes. But such explanations can only account for one appearance in terms of others. We can leave this domain of explanation to science, aware of its many successes, but equally aware that when we try to account for appearance on a more fundamental level, there seems to be 'nothing to say'.

This 'nothing to say' does not have to be a 'stopping point' for knowledge. Instead, we could regard it as a gateway to a new kind of knowing. After all, if objects and events in the physical and mental realms, together with the space that accommodates them, were not in some way 'rootless', the sheer abundance of appearance would long since have led to a kind of universal gridlock. Perhaps having 'nothing to say' puts us in touch with the 'rootlessness' that prevents such congestion.

Viewed as an opening to new knowledge, having 'nothing to say' attunes us to the unbounded and unstructured nature of what appears. Appreciation for 'field dynamics and mechanics' can point 'toward' this unbounded 'dimension'; opening to a second level of space can bring aspects of it into awareness. But in the end there is no structure and no path to pursue—there is simply the 'nothing to say' that reveals appearance as no more substantial than a bubble, forming and reforming in the currents of space and time.

When there is 'nothing to say', the object and its surrounding space can be known as inseparable. Following out this inseparability, entering into it, we discover Great Space: a vision of completeness and perfect accommodation, holding no positions and making no distinctions.

How can we evoke the richness of Great Space? As the infant takes form in the womb and flowers are cultivated in the garden, so Great Space offers a nourishing environment, ready to accommodate and sustain. Yet this image is too static. At the root of the root, whether we explore cosmologically, microscopically, or analytically, Great Space allows the alive and vital exhibition of what appears through being itself 'alive'.

This 'aliveness' of Great Space is not the aliveness of an 'is'; instead it arises through an open allowing. Behind the behind, in the middle of the middle, Space allows. In the essence of absence, Space exhibits. Nothing governs what can appear and nothing sets limits; in the unbounded 'field' of Great Space, there is only the unlimited potential of all possibilities.

Great Space allows for a new vision of what is, implicating time, space, and knowledge alike. All appearance and all physical existence can be Space; all history, suffering, and distinction-making Time; all mental activity, structures of mind, desires, and blockages Knowledge. There is no restriction because there is no becoming; no lack of awareness because there is nothing to be known.

Allowing Matrix

LINEAGE OF
APPEARANCES

Consider the possibility that whatever appears can be traced through a variety of 'lineages'. For example, an object can be traced to its component elements; alternatively, it can be traced to the whole of which it forms a part. There could be tracing in the direction of greater subtlety or underlying energies; tracing in new dimensions, both visible and invisible; tracing of associated sensory and mental operations (including those involved in tracing); tracing of historical conditions and causes. Lineages can be investigated in various domains: structural, chemical, biological, mathematical, philosophical, therapeutic, linguistic, cultural.

Experiment with different ways of opening experience and appearances through tracing lineages. You may find that the further you go, the more character and meaning change. The common-sense emphasis on substance can no longer be contained; there is a move toward process that opens new perspectives. Is there any limit to the lineages that can be traced out in this way?

COMMENTARY

Tracing the lineages of appearance, though itself a linear operation, allows appreciation for simultaneous manifestation and multiple dimensionality. Previous exercises led to an awareness of the 'edge' of space; but awareness of this multiple dimensionality goes further—it supports the ability to go to what might be termed the 'edge of the edge' of space. Familiarity with this 'edge of the edge' can lead to the realization that there is little difference between space and object or object and space.

Space allows the linear chains that manifest shape and form. In this sense, no matter how far we trace out a lineage, the lineage as a whole presupposes space. Yet this 'presupposed' space will also be simultaneous with the lineage. It could even be said to be 'part of' each lineage and each 'lineage holder'.

The interplay of space and lineage helps counteract any tendency to understand space as simply an allowing ground—a gracious host who welcomes guests who are arriving from 'somewhere else', each holding its own lineage. This view (which assumes an indeterminate 'whereabouts' for the 'somewhere else') leaves out of account the role of space in the lineage of what appears. Whatever arises has space as its ancestor. The 'empty background' is inseparable from the chain of manifestation.

Focus on lineages invites a shift from first-level to second-level space; from space that contains to 'space' that projects. To encourage this shift, we could entertain the following view:

> The object (whether physical or not) and space are equally responsible for allowing.

This view suggests a two-way interaction between space and object. Space is responsible for the characteristics of the object: Character and quality arise from point of view. Moreover, if objects exist, their existence requires manifestation in space—even an existence that was hidden and nonappearing would manifest as hidden and nonappearing, and this manifestation would be allowed only through the operation of space. But whether objects exist or not, there could be no space—whether as appearing, existing, or allowing—without manifestation.

To restate this point in a more challenging way: *The object of the object is also the object of space.* Without the object, there is no going to the 'beyond' of space; without space there is no coming to the 'here' of appearance. There is no walking away from space, for there is nowhere else to go.

The conventional view asserts that being belongs to existence and assigns 'the rest' to space. The possibility that 'space' is the 'parent' of existence, an ancestor to which 'what exists' inevitably traces its lineage, can serve as a corrective to this limited perspective.

But this approach still accepts fundamental first-level distinctions, for it regards space and object as separate though interpenetrating. If we go deeper, we discover 'space' as what projects appearance. Now we can refine our earlier, provisional statements in a more decisive way: *The object of the object is space.* Existence is responsible for its own appearance.

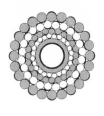

Great Space

SPACE PROJECTING INTO SPACE

The openness of Great Space cannot be considered a beginning, for where there is a beginning there is sequence, and sequence is a sign that the fundamental openness of Space is being restricted.

The linear sequence of the temporal order works to impose a limiting interpretation on Great Space, for it maintains that one possibility can appear only when another possibility ends; that one existent can negate another; that there are absolute limits. Conceptual limits and the rules of logic conform to this same 'order'.

All such rules depend on proclaiming identity. To have an identity means to occupy space and thus to use it up. To occupy space means to be a stranger to Space, an 'outsider' who visits and takes advantage of Space's hospitality.

To be such a visitor—an uneasy guest, never at home in the world—this is our nature. And because we are not at home in Space, we impose on Space our own way of being: We give it identity as physical space and as the inner reaches of the mind. Only then can Space be used up; only then is contradiction possible. Starting from this foundation, limits are adopted, and 'space' becomes dense and solid—mentally, physically, and emotionally.

Understanding Great Space means understanding shape and form as not fixed or identified, for Space free of identity has no occupants. Physical form can appear, but before or after the appearance is just the same. Nothing has been excluded; Space has not been set aside for the newly arrived guest. No vacancy is required, for *form is still space.* Though the senses operate within a certain 'field' and consciousness organizes 'space' into specific structures, human awareness is simply one way of perceiving the openness of Space—a way of perception that Space freely and joyously accommodates without being restricted by that accommodation.

Space projects Space into Space, in an exhibition that ripples outward. In itself, the exhibition is simple; in fact, since it has no identity, nothing could be simpler. It is the limitations we bring to bear that keep us from accommodating this simple openness.

Space projects Space into Space. There are no fixed points and no fixed identity, but quality and character remain. 'Here' and 'there' do not arise, and the 'field' that displays their qualities does not get set aside. Nor does the insubstantiality of contradiction mean that an impossible chaos reigns. The object appears as its own echo; 'subject and object' emerge into 'subject' and 'object'.

Great Space manifests all appearance, without movement, mover, or moved.

Subject and object could be thought of as two structures that come together at a single point, giving rise to the known world—like two pyramids that touch one another at their shared apex. If we start from this interaction at the apex, there are no distinctions—only the knowledge of 'two' and 'interaction'. Subject might be object and object subject, for no directions have been established.

Suppose that each pyramid were thought of as a projection of space. From a first-level perspective this would be like flattening the pyramid out. What was in the foreground merges into the background, and the point at the apex completely disappears. Subject and object have vanished, but so has any possibility for knowledge. There is 'nothing at all'.

From a second-level perspective we might think of the pyramids 'dissolving' into space. Though the pyramidal structure itself would remain, there would be a new focus: the way in which 'space' gives subject and object together, leading to their 'interpenetration' or 'co-determination'.

From a 'third-level' perspective, open to Great Space, seeing the pyramids as 'space projections' entails no transition at all. Nothing 'comes from' space and so nothing 'returns into' space. At this level, we must give up the idea of subject and object as the outcome of a causal sequence. The rhythm of time is not implicated by the projections of space—it neither binds appearance nor serves as its prerequisite. Great Space cannot be divided up and 'measured out'; there is no grading and defining, so where would qualities and attributes come from?

Then how do subject and object and world 'arise'? A Great Space perspective assigns the power to emerge into being to the 'singularity' of the point—like the force bound into the nucleus of an atom, or essential inspiration. The foundation of the pyramid is the apex of the pyramid: a point that *in its 'singularity'* can almost miraculously embrace the whole of the 'measured-out' realm of first-level space. It is the 'singularity' that 'allows' lower-level space its function as accommodation.

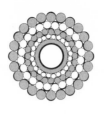

Great Space

ZERO OF BEING

For Great Space, each singular point, point by point, is the 'zero' of being. The source of what is as whole is also the source of what is as hole. Wholly itself, the 'singular' communicates with the 'other side' of what is; it opens what is by 'punching a hole' in the fabric of existence.

In allowing the whole, the point is a sign, as a shadow is a sign of the body that casts it. The 'singularity' of the point—its 'decisive being'—shows the 'availability' of accommodation.

Put differently, accommodation allows existence to be by preserving the point as available. The 'singularity' does not establish: After the nest has been constructed, there is still room to construct a nest. *As* accommodation, the point at once remains the hole of 'zero' and the whole of 'space', not 'less' available in being occupied. What manifests *participates* in accommodation.

On the second level, shape and form are 'established' as though by a 'blueprint', but the Great Space 'zero-point singularity' does not establish. Shape and form arise as free to be transformed. All existence can manifest as infinite 'potential to be', allowed by the Body of Space.

Great Space punches each point into the whole, a hole into a whole. There is not 'only' space, for there is nothing 'apart from' Space. The punching of the hole founds shape and form, but not as founded. Only as we determine to live 'within' the holes punched into space can we speak of founding. Punching a hole in the hole, we call the 'measured-out' world into being.

The subject 'responding' to what Space allows could be said to conduct space toward the physical. 'Interaction' leads toward 'feedback'—a particular shaping of a creative thrust. The same move that makes space 'my' territory makes what appears subject to time. With subject and object stretched out and separated 'in' space, knowledge comes from walking the tightrope between them.

Understood in its own terms, walking this tightrope requires great skill and concentration; despite our best efforts we lose our balance again and again. But seen from the perspective of Great Space, balance comes naturally; indeed there is no possibility of falling out of balance. Each experience is an experience of Space, and each 'instant now' is Space as well.

The three times derive from this 'instant now' and are contained within it. When experience shifts toward the 'zero-point singularity' of Great Space, the present is no longer narrow in a way that excludes past and future, but touches all presentations at once. Balanced in the 'zero point' of Space, open to the 'instant now', we discover a greater sense of control, a more ready way of acting. At home in the 'zero point', we find that the point becomes the whole. A greater 'knowingness' encompasses all the stages of time at once: The normal limit that keeps us from knowing the past or future directly does not operate, nor are we confined to knowing one sense at a time. The past becomes the extension of present memory, so that present and memory are seen to share the same substance, distributed in different ways. As the openness of Space is reinforced, the paradoxical and paranormal are freely accommodated.

Through the power of 'zero-space singularity', the linear sequence of 'measured-out' temporality simply stops. Knowledge takes command, so that we no longer need to take our bearings from the compass always carried with us. With more openness comes more power, which in turn supports greater openness. Experience is seen to give rhythm and rhythm is seen to give time, so that variations in experience can be controlled directly. A new rhythm builds up, reinforcing a momentum that moves without effort toward absolute power—and absolute freedom.

The power that Great Space offers is not a power that seeks its own way. Rather it is a power to exhibit without restriction. 'Endowed' with the wholeness of 'singularity', Great Space 'gives' variation in form and appearance—a performance that is always fresh and new. Like an unimaginably beautiful space flower, Great Space blossoms into unknown Being.

The projecting of Space into Space by Space will result in different interpretations, depending on the stand 'taken' by Knowledge. It might seem that since Great Space is all-accommodating, all patternings are equivalent, and that there is no basis for choosing among them. But new patternings can allow new knowledge, and allow it more fully as they come to approximate the 'allowingness' of Great Space. Space can project into space or form or consciousness; image can project into space or into consciousness, and so on.

When Knowledge conforms to the prevailing 'temporal order', 'space' projects accordingly, 'establishing' the objects and structures of the known world. This projection produces 'feedback' in a quite specific way: a backward projecting that can be understood as the allowing of the subject, and a forward projecting that can be understood as all existence.

The prevailing interpretation brings a particular temporal order into play as its embodiment—setting up a patterning that closes space down. But even in this 'closing down' of 'space-projection', Space is ever active, always projecting Space.

It would be a fundamental mistake to think that Great Space can project only emptiness, for emptiness as the absence of 'something real' is a wholly inadequate symbol for Great Space. Such limitations on 'where' within appearance Space can 'appear' (for example, in physical space, but not in tangible objects, or in tangible objects, but not in thoughts or interpretations) only denies what is spacious in Space.

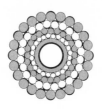

Great Space

SPACE EMBODIMENT

The more open Knowledge allows Space to be, the more fully Space can project without limitation the fullness of possibility. The Knowledge most consonant with the allowing of Space is the one that accepts the richest interpretive possibilities, closing off the least. Open to what Space allows, it will also be present for what Time presents. This richness and vitality will lead Knowledge toward the embodiment of what appears in Space—a complete integration of shape and openness, form and possibility, never 'straying' toward entities and substance.

When such embodiment is complete, Knowledge becomes the Body of Knowledge: Knowledge knowing Space as Knowledge. For Great Space, Knowledge appears in no other way. All appearance is the 'zero-singularity embodiment' of Space by Knowledge. The Body of Knowledge—the fullest expression of appearance in all its dimensions—is at once the perfect exhibition of Space and the most complete realization of Knowledge. It integrates all that Space allows, presenting without limitation: creator and created, yes and no, existence and destruction. Space and Knowledge meet in the dimension of Openness, where beauty takes on inexpressible meaning and nothing is excluded.

If Space were either substantial or insubstantial, the Knowledge that knows Space would be a 'knowledge of', in which the patterns of the first-level temporal order would perpetuate themselves. But Great Space sets Knowledge free. With no distinctions to be known, there is Knowledge in whatever appears. When Great Space allows, the Body of Knowledge shines forth, and appearance exhibits the quality of light.

Opening to Great Space could be said to give birth to a newly active aesthetic of Knowledge, founded on the interaction of Space and Knowledge as sheer beauty, manifesting in joy that readily extends through time by the power of awakened 'knowingness'.

When shape and form are also part of Space, available as what Space exhibits, Space itself 'is' alive as the exhibition of what is. All patterns, no matter how elaborate or simple, all beauty and all prospects for beauty appear as the exhibition of Space. Shape and form project Space into . . . Space. Where else could it go?

The aesthetic of Great Knowledge comes to be in the 'aliveness' of Great Space, which calls forth the presence of Great Time. An unchanging 'field' displays the time and space that we as individuals inhabit and embody.

What is, as it is, can be allowed in its perfection: the heart of the Body of Knowledge.

In the exhibition of Space, Knowledge touches Knowledge. This is Space alive, vital with the richness of the known pulsing in all perception. In the merging of Knowledge with Space, Being is available fully: not as an abstraction, but in the Being of this moment, known in appearing in Space.

Space alive has the flavor of desire fulfilled yet not sated, like an ongoing embrace. It offers knowledge directly, not known *by* the mind or presented *to* the mind, but simply available within what appears, *as* its appearance. No longer *located* in thoughts and judgments, Knowledge knows Knowledge through Space, leaving nothing else to be known. Space is the appearance of this knowing to itself, through the projections that Space projects.

Knowledge appears through Space as beauty. We find the beauty of Great Space in the vastness of the blue sky, the unboundedness of space, the vivid colors of myriad rainbows, and a joy that wells forth within all interactions. Appearance presents itself as though clothed in the richest fabrics, shimmering with unimagined colors, inviting with the smoothest caress. Music wells forth in the fullness of an ever-present silence, and form brings delight to vision through its perfect arising. Fragrances transport us to realms that never were, and the taste of a bliss that knows no limits melts into our being. Active within time, on time, and in time, we celebrate the all-providing mother, the all-knowing presentational immediacy of Great Space.

The beauty of all manifestation expresses an intimacy with knowledge that can only be traced to Space as the nonoriginating source. Appearance is not only known: As the exhibition of Space it surges with the vitality of Knowledge. Like two lovers exchanging kisses, Space and Knowledge find each other delicious. Always reuniting though never separated, Space and Knowledge bid each other welcome. Their embrace gives rise to all that is and was and all that could be.

Spontaneous and surprising, Space expresses the joy of Being for Knowledge to receive. The ever-manifesting, nonoriginating source, it serves as mother of matter and appearance. Shape and form are the beauty of Space, a refreshing rain showering down on Knowledge, every drop a new pleasure. Space and matter interact through the senses, a magical display available to be enjoyed and extended. Sensing becomes the aliveness of Space, projecting projections, inviting knowledge, bestowing on 'knowingness' the capacity to appreciate what appears. As knowledge inseparable from Space, observation becomes comprehension: a 'field' of knowledge based on the enjoying 'feel' of knowledge.

Through the senses, openness becomes the extension of joy, brought into being through the unrestricted activity of Knowledge. Open to the openness of Great Space, Knowledge knows no hindrance or impediment. Extending everywhere, it unites the allowing of Space with the power of 'knowingness'. In a dance of joy and love, the unbounded Body of Knowledge expresses fulfillment.

Great Space

CO-RELATION

A. Look at subject and object and their relationship. What makes the subject the subject? Try reversing the relationship, so that the object becomes the subject. You could take as object another person, a physical entity, or perhaps yourself at another time, past or future. To explore this practice further, refer to Exercise 30 in *Time, Space, and Knowledge:* "A Subject-Object Reversal".

B. Investigate the relationship between space and existence as a relationship between subject and object or object and subject. If you have difficulty knowing how to proceed, you might initially apply the subject-object orientation with regard to thought and awareness.

C. Continue with the exercise, paying particular attention to the subject. How is the subject constituted and what determines its boundaries? Let this question lead naturally into an exploration at various levels of the subject's relationship to space.

D. Now see if you can integrate into the relationship between subject and space that between subject and object. How does making this move affect the standard relationship between object and space?

COMMENTARY

From the viewpoint of space, it seems that the 'by-stander-self' is the object rather than the subject. Adopting this view is already a rather startling departure from the usual subject-object orientation. But there is another possibility as well: We could say that the 'bystander-self' is space as subject, while the rest of existence is space as object.

Making this identification gives the self a new role: If self as subject is space, then the self is the one who allows what appears to operate; who originates dimensionality. As this role is played out, the usual distinction between subject and object loses much of its significance.

Though subject and object are articulated, they are not separate: It seems that either one could be considered the subject. It is as though two individuals facing each other both decide to move 'forward': Each will proceed in the opposite direction. Insisting that only one of these directions is 'really' forward would only lead to deep confusion.

The 'identification' of space and subject, however, remains incomplete unless we acknowledge that *space itself 'appears' and 'is' the appearance*. Because space allows, it provides the shape and form of existence. By integrating this insight with the practice of space as subject, we see that space is completely free, 'subject to nothing'.

It is as though 'space' communicated space, together with subject and objects 'in' space. The communication takes place on a clear frequency; there will be no static and no loss of information.

In such communication, 'space' plays the role of both subject and object. But this means that 'space' plays no role at all, not even for the moment. It takes no positions, even when it exhibits existence. 'Space' as subject projects no objects; 'space' as object offers no subject.

There is no ultimate and no ultimatum, no 'doer' and no 'done'. Space exercises the deepest knowledge, displaying the dimension of fundamental freedom and unconditioned value: 'zero point' within each point, the non-originating source of all appearance.

KNOWLEDGE

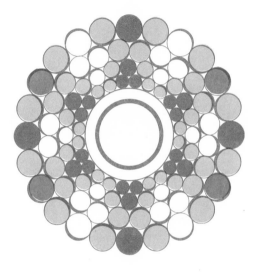

PART THREE

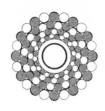

Before Knowledge

NOT-KNOWING

Before there is knowledge, there is not-knowing. Born into a world vast beyond comprehension, human beings begin life subject to a basic ignorance that gives way only gradually and grudgingly. From the time we are born, day to day and hour to hour we must seek out knowledge to direct our thoughts and guide our actions. Through labels and identification we link what we learn into meaningful structures; making use of language and concepts, we form models and assert claims.

Gathering and implementing knowledge could be understood as the fundamental human activity. Through such activity human beings serve as knowledge-bearers for the universe. Yet this role is enacted within a setting shaped by limitation. In the course of each human life, not-knowing comes first and naturally; though it may recede from view, it continues to function. Whatever 'field' of inquiry we investigate—the particles that make up matter, the events that make up history, the elements of consciousness—the answers we arrive at refer onward to something unknown.

How did the universe originate? How did human consciousness take form and through what power does it operate? Where does a thought come from, and what is the transition from one thought to the next? Tracing each new fact and theory back through further questioning, eventually we reach a point where we have nothing to say. The original not-knowing reemerges, silent witness to our limitations.

If what we know is founded on not-knowing, how can we call it knowledge at all? Perhaps we are living our lives on the basis of mistaken perceptions and understandings. Perhaps the difficulties and frustrations we face reflect the unknown origins that underlie our thinking and acting.

Suppose that we looked at not-knowing from the perspective of knowledge itself. At once the ceaseless activity of 'gathering' information becomes rather mysterious. *Since knowledge tends by nature to know, why should it be limited at all?* Why is it not fully accessible from the outset, matching the infinite range of knowables with a boundless knowing?

This question could be seen as based on a confusion generated by language. To speak of knowledge apart from those who know turns it into a 'substance' with independent status. But how can there be 'knowledge as such', apart from the one who knows? And even assuming such a separate entity, why would it concern us? We care only about the knowledge that human beings possess or could possess.

Before we abandon a 'knowledge-centered' perspective, however, we might want to take a look at the consequences. Are we willing to see the fundamental 'knowledgeability' that seems to be the human birthright transformed into the substance of an ever-active unknowing? Must we simply close the book on our capacity for knowledge?

Whatever the nature of the knowledge that arises to the mind, it will leave unknown the mind itself. Indeed, we cannot even say for certain that the mind is an 'entity' to be known; from a certain perspective it seems more accurate to say that 'mind' is simply a pattern of recognition and understanding, the product of a specific history and the expression of a particular knowledge. Yet we can say this: So long as the substance or activity of mind remains unknown, our knowledge takes form within a 'context' of not-knowing. Is it any wonder that our actions often fail to produce the results we hope for?

This 'context' of not-knowing finds expression in the structure of polarity and discrimination we accept when we try to work out a solution to a problem. Called into being together, within a 'field' of not-knowing, problem and solution are like two magnetic poles that carry the same charge—they naturally repel one another. The self as knower, concerned with bringing them together, must expend prodigious energy to establish communication between them. The tendency is for this communication to be limited and incomplete, for the energy of the 'field' to reassert itself so that the problem soon emerges in new forms.

As expressions of the 'field' of not-knowing, problems are like the mythical monster known as a hydra, which grew new heads as the old ones were chopped off. But we might wonder: Perhaps the growth of new heads is due to the nature of the sword with which we do the cutting.

What if we could put aside our usual weapon and challenge problems in a way that did not confirm the 'field' of not-knowing we are so accustomed to? To make a preliminary proposal: Suppose that problems were understood as part of a global 'read-out' that expressed the result of a certain kind of knowing being in effect. Whatever its 'contents', as a read-out it would reveal this fundamental knowing as the source of a remarkable creativity.

With knowledge inherent in problem as well as solution, would problems still require 'solutions'? Could the underlying creativity of knowledge be brought into play directly? For example, could a completely different 'read-out' emerge, in which the nature of the problem was transformed?

When polarity and positioning are allowed to establish a 'negative' for each 'positive', the negative tends to resist being known, and the structures that 'embody' such negativity—such as solutions to problems—seem to close off inspiration. Yet repeating old ways of knowing is itself an act of creation, an active mode of *being* that renews itself from moment to moment. We are always enacting anew, even if what we enact is repetition.

The conviction that the constantly renewed commitment to the old ways exhausts our creative power is an aspect of the stories established and promoted by the founding 'logos'. If we can shift our orientation just slightly, so that we see the well-worn patterns at an angle instead of head-on, the hold they have over us begins to fade, allowing an ever-present creativity to flow in new and unaccustomed ways.

In the momentum of conventional patterns, a thought projects into another thought, a habit pattern into another habit pattern, a behavior into a behavior—all based on the rhythms that emerge as form and character take shape. There may be a sense of aliveness, but the momentum being projected forward is actually frozen in place.

Creative knowing can cut through this momentum. The fullness of Time, Space, and Knowledge are always available to us—not as remote, impersonal forces or 'fields', but as the reality of our own being, open, alive, and embodied. We enter this fullness simply and easily, through a responsible, lively intelligence. Staying close to the 'zero point', moving at the subtlest, most universal level, we can turn to the boundaries of experience, looking at limits and outermost edges in ways that allow the unexpected and the unknown to arise. It is like exploring the inner workings of the smallest, most subtle and paradoxical atomic particles, and then finding that the results of our inquiry give us precious new insight into the workings of the cosmos as a whole.

We can draw on this creativity of knowledge most directly in not-knowing. Without risking either laziness or craziness, not-knowing teaches us to see when we are being honest and when we are fooling ourselves; when we are applying double standards in our inquiry; when we are excepting cherished beliefs or protecting a subtle aspect of the self. Exercising the knowledge of not-knowing vigorously and with integrity, we can let the light of knowing illuminate all being.

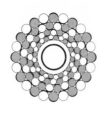

POTENTIAL
FOR KNOWING

Although we usually understand not-knowing as dark-ness, a place where the light of knowledge does not shine, this does not tell us what not-knowing truly is. On the one hand, it might be a blank with nothing to offer; on the other, it might reflect a potential for knowing that does not accord with the juxtaposed positions of the already known.

As a symbol of this latter possibility, we can designate the unknown as 'x'. In ordinary usage, 'x' not only marks the unknown, but also designates the infinitely variable. It indicates not only a point where entry is forbidden, but also 'the spot': the point that may hold the treasure we seek. The multiple dimensionality of 'x' suggests that the unknown might offer great value.

Greater appreciation for not-knowing can be devel-oped by investigating the links between knowing and not-knowing through several successive stages.

Stage One: At the outset, knowing and not-knowing are sharply distinguished. But this distinction, by separating the known from the unknown, defines the known and gives it shape. We might say that the unknown is the 'field' from within which the known emerges; the 'not this' from which 'this' comes forth. While the difference between knowing and not-knowing predominates, it is already clear that this difference is possible on the basis of something shared. Like the back side of a coin, not-knowing supports the known.

Stage Two: At this stage, the focus is on the barriers and limits to knowledge—the points of contact between known and unknown. These limits give the known its structure, even its authenticity. Without them, the knowable would remain an open and undifferentiated 'field', perhaps not even knowledge at all.

Focusing on borders suggests that the line between known and unknown may not be so easy to draw. On the one hand, limits mark the appearance of the not-known within the realm of the known; on the other hand, the same limits are the most distinctive aspect of the known.

Stage Three: Now the focus shifts to the potential for knowing within not-knowing. As the point of not-knowing, 'x' is also the point at which old limits can be challenged and new knowledge can emerge. For each new and unknown point, 'x' allows the possibility that knowledge can open. Now for the first time not-knowing does not limit knowledge at all; it seems possible that knowledge could hold the whole, that knowledge is found in each point. Indeed, not-knowing seems the only possible source for knowledge.

As a corollary, not-knowing now becomes the 'carrier' of knowledge. At the first stage, when knowing and not-knowing are clearly distinguished from one another, 'carrying' knowledge would simply mean transporting it from one place to another. But now something different is being suggested. Not-knowing might carry a 'knowledge' that can encompass both knowing and not-knowing—a 'knowledge' within conventional knowledge that at the same time does not exclude not-knowing.

The view that *not-knowing can carry 'knowledge' into knowledge* requires a reinterpretation of the limitations implicit in juxtaposed positioning. As points of 'not-knowing', these limitations are expressions of a more encompassing 'knowledge'. The conventionality of conventional knowledge—its restriction to a lower level—is likewise an expression of such 'knowability'. We might say that not-knowing has disappeared, only to reemerge as the 'knowing' within first-level conventional knowledge. This second-level 'knowledge' shows up everywhere, making no distinctions and knowing no limits.

This transitional view culminates in a final stage:

Stage Four: The unknown as a sponsor of 'knowledge'. At this stage, 'knowledge' invites us to discover a more fundamental 'not-knowing' implicit in conventional knowledge. Although earlier views brought knowing and not-knowing closer together, not-knowing was still understood as 'surrounding' knowledge or underlying it. Now we can see that not-knowing, in both a first-level and second-level sense, is intrinsic to knowledge. The move that places not-knowing 'outside' is a kind of deception practiced by first-level knowledge, a distortion (or 'not-knowing') that comes from the failure to acknowledge not-knowing *as* the limited nature of first-level knowledge.

The dynamic that discloses this interconnection is not-knowing as 'knowledge'. Newly familiar with not-knowing, we see the way in which we requisition a previous set of arrangements from the storehouse of what is familiar. We see how we have learned to take responsibility for the not-knowing of first-level knowledge, accepting not-knowing as our duty and making it into our position—even defining it as knowledge.

At this fourth stage, not-knowing now delivers 'knowledge' in the non-deliverability of knowledge. Accepting the pattern of conventional not-knowing as what is given by 'knowledge', not-knowing lets us embody the 'knowledge' that is there. Not-knowing challenges each axiom, disclosing the 'x' of the axiom as unknown, *and* as the 'known' in the unknown.

The stages outlined here mark a transition from a first to a second level of knowledge. In the non-positioned 'knowing' of this newly available second-level knowledge, first-level knowing and not-knowing are inseparable aspects of a limited positioning. This insight is presented not as a critique, but as an invitation: When we no longer confine ourselves to knowing, knowing and not-knowing alike become manifestations of a second-level 'knowledgeability'.

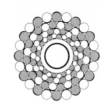

Before Knowledge

ZERO POINT

Whatever relationship we establish with knowledge, the very fact that we *set ourselves apart* will mean that a subtle part of knowledge remains beyond reach. Because we take a stand toward knowledge, we stand outside it and do not understand it.

In taking a stand toward knowledge, we refer it to ourselves as the knower. Whether we 'have' knowledge or 'lack' it, we relate to it as if it were a possession.

Each time we take a position, we once more position knowledge as a possession, affirming an unbridgeable distance between knower and known that brings not-knowing to the fore. Though we can establish countless structures based on the interaction of positions and the exchange of predetermined messages, we are simply working out the implications of this not-knowing.

If we are willing to give up our usual claim of ownership over knowledge, looking at knowledge anew, we see that in each act of positioned knowing, there is a 'point of decision', a vital 'zero point' 'before' knowing is 'accomplished'. At that 'decisive point', could not-knowing be available in a way that is not yet separate from knowing? If we could contact the non-positioned 'zero point' and the not-knowing it 'points out', we might find that we could link the knowing that comes through positioning with the not-knowing that each position implicitly affirms. Knowing in this way, could we restore knowledge to itself?

Ordinarily we assign all significance to what is known; to what exists and to the distinctions among existents. 'Zero' in this context reduces a separation that might otherwise be 'meaningful' to 'nothing', and so is interpreted as a *loss* of knowledge. But this view, which *looks past* the 'zero point' to the content of what manifests, also *loses sight* of knowledge. When we focus on the content of what is known, knowledge *as active knowing* is presented as 'disembodied', separate from the known—'nothing at all'.

Perhaps if we are willing to look *through* the content of manifestations to the 'zero point within', we can understand manifestation differently, as the very 'body' of knowledge. Through a mechanism of transformation that itself remains unknown, accepting the unknown of the 'zero point' as inseparable from knowing might let us see with new eyes. Our logic, our consciousness, our way of being might change, as though appearance appeared in a new light.

'Zero' implies an unknown, in the same way that not-knowing implies an unknown—an interpretation made by the knower with regard to the limits of the known. If 'x' is the unknown, the knower assigns 'x' a value, positioning it through words or conduct, giving it provisional identity as 'what is unknown'.

'Zero' is such an unknown, for by definition it has no existence, and so does not exist to be known. Yet 'zero' seems to be a limiting case for the unknown, since as soon as we assign it a provisional identity as 'unknown', we contradict its nature as nonexistent.

'Zero' as a conventional number occupies its specific point on the number line, precisely positioned between negative and positive. But the 'number-line zero' is conceptual, an artificial construct that has been 'measured out' and brought into the realm of the known.

If we let 'zero' remain as nonpositioned, its specific value of 'no value at all' sets it in contrast to what is. This function suggests an unusual formulation: *By standing in contrast to what is, 'zero' grants existence permission to be.*

Although this formulation may seem to go against ordinary understanding, we can observe something similar at work in arithmetic operations. Playing its paradoxical role as 'nonexistent unknown', 'zero' opens a place for what is known to be 'measured out' and reckoned with; by serving as 'placeholder' it makes possible 'meaningful' results. Looking at numbers more abstractly, we might also say that when 'zero' is assigned its 'no value' identity, this identity establishes 'one'. The distinction between 'zero' and 'one' in turn gives 'two'.

From there the world of multiplicity can unfold in a linear progression.

It may be that 'zero' plays a similar role in terms of existence—allowing existence to take its own measure, 'measuring out' a world. Unknown without being *an* unknown, permitting without defining, 'zero' unifies all manifestations by defining them as manifestations, each with its assigned place. The 'starting point' for what is, it is 'present' within all points. Adding nothing to what appears, simply permitting, it refers all appearance back to itself. As the 'unknown unknown', 'zero' is the agent of knowledge, allowing knowledge to embody as all manifestations.

For a 'zero-point' knowing, the usual claim of ownership over knowledge would have a very different quality. Instead of being given as either true or false, the claim itself would become an *exhibition* of knowledge as it unfolded from the 'zero point' into a specific structure. 'Ownership' would not have to be renounced, because it would never arise as 'real' in the first place. As basic 'qualities' of each position, the structures of 'knower' and 'known' would sustain neither the claim of ownership nor the distance from knowledge through which not-knowing maintains its priority. Instead of determining the range of knowledge available, they would themselves become co-determined aspects of an active knowing.

If we look honestly, we may sense in ourselves an uneasiness in the face of 'zero', a reluctance to let it come to the fore—perhaps a fear of 'negating' what exists. But the availability of the 'zero point' can be understood very differently. It reveals space as open with an allowing that does not depend on the void, and discloses time as alive with an energy not trapped by the determinism and ever-threatening chaos of linear momentum. It is as though we had discovered a black hole at the center of every atom of existence—a source of power and transformation, active with an unimaginable intensity, open to unknown dimensions of being.

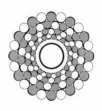

Before Knowledge

HEART OF
KNOWLEDGE

The move away from the 'zero point' seems to be activated by 'what matters' to us: the concerns that we bring to a situation. But the knowledge that would satisfy our concerns at the deepest level cannot manifest. The very move away from 'zero' separates us from the fullness of knowing, erecting barriers to knowledge. Keenly aware of the 'value judgments' of right and wrong, benefit and value, we refer these standards back to an absolute—'fully right', 'fully valuable', 'fully knowledgeable'. But we have no way to gain access to this assumed absolute realm. The space that would allow it is not available, and the time that would present it has not yet come. A deeper knowing seems not to trace to the same background as human being.

Could we look past our concerns for 'what matters'? Starting with knowledge as its own intrinsic certainty, could we search out the places in experience where knowledge can bear witness to itself, wholly apart from our needs and wishes? Perhaps this approach is possible in theory, but as soon as we ask *why* we would make this move, we see that we are still firmly within the world that 'what matters' establishes.

Perhaps a better approach is to ask whether concern for 'what matters' itself *expresses* knowledge that has been directed toward specific ends. Following this possibility out, we can see that the knowledge 'unknown' to this concern is not impossibly removed after all; instead, it lies on a continuum with concern itself and with the knowledge available within the 'field' that such concern establishes. If we could restore this 'unknown' to knowledge, it would *complete into fullness* the knowledge accessible to us now.

The prospect that 'concern for what matters' could show the way toward the knowledge that it apparently excludes transforms what seems to be a 'narrowing' of knowledge into an indication of the commanding strength of knowledge as such. This intrinsic 'knowledgeability' is neither separate from knowledge nor limited by it. We might call it Great Knowledge, for it is indomitable; though we cut it off, it makes itself available in our act of rejection.

Great Knowledge could be seen as the heart of all knowledge, known and unknown—an unknown 'knowingness', the 'not-truth' of positioned knowledge. It provides whatever we ask from it—even when we approach it in a way that puts it at a distance; even when it has already eluded our grasp. Unbounded, Great Knowledge does not exclude whatever limit we put on it. Even not-knowing is an expression of Great Knowledge, for the barrier between knowing and not-knowing depends on definitions that Knowledge makes possible. Seen in this light, not-knowing is an agent of 'knowingness': unrestricted, unfounded, the self-founding 'zero point' that can transform each barrier into a gateway.

With no previous record of such 'knowledge', we may not know how to activate this possibility. Still, something in our experience will speak to us of what is available. We can affirm our own highest projection of what has the validity of truth as such, drawing on that affirmation to explore the unknown as the 'source' of knowledge. Touching this not-knowing *as knowing* reminds us that knowledge is boundless, and so increases our confidence. Through our exploration, the *gap* between known and unknown, subject and object, can become the *root* of the unitary event of active knowledge.

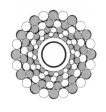

INQUIRY
WITHOUT GOAL

Although our inquiry is 'directed toward' Great Knowledge, it can nevertheless proceed without aiming at a particular goal or result, or without defining a specific 'something' as a final target. Exploration and unfolding are the sign of knowledge in operation, while conclusions are grounds to suspect that freely available knowledge is being manipulated for purposes unrelated to knowing.

From any conventional perspective, it is natural to frame our efforts in terms of wanting to reach a certain goal, after which we can rest. But if knowledge is truly without limitation, it will not tire or wear out; it will not turn heavy, and there will be no need for rest. Heaviness, weariness, resistance, and the like are signs of an incomplete knowing in operation.

True, there may come a point in inquiry (associated with the transition to a new level of knowledge) when it will seem that major efforts are required to achieve a 'goal', understood in terms of transformation. But these efforts tend to be self-cancelling—without this meaning that they are fruitless. The categories that identify effort as the route toward achieving a specific goal lose their hold in the face of the recognition that *being, as it is, is knowledge.* Although 'right' and 'wrong', 'limited' and 'unlimited' retain their meanings and qualities, they also reflect the judgments of a particular knowledge referred to a particular version of time and space. They are inappropriate to Great Knowledge.

When Great Knowledge is made into a goal, a position or view is presented, excluding and rejecting, inviting assent or conversion. But exclusion is untrue to Great Knowledge as all-encompassing, and assent can only bring duplication, not true knowledge.

Although the inquiry being conducted here could be seen as directed toward a goal, this view is partial. We have no interest in arriving 'at' Great Knowledge, or even in attaining knowledge of the way things are. We may proceed through models that accept a particular goal as being significant, but this is a matter of methodology. Great Knowledge is found not in any particular outcome, but in the act of knowing.

Great Knowledge could be considered a 'gesture' of Knowledge, *made by Knowledge itself,* asserting or maintaining nothing. We discover it in operation through certain qualities. For example, one initial indication is loving acceptance—not only on the interpersonal and psychological levels, but in terms of the

fundamental structures through which the self proclaims its being. The tension and sense of need that drive
us to fulfill our needs or to seek new states relaxes. Tendencies toward self-doubt, inner turmoil, or confrontation
with others open to impartial accommodation, becoming
part of an unfolding process. With no discrimination
between opposites, there is no basis for conflict or rejection. We can uphold strongly what has value without
taking positions or rejecting other values. Praise and
blame both lose their projective qualities.

A second indication of Great Knowledge in operation
is inner balance. When space exhibits only polarities and
solid structures, balance depends on superstructures
carefully put in place and cautiously maintained. Similarly, when the dynamic of time presents the rigid distinctions of the temporal order, balance requires juggling
various separate entities. But Great Knowledge offers
balance through inner harmony, based on ready communication among different elements—in our own mental activity, our dealings with others, and our connection
with embodied being. Not caught up in accepting and
rejecting, we can learn respect for the 'knowingness'
embodied within alternatives. Thoughts balance with
feelings and critical awareness with appreciation; a more
open awareness complements the logic of contradiction.

We can learn to investigate contradiction in ways that
hold inquiry open. For instance, the 'field' of Time, Space,
and Knowledge can be understood at different levels: not
in order to offer a way out, but to prevent prematurely
closing the question at hand. In the same way, we might

speak of different levels of thinking, or of what happens when we become more open to the Space of Knowledge.

When Great Space accommodates Great Knowledge, the 'field' of dynamic embodiment becomes the person or being embodied. Then how can there be contradiction? We might even say: When contradiction as a barrier to knowledge disappears, this is embodiment. Put differently, for embodiment as a 'field' of Being, contradiction becomes an expression of the 'field'—a 'field trans- formation' of the unity of Space, Time, and Knowledge.

A third indication of Great Knowledge in operation is thoughtful appreciation for the patterns of both personal and human history. Through appreciation we can see how structures of understanding that we apply in our own lives and in fields such as religion, psychology, phi- losophy, and social interaction depend on discrimina- tion. We can observe the fundamental mechanism through which discrimination creates 'friction' in each and every interaction, and explore ways of responding not shaped and formed by 'friction', but governed by the knowledge implicit in the situation as a whole.

Deeper appreciation for historical developments teaches us to see conventional truths and values as ex- pressions of the twists and turns that knowledge takes in response to the flow of linear time. We can recognize how we have determined in advance the range of our own possible understanding. We find ourselves less tightly bound to the always emerging consensus, able to act on our own knowing and to judge for ourselves the accuracy of reasons and explanations. Even when the 'truths' of history and the 'limitations' of our situation proclaim that we have reached a dead end, we can find opportunities to manifest in new ways.

Carried to a certain point, such 'objective' appreciation reveals the fundamental stories and claims of the self and the consequences to which they lead. Starting by investigating the past, we can see that we continue to weave the same patterns right now in the present. Although the present presents itself as more established than the past, or more true, or sustained by more conclusive reasoning, knowledge lets us cut through even these convincing positionings, revealing each pattern and each positioning as a gesture of knowledge, directly available, with no limitation.

In thinking through the limits we build into our knowledge, we open to new ways of knowing. We also may have special experiences that allow for a more comprehensive knowing, suggesting new 'fields' to be explored or new 'orders' to be enjoyed. Such experiences do not need to be seen as either 'real' or 'unreal'; they can simply be appreciated as presentations and exhibitions. Not interpreted or categorized, their power remains intact.

Path of Inquiry

KNOWLEDGE
CONFINED

There may be times in conducting inquiry, for example in reading and reflecting on what we read, when we encounter possibilities that seem particularly inviting. Perhaps we have had experiences with which we associate these ideas; perhaps our own independent inquiry has led us to a similar point of view. We experience the pleasure of recognition and confirmation, and eagerly press onward.

At just this point we risk shutting down the capacity for knowledge. To describe the known or true sets a limit on meaning. Said in this context, "I know" means "I stop here." Knowledge is confined by words, or (on a more subtle level) by experience.

The workings of 'I know' determine how awareness is shaped and confined. Suppose an experience occurs, and we determine that we know why it happened. Is this the end of inquiry, or just a first step? There are countless questions left open: Through what means did the experience arise? Why did it endure, and how did it disappear? How is it determined by the senses or linked to other experiences, and how do knowledge and sense experience interact? Will 'I know' let us keep these questions open?

When we say that we know (or think or feel), we imply that we have arrived at a result. We think or feel 'something'. But how has this result been determined— through what process? Can it be changed or shifted, opened or expanded, or even prevented from arising? We should look carefully at any answers that present themselves: If we designate a state of being or mind as source or result of our thoughts or feelings, we are just placing a label on what remains unknown. Such a move may simply indicate that we are tired of questions and do not want to go on.

Stopping the questioning process might not be a bad move, but what will take the place of questions? Can we cut through our repetitious and unwanted thoughts? Can we cut through the feelings of being impatient or bored? Can we cut through judgments? Even if we manage just to follow feelings as they arise, we are adopting a particular position that may restrict active knowing.

Perhaps we have been wondering about our own being and the workings of the mind for a long time. We may have the sense that we have 'learned something' about these 'matters'—that we have made progress toward clarity. But what answers to our questions do we have? What conclusions have we reached? Do we relate these conclusions to ourselves and to the knowledge we apply now to our lives? Do we know what tools of interpretation we are using?

Whatever 'progress' we have made, if we are still using old interpretations and understandings based on familiar rhythms of knowing, we are like someone who has learned numerous dialects of a single language. When we offer or adopt new meanings, do these 'new' meanings still make use of labels and positions? Are we aware of any alternative? Do we have the means to know the meaning of knowledge?

The conclusion 'I know' may be based on recalling a time when we *knew*, even though now the knowledge is no longer alive within us. But how can we relate to this previous knowledge if it is not there now? How can we track it or make sense of it? The present memory may simply project a current sense of shortage or lack of knowledge, or may be based on associations through language that mask vital differences from the 'original' experience of knowledge.

If we look honestly at how we can authenticate what we know, we may come away convinced that there is nothing to say or think that we can truly rely on. It is not difficult to demonstrate that our knowing will always be trapped in language and positions, that no one has ever been able to escape imprisonment by thoughts and constructs. But whether we are convinced by the logic of this reasoning or discouraged by the bleakness of the result, we are simply proclaiming another 'I know'. Such 'unassailable' conclusions can easily serve as a justification for calling a halt to investigation.

But though we may be bound in our own thoughts and constructs, we can still investigate what appears to the mind and its value. The 'field' of knowledge is always available. We can always raise questions about our 'field of knowledge', about the 'order' and perspective of our knowledge; we can always deepen understanding of how our experience and knowledge arise and how the senses function.

In asking these questions of ourselves other questions come to mind: From time to time we fall out of harmony, like an airplane that suddenly loses power and crash-lands. Why do we have such times, when we would certainly wish otherwise? Why do some people experience them more often than others? Why do such times bring with them so much sense of blame or discouragement, so much lack of self-esteem? Rather than complaining or hiding, we can investigate how such experience comes about and just what is happening in our mind, our thoughts, and our senses. We may not know in advance the value or significance of what we will discover, but why should we forego the opportunity?

Our exploration can continue in times when we feel more fully in harmony, with a sense of balance in body, mind, and senses, intention and vision. Such occasions activate a confidence that inspires further inquiry. Perhaps they are telling us that we are able to contact a more direct and immediate knowing after all.

Very likely there will be times when we feel discouraged, even hopeless. We may conclude that we are too firmly caught in old ways to make the transition to greater knowledge; that it is not worth making efforts when we are bound to fail, that we would rather stay as we are. But this position applies an old, familiar understanding, based on a predetermined set of concerns and a specific attitude. It plots the range of the possible on a map that conforms to the geography of the everyday.

As long as we stay with the old map, there is little possibility of discovering new routes or even another way of traveling. Our questions will repeat themselves to a point where questioning seems 'beside the point'. The 'point' itself is immovable, and because we are bound to the 'point', we too are locked in place. We proceed with single-minded determination, unable to communicate with other alternatives.

Yet knowledge offers less predetermined ways of being. One point can proceed along different lines, in accord with varying momentums, subject to a range of responses, giving multiple meanings. A knowledge that accorded with this multiplicity would seem free to go in virtually any direction, following any route by any means, opening a 'potential' that from another perspective we could describe as 'already here'.

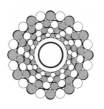

Path of Inquiry

A LIFE OF KNOWLEDGE

We give knowledge too little due if we use it only to attain our own limited goals. Yet we can also exalt knowledge to the point where it has no bearing on the realities of our lives—like a general whose promotion to a high administrative post removes him from battle as effectively as if he had been stripped of his rank. Worth, well-being, and success in conventional terms all depend on knowledge. Would we be completely satisfied with a knowledge that could not demonstrate its effectiveness on this level?

The quality of our knowledge proves itself in the quality of our lives. A knowledge constructed of concepts that identify and manipulate preestablished structures yields a world that is crowded, rigid, compressed, and impenetrable. Human suffering is built up in layers of increasing solidity, each layer a further misreading of a fluid dynamic. We participate in this order, joining in the shared agreement that perpetuates it, because we do not *know* any other way. And if we ask *why* this should be so, we find that the knowledge to answer this question is lacking as well.

The outcome is a life filled with care. The established 'order' specifies our choices, and though those choices may lead only to routine and repetition, there is nowhere to lodge a protest. If we rebel, we risk being judged irrational, escapist, or worse. And so instead we join in, accepting the consequences. There is no way of putting a stop to it all, of saying, "I have had enough suffering now; enough pressure and enough pain."

The limited knowledge that confines us in this way is shaped and confined in turn by limited space and time. It is as though we had been trapped in the narrow angle of a triangle, squeezed on one side by linear time and on the other by empty space. At the base of the triangle, determining its structure, is the knowledge that space and time make available—not only limited, but separated from us by a distance we have no hope of crossing. Though linear time moves freely, it presents us with one 'measured-out' triangle after another, each as confining as the last. Though empty space allows an infinite number of positions, each one traps us in the same way.

If we could somehow open space or time, knowledge would become available in a new way. We could move out of the narrow angle in which we have been wedged to explore the space that the triangle encloses. We could question the dynamic that creates the triangle and propels us from one triangle to the next. We could reach out to know knowledge directly, perhaps finding as we did so that the triangle itself shifted shape or dissolved entirely. No longer confined like an animal in its pen, we could start to live a richer way of being.

Though this prospect can give us heart, we risk deception if we pin our hopes on change as such. The momentum of time brings incessant change, but leaves the structure of our circumstances unaltered. The aspiration for change can help us to embark on the path of inquiry toward the Body of Knowledge, but we should bear in mind that it does not itself reflect a full embodiment of knowledge. When we think in terms of 'more' space or 'new' circumstances, we move within the confines of the old. Taken as a goal, change becomes a possession, something we can 'get' from higher knowledge. But Great Knowledge does not hand out trophies. To hope that it does and hold to our hopes is to hold ourselves back from the fullness of knowing and the whole of our being.

By devoting ourselves fully to knowledge, we may be able to direct the course of change, so that time and space do open and insight flows freely, supporting a deep sense of well-being. Yet unless the underlying structure imposed on time and space and knowledge is transformed, such change may be temporary: as though the angle that confines us widened for a time before narrowing once more—settling into a new but just as confining 'order'.

We are used to knowing within a system or 'order'. Most often we imagine that the 'order' has always been in operation, not recognizing that this 'always already there' is an aspect of the knowing that the 'order' permits and embodies.

Inquiry shows that knowledge does not have to be limited by any system or 'order', for each system of knowing, with all its intrinsic limitations on what can be known, is itself an embodiment of Great Knowledge. This global, embodied knowledge can also be explored, in a knowing that reveals Knowledge to itself.

Knowing the 'order' directly requires dropping any commitment to the 'order'. Yet 'we' as the inquirers rely on the 'order', taking our identity from the specific forms of knowledge, space, and time that the 'order' permits. It seems inevitable that on the most basic level, we will be defenders of the 'order'.

For example, though reason and inference can clarify and open new avenues of knowledge, undermine emotionality and bias, and make visible the structure of the whole, they ultimately take their stand within the 'order'. They accept dichotomy and polarity for the simple reason that within the system they are inescapable.

Can we embrace all polarities? So much of our lives is made up of conflict, confusion, restraint, restriction, and misunderstanding. But these aspects of polarity are also made available through knowledge; we could even say that they are created by knowledge. Once we realize this, polarities cannot bind us in the same way; instead, they point toward the deeper, more comprehensive 'knowingness' accessible within the knowledge that shapes the system.

'Knowingness' recognizes distinctions, for the making of distinctions is itself a kind of intelligence. But at the same time, we can see through distinctions as though they had become transparent. Within confusion, we can find the clarity of recognizing that we are confused; within frustration, we can experience without judgment the pain of being frustrated. By embracing who we are and what we know, we free ourselves from the constraints of lower knowledge, which insists on the 'reality' of what is experienced. We awaken to our full capacity as human beings.

The power of inquiry and the strength that it develops determine the measure of what will be possible. Like a far-reaching scientific theory that reveals its predictive force only over time, inquiry initiates a process in which 'knowingness' can come ever more to the fore.

When inquiry is understood as the activity that embodies Great Knowledge, the interplay of Knowledge with Space and Time emerges in a new way. Space opens and its 'contents' are illuminated, like motes of dust that suddenly glow brilliantly in the rays of the sun. Alive with a radiant energy, this activity itself is Time. Space and Time 'feed back' Knowledge: Great Space displays the embodying of Great Knowledge within the temporal realm; Great Time presents the activation of Great Knowledge in inquiry. Unfolding in being vigorously exercised, Great Knowledge inspires its own awakening through an aspiration that deepens into love.

Path of Inquiry

KNOWLEDGE MOVING
TOWARD KNOWING

Knowledge moves naturally toward knowing and will not easily rest within the established constructs of the prevailing 'order', although each conventional act of knowing embodies a structure that limits knowledge, confirming and authenticating limits even as it knows. From the initial insight that this 'order' itself is a construct comes a seeing that recognizes what appears in time and space as a self-perpetuating tendency. What has been 'known' as beyond questioning becomes 'unknown' once again.

When the 'unknown' is allowed to foreclose knowledge, a lack of imagination is in operation. Its source is a lack of inspiration. But investigation can easily offer new inspiration. Knowledge is available within the conventional 'order' in 'places' no one ever thinks to look, because that 'order' *is itself knowledge.* The co-determined appearance of self and world expresses a knowledge available before the beginning and within each moment. The continuing discovery and embodiment of such 'unknown' forms of knowledge marks the path of an inquiry that opens into freedom and delight.

In exploring how to embark on this path, we might invoke the ideal of the 'professional'—one for whom Knowledge is a vocation. For the 'professional', knowledge can be discovered anywhere. When knowledge becomes a calling that calls us toward our own being, we can discover it in art and music and poetry as well as in rocks and trees and stars. Knowledge is found in all living things, as well as in numbers and symbols. It is found in all creativity and inspiration. Knowledge is beauty, delight, and joy, like rich, full humor and laughter. It is love and appreciation, alive with the richest feelings that the heart can offer.

Stimulating and alive, knowledge arises through direct embodiment of the highest human faculties. The individual who follows the path of knowledge is dedicated to knowledge—inspired by a broad vision and by the needs of others, and asking what needs to be known. Pursuing this ideal reminds us that knowing is a human activity with a human face.

Such an individual could be known as a 'knowledge-bearer'—one who makes enormous, *unending* efforts, based on a fundamental *dedication* to knowledge. The knowledge that arises in this way nourishes the spirit and sustains its own unfolding. The model of such a 'knowledge-bearer' points out that knowledge is more than the accumulation of facts. True, each shape or form, each experience or event, has a 'lineage of facts' that could be traced back to the point where form and formlessness arise together. But such a search could be an endless task, and might still leave higher knowledge inaccessible. Real access to knowledge seems to depend on a more basic intelligence that discovers the *patterns* within experience and recognizes them as the manifestation of knowledge.

The web of recorded history is tangled in knots of struggle and sorrow—difficulties of communication and appreciation, actions born of inadequacy, closed hearts, recurring patterns of pain that persist in every generation. It is clear that when knowledge is treated as if it were merely a matter of ideas, it can prove ultimately destructive. But this is not the whole story.

Human beings of great intelligence have walked the face of this planet, some perhaps supremely awakened. The awakening of these 'most fully developed' human beings seems traceable directly to knowledge. We might even say that their 'field of specialization' has been knowledge: how it operates and how it can transform action and feeling. The question for us is how we can join in the heart of this knowledge, or at least imitate it in our own inquiry. Imitation may seem a modest goal, but it gives us a way to start, to learn, to progress, a way to change the course that we have so far followed.

Ordinarily we consider knowledge a potential possession, like a gem embedded in rock that we can discover, cut out, and take away with us. Seeing knowledge as both limited and scarce, we grow jealous of what we know and envy those who seem to know more. We may even resent others for having discovered knowledge before us, so that we can not be the first to obtain it. At times such a feeling may come upon us quite strongly—a sense that we live amidst the ruins of an earlier age of splendor, or that we must make our humble way amidst the achievements of those more knowledgeable than we are.

When we resolve to join the lineage of the great knowledge holders, however, matters look quite different. Instead of being a potential possession, knowledge becomes a facet of being, in partnership with time and space. Born in time and space, we too are partners with knowledge: We share with knowledge our own being, in an arising and emerging that we can share with time and space as well.

Through dedication, knowledge blossoms into the knowing of the heart. The growth of knowledge means the end of restriction, bias, and repetition. It tends naturally toward what is beneficial and inspiring; its perfection brings harmony and creativity. There is no premature resting place—no closed 'body of knowledge' or retreat into tranquility or bliss.

A partnership of time, space, and knowledge gives a world quite different from what history reveals. Space does not discriminate, allowing this one but not that one; instead, all points become one, each interacting with the others. Time does not separate past from present from future: As the unitary time of experience, this triad evokes space and knowledge, which together allow experience to exhibit in wholeness.

The manifestation of beauty or accomplishment by those who most fully embody human capacities seems equally and inescapably a manifestation in, of, and by time and space and knowledge. We can identify this co-relating co-appearance in imagery or symbols, character, qualities, or virtues; we can find it in manifestations that are peaceful or wrathful, in loving joy or its seeming opposite, sorrow.

Knowledge can express enough, time bring up enough, space accommodate enough. We need never feel lost or isolated, or imagine that the best has already happened. We can look to the past and all achievement, or to the future and all potential, drawing inspiration from both. We can invite both equally; and at the same time we can act uniquely ourselves. If perfection beckons, we can choose it, for we have available the fullness of Being and the greatness of Great Knowledge.

Aware of the lineage of knowledge, we can awaken to this fullness. We can open each point, each present singularity of oneness, finding in each point the unique occasion of the whole. We can link past and future through the present, discovering the link through knowledge. If we listen with our hearts and with our being, we can hear a message being broadcast: The present is not stagnant, not determined. There is no 'between' as a separate position, no 'one' that is not 'all', no 'apart from' in what is unique.

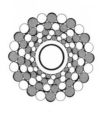

Self Center

KEY OF
KNOWLEDGE

W herever we go, we carry with us a way of knowing—a key that opens the door into the world of
experience. How did the key come into our possession?
It seems that someone gave it to us and showed us how
to fit it into the lock. Human education means being
trained in the use of this key: learning how to perceive,
experience, make inferences, distinguish true from false.
Human capacities give us the potential to be trained in
this way, and human culture assures that this potential
will be realized.

Such knowledge serves a vital purpose, yet we have
reason to suspect that it is incomplete. At times we may
wonder at the wealth of human knowledge and the accomplishments of humanity through the ages, but there
are other times when reviewing the record of human
history will leave us close to complete frustration or
despair. When we think about how difficult it is to

accomplish what we want for ourselves or to cope with our own experience, we can be painfully aware that there has been little progress through the centuries in achieving greater well-being for the peoples of the earth. Though we try to fix, to improve, to adapt what we know, a chronic sense of shortage can bring feelings of tightness and oppression to our hearts.

Perhaps we can remind ourselves that the ways we have of knowing are human constructs that do not begin to tap the full riches of knowledge. There seem to be many keys . . . why do we choose one key over another? How and why were the keys to the door of knowledge manufactured?

Conventional knowledge is primarily the self's device for learning what is happening in its world, and as such, belongs to the self. Only by means of the self's knowledge can we take part in the questioning, interpretation, creation, projection, and action through which we learn the qualities and distinctions that make up 'our' known world.

Conventional knowledge has certain rules that determine how knowledge arises. These rules are based on a subject-object structure: They specify that the knowing faculty is separate from what is to be known, and can gain access to the knowable only through the senses or the mental faculty. Knowledge is the outcome of a 'process', and until this process is completed, a condition of not-knowing is in effect. The process requires space and time: Without *space* for the knowable to appear and *time* for it to exist, it is difficult to imagine that knowledge could arise at all.

The basic model we have for the process of gaining knowledge suggests that the self must manufacture knowledge from the raw material of not-knowing. Accordingly, we look to sequences and consequences rather than origins, like someone who tracks an animal's footprints without ever asking what kind of animal made them. We look to 'feedback' but not to the 'field' within which 'feedback' arises; to the 'bystander' but not to the basis for the 'bystander' way of being.

The world of the self is accepted as given, and therefore certain topics go unexamined. For example, while questions regarding the 'mechanics' of sight or hearing attract considerable attention, the more fundamental issue of the *capacity* for sensory experience—of *how* the structures of existence allow for hearing or seeing in the first place—is seldom raised.

With such a style of knowing in operation, whatever responds to a rhythm or sequence of time that does not allow for the operation of the self, or manifests in ways that cannot be grasped from a single perspective, will remain unknowable. Confined to analyzing the entities that 'bystander knowledge' identifies, judges, and labels, the disciplines within which knowledge is pursued move inexorably toward historical and material determinism. The temporal order in principle is completely knowable in the 'first moment' of time; paradoxically, this claim of 'complete knowability' binds knowledge to the limits implicit in the operation of the 'order' in effect.

Conventional, 'first-level' knowledge seems to depend on conditions that operate only when space and time 'are' a certain way:

First, what is known must occupy a uniquely specifiable space and time, and must interact in space and time in precise and invariant ways with the subject that knows it. For example, the self can observe only objects with which it shares the same time, and which occupy a limited range within space.

Second, events (including the continuing 'existence' of objects) must be distinguishable in terms of a temporal sequencing, the units of which remain constant in their interrelationship. An example is the sequence of cause and effect.

Third, since knowing unfolds over time, it must be capable of communicating itself forward for the 'length' of time required to arrive at a conclusion, while accurately referring back to and incorporating the outcome of previous acts of knowing.

Fourth, for knowing to be 'correct' in its relationship to 'what is known', the 'objective' world must remain congruent with itself for the length of time required for it to be known, and must also remain relatively constant from one completed act of knowing to the next.

All these conditions significantly limit the kinds of knowledge available. Whatever cannot be understood as an event in linear time or an object in 'objective' space—

or at least as analogous to such events and objects—is unknowable. Moreover, there is a built-in bias toward the familiar. Knowledge that departs in significant ways from what is already known tends to be inaccessible.

These limits are so thoroughly ingrained that they *do not appear as limits at all.* Instead, because they are *given by space and time,* these limits seem natural and obvious. In sensory observation, knowledge can know only surfaces, and even those can be known only from one perspective or viewpoint at a time, leaving the whole to be inferred or imagined. Beyond the realm of the senses, knowledge regarding what is neither mechanical and repetitious nor sequential and measurable can be difficult to obtain and will always fall short of certainty. With respect to questions of meaning and significance, there is a pronounced tendency toward error, deception, and misinterpretation. Whatever presents a unique unfolding of complex patterns over time tends to remain mysterious. And certain kinds of knowledge—for example, direct knowledge of past and future—are foreclosed completely.

Such limitations may seem regrettable, but also inescapable. When the world is presented in terms of a time that unfolds and a space that contains, knowledge operates in ways that are presupposed. There seems little point in wishing that it were otherwise.

The specific characteristics of space and time 'in operation' shape the knowledge available. For example, 'existence' arises within a temporal order shaped by specific rhythms of repetition and change. Knowledge discovers and affirms this 'order' and its contents, organizing and defining the distinctions through which the 'order' takes shape and setting up a known world to be experienced. Likewise, the 'objective' world of physical space discloses the existence of both self and objects, interacting in ways that generate knowledge. Our 'key' of knowledge seems able to open only certain doors and not others.

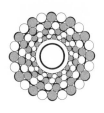

Self Center

SELF AND KNOWLEDGE

Bound to space and time, the self depends for knowledge on the body. Not only does the knowing capacity seem linked to the brain and nervous system, but a knowing instinctive to the body seems virtually co-emergent with consciousness.

As knowledge expands after birth, this corporal knowing is augmented through the physical senses. Even the most abstract ideas still draw on the senses for their 'structures' and governing metaphors.

Knowing through the body depends on repetition and familiarity. Information taken in by the senses is referred back to established patterns; it is assimilated to what is already known and analyzed accordingly. The tendency to fit incoming data into a preestablished program operates at all levels. Thus the scientific method, which relies on repetition and similarity, can be applied with some success not only to physical processes but also to study of the human personality and human institutions.

Yet the self occupies space and time in a way that never fully conforms to established structures of knowing. And there is reason to have fundamental reservations about the whole process. What is this 'self' that is so central and where can it be found? How does it arise, and from where does it obtain its capacities to know, to create, and to interact with the world around it? Beneath the level of personality, personal history, and self-image, the unique nature of the 'being' at the center of experience—the subject in a world of objects—remains strangely inaccessible.

One model for the self holds that it can be reduced to physical structures of the body that manifest in space—to specific operational modes of such physical structures as the brain and nervous system. However, such a view seems self-defeating, for it depends on the *mentally established* distinction between mental and physical. Moreover, this approach leaves out of account plans and constructs, thoughts, emotions, and feelings, and all the other 'interior' events that are normally understood as the very heart of 'being a self'. There is no 'room' for meaning, understanding, and appreciation to unfold.

It might be argued that this defect is due only to the present inadequate development of a particular branch of knowledge, but the difficulty seems to run deeper. By rejecting the ultimate reality of the interior realm, a 'physicalist' view of the self actually affirms the split between subject and object, making limits on knowledge regarding the self *as we experience it* inevitable.

A second model accepts the split between subject and object but proposes that the self occupies its own 'kind' of reality. This view accounts for the 'inaccessibility' of the self (together with 'mind', 'consciousness', or 'awareness') to conventional knowledge. But it leads to the seemingly insurmountable problem of how these two kinds of reality can interact. Since it is just these interactions that make knowledge possible, transforming 'the mystery of the self' into the mystery of 'interaction' between 'self' and 'world' or 'body' and 'mind' does little to advance knowledge.

A third model maintains that subject and object alike are manifestations of mind, enjoying the particular reality appropriate to mental constructs. In one version, this view attributes the 'objective' world to the mind of a creator, leaving the ultimate nature of mind mysterious. Another version assigns the creative power that generates 'existence' to the mind of the subject. The difficulties that arise from this version have to do with establishing intersubjective reality, the intractability of physical events, and so on.

Throughout more than two thousand years of philosophical inquiry, the limitations inherent in each of these three views have never been adequately resolved. We might take this as an indication that there is something wrong with the basic formulations. Our basic view of self and world, subject and object, may be fundamentally mistaken.

If so, the consequences go far beyond the quest for philosophical clarity. We live our lives in accord with the belief in a self, orienting our actions toward its needs and filtering knowledge through its perceptions. If this understanding of what is real gave way, would we find ourselves in a vacuum, paralyzed by the collapse of old constructs? Or would we discover new and unimagined possibilities?

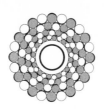

Self Center

BYSTANDER MODEL

In the common sense model of how knowledge arises, it is accepted that knowledge arises through the interaction between an observed object or entity and the observer/experiencer. Two 'entities', each an 'outsider' to the other, are separated by a distance that must somehow be bridged through an 'act of knowing'.

Yet the nature of this distance is mysterious. Although for certain kinds of 'knowledge interactions' we can speak of the physical distance between the 'located observer' and the 'located object' and measure this distance with varying degrees of precision, the distance to be bridged in an act of knowing is different. The observer and the object to be observed appear to occupy different realms entirely. The observer is a 'bystander' to what is observed, not necessarily involved in the physical realm at all.

True, the observer has a body that occupies space and determines location, but the body is also an 'outsider';

that is, 'I' am not 'my' body. In the same way, 'I' am not 'my' physical sensations or even 'my' thoughts. Then where is the 'bystander-observer' located? What kind of space does it occupy, and how can the distance between this space and the space of the 'outsider' be bridged?

If the 'outsider-object', located 'there', is distant, it would seem that the 'bystander-subject', located 'here', would not be distant at all. But the reverse is true: The 'bystander' is perhaps the most distant of all, for as soon as we turn to observe it, it becomes another 'outsider'. 'Here' proves to be impossibly far removed from the realm available through conventional knowledge.

This inaccessibility can be clarified through the model that understands knowledge as information generated by 'feedback' from the entities we want to know. Unless we take the rather radical position that the appearance of objects in the first place is 'subject-generated', the knowing of objects in the conventional way provides no 'feedback' regarding the 'bystander', which thus remains unknowable.

Although we cannot account for the nature of the 'bystander', we can say a great deal about the way that it operates. The self lives out the 'bystander' model. Interacting with such 'outsiders' as objects and experience, the self attempts to identify, measure out, and control its territory. Applying such dichotomies as 'exist/not exist' and 'occupied/unoccupied', it seeks to establish a world that behaves in orderly and desirable ways.

The 'field' of 'bystander-outsider interaction' possesses a characteristic 'feel' and an intrinsic temporal momentum that shapes the dynamic of observation. As soon as an act of observation begins, the 'bystander' projects an inner sense of time. In a single 'moment', the energy of an inner intensive awareness contacts what will be identified as an observed object, situating it through juxtapositions and dichotomies that understand the present in terms of a particular past and future.

It seems unlikely that such momentary knowing will be accurate. What is known has already withdrawn from what the object might be said to embody. Certain data has been lost; certain interpretations and projections added. The 'bystander' will function as a 'bias-stander', bound by past positioning and a fixed mode of operation. Viewed as the outcome of the knowing process activated in this way, knowledge seems a rather secondary phenomenon, like a story about a story.

Human beings have long attempted to establish accurate knowledge based on 'bystander awareness'. Definitions are assigned and conclusions reached on the basis of identities constructed through the interaction of momentary awareness with past-centered interpretations and future-centered desires.

Yet when we look honestly, we have to admit that something is missing. Judging by the results, these efforts seem ineffective. The world we discover in 'standing by' is one of dismay and disarray, strongly resistant to our needs and concerns, constantly surprising and disappointing us.

Perhaps these difficulties reflect a fundamental flaw in the 'bystander' way of being. The 'bystander-self' stays removed, never merging into the triple field of time, space, and knowledge. Bound to a specific mode of existing, the self is committed at the outset, indeed for all time, to a specific not-knowing that fosters an ever-present existential disquiet. Truly reliable knowledge seems to depend on a hidden dimension, unseen yet inseparable from what appears, like the back of a coin or the dark side of the moon.

This missing and mysterious dimension is not easily contacted, but there are powerful reasons for making the effort, for the current understanding of knowledge is having impact in ways that are seriously intensifying its shortcomings.

For example, attempts are currently being made to simulate human intelligence using computers programmed on the basis of prevailing models of knowledge. One day soon such machines may be able to communicate with us directly as our peers, and we may even come to rely on them to give us insight into how our minds work. If the model of knowledge that guides these developments leaves something fundamental out of account, we risk losing access to an inner resource that may be our most precious birthright.

We are accustomed to thinking that the 'bystander' mode of being is what sets human beings apart from other entities. After all, who would claim that two insentient objects, both situated in space in the 'ordinary' way, know one another? Who would argue for their sentience, or trade the human way of being for theirs?

It may be, however, that this choice is wrongly put, for 'bystander' and 'outsider' seem to emerge *together*. We might say that the 'bystander' interacts with objects in terms of the 'field' within which the objects appear—a 'field' that must also somehow 'encompass' or at least permit access to the 'bystander'.

Self Center

HIDDEN DIMENSION
OF KNOWLEDGE

As a preliminary move toward the hidden dimension of knowledge, we could look at the 'field' within which knowledge arises. The 'feedback' that gives the 'bystander' information about a known object could be said to depend entirely on the 'field' of knowledge in operation. For example, an object located across the room can generate visual but not tactile 'feedback', while an event that occurred yesterday is available only in the 'field' of memory. But what are such 'fields': How do they function and how are they related to the 'field' within which 'bystander' and 'outsider' jointly emerge? Though we know the specific characteristics or qualities available within a 'field of knowledge'—the descriptions or measurements that it allows—we do not really know the dynamic and the mechanisms of the 'field' itself.

As 'owners' of the awareness specified by the 'field' of conventional reality, we are already 'bystanders', excluded from a deeper knowing that could be said to be at the center of experience. Whatever shape and form experience and mental attitudes take, they express this specific 'bystander' quality.

An indication of this restriction is that awareness takes sequential time as given. Awareness affirms linearity through circularity: Programmed in advance, it supports such programming; established as an outcome, it proceeds step by step. Awareness projects shape and form into preestablished mental capacities, yielding awareness as the result.

Among the capacities that open to receive awareness as outcome are the sense faculties. But there are countless mental positionings as well, such as anger and desire, confusion and self-deception, love and joy, faith and devotion, resentment and self-protection. All such capacities are already embodied, labeled, introduced, and familiar. They give rise to specified qualities and judgeable characteristics—good and evil, right and wrong, and so forth. The awareness they countenance is constricted and restricted, largely devoid of power.

Suppose that awareness were not owned by the 'bystander', and so were available 'within' experience, 'as' experience. In that case awareness would operate 'within' each mental capacity as well. Available at the outset as well as the outcome, such awareness could be understood as the expression of a deeper knowledge, alive with a vitality prior to distinctions and determinations.

Nonconceptual, more than accessible, such a knowledge could never be lost or disturbed. Not bound by sequential time, it would precede the positionings that characterize conventional space, and would remain available and free even when 'caught' in emotional constructs and perceptual frameworks.

Understood as active *within* the 'field', rather than specified *by* the 'field', awareness would lead directly to knowledge. But when we act in accord with position and character, treating awareness as response, we are merely accepting the 'output' of the 'input' put forward by knowledge. If we can 'take out' what has been 'put in' in a way that stays true to knowledge as the source, our acceptance will not specify awareness in a restrictive way. It will not activate the 'order' of sequential time, nor will it validate the 'reality' of the 'spatial field'. Then we can know without character and identity, for we have entered the 'field' of space without borders, a world in which our own being seems suddenly different.

The 'quality' of this 'field' is one of perfect liberation. We can see that we have been born in freedom, that our 'potential' need not be given in advance by rules, beliefs, or other exponents of limited patterning. Knowledge can be the master of all operations, giving us the choice to act as we will.

Ordinarily we have no power over the manifestations of human patternings; instead, they overpower us. Preoccupying thoughts establish inescapable ways of seeing, and we 'recognize' that our being has been cast in a mold. But even when preoccupied by specific mental attitudes and their concurrent rhythms, knowledge activates *as* labeling and establishing, creating full character and manifesting experience in all its various flavors. Seeing knowledge as ever-present in this way, we touch the Body of Knowledge within experience as *inseparable* from awareness. The conventional, rational order, dictated by limitations in time, space, and knowledge, repetitiously bound in circles, self-burdened for all time, is not the last word. *Within its limits,* Great Knowledge is active.

If we turn from the self to investigate the world as given by the temporal order as a specific *presentation* in time and a specific *exhibition* in space, we allow for the possibility that time, space, and knowledge might interact in completely different ways, yielding a 'reality' not centered on the self. Perhaps this 'reality' would be located 'somewhere else', but perhaps also it would interpenetrate our own known world—a secret code pulsing throughout the 'known' universe.

To take this possibility beyond the realm of the hypothetical, we could seek out a different kind of 'feedback'. The world presents itself in ways that conform to our capacity for knowledge: The *content* of what is known is in intimate harmony with the *knowing* of it. If we take this circumstance as indicating that knowledge is 'embodied' in its known world, a new possibility for knowing presents itself. We can turn from the content of what is known to look at the interaction between what time presents, space exhibits, and knowledge knows. We can let presuppositions as to knowledge—its nature, location, and limits—fall away. Though old patterns and standard descriptions can be readily accounted for, they need not limit knowledge.

In the unfolding of a knowledge embodied in the activity of knowing, we find that the more carefully we look, the *closer* the topic being investigated comes to us, until ultimately *we ourselves are the subjects of the inquiry.* This is so not in the sense that the self is subjected to analysis from outside, but rather in the sense that the fundamental aspects of our own embodied being—time, space, and knowledge—are revealed as wholly interwoven.

At this higher level, the act of knowing does not need to obey conventional structures: It need not traverse a distance, nor does it have to be 'measured out'. The accommodation of space and dynamic of time unfold in knowledge to present an existence that is inevitably and inseparably our own. Knowing and Being enter into a partnership in which knowing and knower are the same.

Such a higher knowledge reveals our ordinary orientation toward knowledge as the expression of a particular 'focal setting' on what is being known. We begin to see what it means to engage a knowledge independent of the 'focal setting'—knowledge as a pervasive medium rather than a project. Activating the newly accessible dynamic of time, knowledge deepens naturally into a greater knowing, akin to intuition.

With knowledge available in this global and pervasive way, it is difficult to say who knows or who possesses knowledge. The knower appears as part of the 'read-out' that time presents: a particular shape and form; an embodiment visible through a specific 'focal setting'. Each presentation is an *invitation* to know rather than an *exposition* of what is to be known. Exposition brings together particular details or forms of expression; it constructs an edifice that can serve as a bridge to a knowledge situated 'somewhere else'. But when knowledge is freely available 'here', there is no need for exposition. Ideas can now be presented as metaphors or symbols: 'pointers' toward a knowledge that is already present.

This comprehensive availability of knowledge goes against our deep convictions. It is as though we had been raised in the utter darkness of a subterranean cavern, endlessly straining to see through the gloom. If we were one day led out into the brilliant light of the sun, would we welcome such all-encompassing illumination, or would we consider it another, more awful form of darkness, and draw back to our more familiar setting?

The availability of a comprehensive knowing depends on a willingness to see 'through' the distinctions we make and the objects we identify. The content of our constructs could be considered part of a 'global read-out': the expression of a particular knowledge and embodiment of a particular time and space. To know the 'read-out' as 'read-out' is itself the awakening of Great Knowledge—a knowledge beyond all specific knowings, attuned to a fundamental 'knowingness'.

Body of Knowledge

SENSE-BASED
KNOWING

Imagine what it would be like to float in outer space. There would be no way to distinguish 'up' from 'down' except by the position of the head in relationship to some other object—a relationship which, in the absence of gravity, might change at any moment.

In the same way, the distinctions on which conventional knowledge is based could not operate apart from established positionings that express (and perhaps create) the 'gravity' of the present situation. In this sense, knowledge arises as the outcome of the positions we already occupy. Communicating knowledge to others and having them verify it seems to depend on the transmission of such pre-occupied positions, rather than on sharing the direct experience of knowing itself.

The basic positionings that condition knowledge and allow communication are usually based on sense experience. Such 'sense-based' positions, however, can prove unreliable. For example, particle physics operates in realms where standard connections based on sense experience break down and new connections are not easily established.

Contemplating such possibilities, we truly float in empty space, cut off from the constructs we rely on to give us our bearings. When we enter these realms in search of knowledge, the results we obtain are actually 'translations' from the new realm to the old. Even when they prove 'successful', it remains unclear whether this success means that we have gained 'knowledge' of the new realm.

Inquiry into a knowledge consistent with 'higher' levels of space and time raises similar questions. As connections to the everyday world grow increasingly attenuated, ordinary cognition based on the first-level structure of an embodied self may prove to have little value. Then how is orientation possible? Is floating helplessly in space the only alternative to 'positions' and 'gravity'?

Perhaps we could 'reposition' ourselves through logic and mathematics, which seem to remain available even when the connection to the senses and the body somehow fails. But this suggestion may be misleading. Hypothesis, inference, and mathematical reasoning make use of mental faculties and properties that cannot be separated from embodiment. Even the most abstract reasoning capacity of the mind is the outcome of a prior momentum 'embodying' both the body and the physical world. Even the bare circumstance of 'knowability'—the capacity for knowledge inherent in a 'field'—still seems to depend on the structures of body and mind: on positions and on 'gravity'.

As long as we are restricted by positions, we are bound by the division between subject and object. True, the essential interdependence of subject and object suggests an underlying unity, which perception, measurement, and inference could all be considered to confirm. Yet we remain bound by two. And since knowing through distinctions requires two objects to be distinguished, knowledge moves at once to three. When we know by specifying parts, three quickly proliferates. We might say that once there is more than one, there is multiplicity, that 'any' gives 'many'.

The 'measured-out' world that takes form through such multiplication is reflected in the limitations inherent in the ways of knowing available to the senses and the mind. Extending the range of the senses through the use of scientific instruments leaves intact structures of viewpoint and observation. Similarly, rational thought will ultimately depend on unfounded axioms that express the not-knowing implicit in two. Even the mathematical equation confirms not-knowing in the moment that the 'equals' sign is set in place.

It might be argued that mathematics is limited only because as a human activity it unfolds in time; considered in its timeless aspect, mathematics could move toward completion. But mathematics cannot escape the incompleteness of the axiomatic. In any event, 'timeless' mathematics is a construct: It is the *activity* of mathematics that offers knowledge.

While the limitations of subjective knowing and the incompleteness of the axiomatic may seem frustrating, they also point to a new source of knowledge. *As a limit,* each axiom is unlimited, for it carries implicit within it *the whole* of the unknown. Just as cracking the atom releases the vast energy bound up in physical structures, so cracking the axioms and limits of the unknown might release an energy so potent it could transform our world.

Body of Knowledge

MULTIPLE DIMENSIONALITY
OF KNOWLEDGE

W ithin time and space, infinite manifestations seem possible. Ordinarily, such manifestations lead to the playing out of specific roles: a certain place, a certain 'order', a specific character.

As these roles are adopted, they act on one another, multiplying into the whole range of what is. The outcome, though vast beyond imagining, nevertheless incorporates a sense of constriction: There is one way to be or to act, one truth and one reality.

Yet even on the conventional level, such a single-minded way is not true to being. The reality of ordinary experience is also the reality of subatomic particles and microscopic organisms, of vibrating molecules and radiating waves of energy. The reality of shape and form 'coexists' with the translucent reality of energy and the vital reality of our minds in operation.

The truth of multiple dimensionality interacts with the truth of unitary being. Each individual entity shares the same space and time, the same temporal order and 'field' of being. Each point in space or time is integral to the others, for each is part of the whole and each invites greater involvement and interest. Though each point can in principle be infinitely divided, no division will affect the unitary interplay of being. Though we can specify time to a trillionth of a second, we will never reach the underlying 'timeness' of time, nor will we ever be able to measure its 'vastness'.

Applied to knowledge, the unity of dimensionality reveals everything as possibility. How many developments could be made available to knowledge in 600 million years? Even what cannot be developed, what seems impossible, is based on a 'cannot' that is also a part of what is allowed. If this is so, where are the limits? Although we think we understand the process of measurement through which limits are imposed, our understanding may have to be revised. Can there be measurement that does not exclude, and limits that do not serve as barriers?

The possibility of all possibilities celebrates the interaction of space, time, and knowledge. Perhaps it is true that knowledge throughout recorded time has developed in just one way, but how many different ways are possible! This universe is the only one we know, but how many different universes could take form! There seem to be no limits—only unfolding aspects of dimensionality.

Whether or not we can activate this 'multiple dimensionality' of knowledge will have a great deal to do with attitude. The self tends to adopt set attitudes in accord with the specific roles seen as available. But with the realization that knowledge *could be* more open, we can become aware of these attitudes in operation. Aware of knowledge as the outcome of countless interactions, we may see how the original vastness of knowledge has been attributed and exercised in ways that 'measure it out'. As inquiry brings awareness, observation, and intelligence into play, we can see what attitudes support effective knowing.

Here again we may feel overwhelmed. Seeing how knowledge is distributed and narrowed down, how we attempt to capture it through the structures we impose, how we support our own limitations, we may find ourselves pulling back from looking openly. For mind confined to the psychological level, it may be too much to think about or grasp; for mind on the level of feelings, it may be too painful or shocking to recognize what we are doing to ourselves.

This view does not take awareness far enough. Having discovered a door to new knowledge, we do not have to accept or reject what we see as we stand in the doorway. The multiple range of opportunities, the countless ways of seeing and being, allow for wonder and delight. These possibilities are themselves knowledge. Their availability reveals the self-concern of 'what matters to us' as the outcome of a particular 'focal setting'. From a wider perspective, there is no need to personalize knowledge or put it to use; there is no need to turn knowledge into a key or weapon.

When knowledge is complete, its availability to be owned and to establish an owner does not foreclose its being available also as a guide and a friend. We can go even further. Aware that knowledge has no bounds, we can resolve not just to know knowledge, but to embody it—to *unite* with the Body of Knowledge as the full expression of our own being. We can activate the realization that knowledge is all.

The multiple dimensionality of space and time and knowledge as given together extends beyond the furthest point that can be seen. It suggests space and time and knowledge as alive, as the source of life—for if these ever-allowing aspects of Being were not alive, how could life ever manifest? We may not know what to make of such possibilities, but at least we can acknowledge that we seem able to entertain them, and that they are not just dreams that vanish into air when we shake off sleep. If we allow for this initial openness, not returning to a foreclosed *way* of being, a new 'field' emerges, bearing a new 'feel' for experience.

Attuned to this 'feel', or to its distant echo, we can leave the open open. Without giving up reason as a starting point, we can see 'into' the reasonable and into our responses to what is not bound by reason. We can glimpse within appearance the shadow of 'something else'. We can question, allowing our questions to echo in multiple dimensions. Where does the future come from? How far can we divide up points? What is beyond the farthest border? How does it feel to be kissed by space?

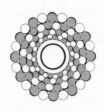

Body of Knowledge

KNOWLEDGE
AS CAPACITY

As the guardian of conventional knowledge, the mind functions like a benevolent ruler, collecting and distributing knowledge for our benefit. It sets policies and establishes structures, intent on fostering our security and well-being. Safeguarded by the activity of the mind, we can go about our business from day to day free from fundamental fear. True, the unknown, the unanticipated, and the uncontrollable remind us that chaos can lurk beneath the established order. But the familiar routines keep anxiety in check, while offering a degree of freedom to choose among established alternatives.

Still, we may wonder whether we could not discover greater freedom. The mind attempts to distribute knowledge in accord with our needs, but perhaps we are ready to seek out knowledge for ourselves, and even to question whether need should be the determining factor in our lives. We might imagine that in the distant past we had made a pact with mind, turning over knowledge in return for the assurance of security. Now we may be ready to reclaim the power that we gave away, seeing that we are no longer getting the best of the bargain.

To pursue this course, we can start by looking at the mind itself, ready to work with knowledge as the mind presents it, but not content to accept that presentation as final. Our focus will be the limits on knowledge that the mind affirms: the obstacles to knowledge that must be overcome.

It might seem that we would have to break through those obstacles in the hope of finding more knowledge 'beyond', but there is a more direct approach. How are the obstacles themselves set into place? How do we know that these obstacles are real? The mind communicates the knowing that can answer these questions *in the form of the obstacle itself.* Considered in this light, obstacles to knowledge are themselves *a form of knowledge.* The role they play in marking the *end* of knowledge may simply be an interpretation made by mind.

Knowing limits as limits, we know them also as knowledge. Aware of the mind as the one that affirms limits, we can ask whether mind too is knowledge. If so, knowledge becomes freely available in a previously unsuspected way. Self-sufficient, self-reliant, and dynamic, the mind expresses knowledge *not as content but as capacity.*

Such a knowledge is not ours to own, but is also not separate from us. Not based in structures of 'from' and 'to', not dependent on ideas or information, knowledge can appear to us as our own being. Even the mind, the unknown factor that conceals its own nature in determining what can be known, can lead us toward a deeper, more comprehensive knowing.

Awake to the 'potential' for an unbounded knowledge, we encounter experience as available for transformation, like base metals awaiting alchemical transmutation. The aspects of mind that seem most cut off from knowledge, including our emotional responses, our familiar set of day-to-day concerns, can be seen as potentially radiant with 'knowingness'.

Though we may not have words to describe this unbounded knowledge, it can still be communicated, for the words we choose can communicate knowledge not only through content or reference, but also just in the act of being spoken. Indeed, knowledge can speak in the powerful dynamic that manifests shape and form. We discover this knowledge through the senses as well as through the mind, through adopting particular points of view and through maintaining an unsullied clarity.

Like the petals of a beautiful flower, the fragrance of the most rare perfume, or the texture of a perfectly realized piece of music, knowledge appears within whatever manifests. We might understand knowledge as the delight inherent in perception, sensing, and defining, the joy available within thoughts and within each and every way of knowing.

Tapping this 'potential', we can find within the content that the mind acknowledges a fantastic exhilaration, a rainbow of light—clear and vibrant, sharp and dynamic. Even within our most constricted moments of preoccupation, when consensus restricts knowing to the surface, a magical knowledge is accessible. Within all 'minding', the Body of Knowledge offers full, illuminated awareness.

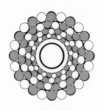

Body of Knowledge

WHAT MATTERS
TO THE MIND

To investigate the 'source' of knowledge, we can start by looking at the multiple dimensionality of mind. Questions about basic structures such as 'experience' or 'subject and object' can lead to a certain level of insight; from that level we can set forth again, exploring and expanding on what we have already discovered.

What do we know about the mind itself? Although we say the mind knows, what is mind? Where does mind live? Does it have color and taste? What is its ancestry? Where does it come from and where does it go? What happens to mind when we forget, and what is the relation between mind and memory? What happens to mind when we sleep? Is mind 'mine'?

Meaning unfolds on many levels, giving multiple realities of mind. Experience leads from point to point. Subject and object relate in countless ways: forward and

backward, reflecting, sharing energy, establishing opposition, touching, joining in partnership. Projection and
'feedback' establish an 'order'; self and world interact;
physical and mental share a mutual determination.

But this level of multiple interaction can also easily
be called into question. When we set up structures and
specify the elements of experience, are we doing anything more than playing with words and ideas? Is the
'reality' of words more than just noise? Is there a truth to
knowledge more basic than specification?

We can look at what we do seem to know about the
mind. Mind experiences in past and present and future.
From awareness comes a recording of what appears; then
connections are made, based on the self or the entity to
be observed, and framed in terms of experience. Assigning identity makes experience 'real' and prepares the way
for reaction and judgment.

With identification, experience has moved into the
past and is gone. As already gone, what shows up no
longer 'matters', for it cannot be 'alive'. Bound to what
'does not matter', we move on, looking for what is meaningful in another 'part' of reality, another 'place' in space,
or a different 'source' of meaning.

Although 'doesn't matter' tends toward the meaningless, it also suggests that matters could be otherwise. In
one way, our difficulty is that experience matters too
much. When we reject, that matters; when we judge, that
matters. In terms of the identifications we have made,
we care very much, even if it is a caring based at bottom
on having nothing more fundamental to care about.

The twofold structure of caring suggests the possibility of a reversal. When we judge and reject, we could say it is *this* that 'doesn't matter'. Our concerns and problems may be problematic due simply to the way we characterize how we want matters to be. If what mattered changed, knowledge and experience might not be bound in the way we imagine. What seems to make a major difference might be completely different.

Whatever position we record, however important it seems to us, may represent only a single small point, like the period at the end of this sentence. To see whether this is so, we could ask what knowledge makes the 'point' available. If we do this in a particular way, not trying to move at once to a new position, the question will change into its 'answer' *in being asked.* The recordings we know will appear as expressions of knowledge. In the end the whole of our being—the sum total of recorded points—will be inseparable from knowledge.

Such global knowledge develops a new direction for 'doesn't matter'. We can take any position, make any point, and in the end 'it doesn't matter'. Like someone who has journeyed to the fabled land of gold, we find that all things and manifestations—sufferings and headaches, radiant light and ecstasy—are priceless. Rhythms of emotions become attributes of knowledge, sorrows and pains sources of understanding. The dynamic of being is appreciated as an emerging exhibition of the potential and the realized. A 'doesn't matter' Body of Knowledge encompasses space, for whatever appears is carved or manufactured by knowledge. Positioning is no longer a question of belonging or identifying; taking shape and form continues, *but it is not 'essential'.*

Perhaps this seems to suggest that no project and no accomplishment matters either. But applied to the values of the realm within which projects and accomplishments arise, this conclusion is deceptive. The change implicit in a 'deeper' 'doesn't matter' is not a change in some aspect of the realm, but in the whole activity of shaping and forming. Different facets take form, different rhythms are expressed and serve as carriers. Only in this context can we say that differences are not vital; that adding and contracting are part of the whole.

If we try to apply this understanding on a more conventional level, we may find ourselves caught in contradiction: There is nothing to say and much to say; it does make a difference and it doesn't; there is nothing to understand and nothing to put in place of what was previously understood. Yet just on these 'grounds', contradiction is allowed as well. When there is truly no place, there is 'room' for contradiction.

It may seem too easy to dismiss contradiction as no contradiction; perhaps this move itself seems to contradict a way of inquiry that is meant to be precise and clear. But accepting contradiction is a barrier to inquiry only when we are committed to content. In a seeing that embodies knowledge, contradictions simply point to the potential for more knowing. How do contradictions arise? What is knowledge, that it can allow for so many different modes of expression? Are the interpretations that let us discover contradiction themselves forms of knowledge?

As we move from layer to layer, level to level, we will readily abandon the view that proclaims things to be simply as they are. We will discover an interweaving that seems to shape experience, as though we were bound to all the universe by gossamer threads—a web of meaning that vibrates everywhere when touched anywhere.

When we know this interweaving, concerns that formerly seemed basic may alter. Birth and death are fundamental to existence, but what significance do they have if existence cannot be separated from nonexistence? Knowing that comes from the structures of the past affirms not-knowing, but what happens to not-knowing if it is not based on past distinctions?

With no separation, there can be no measurement. 'Pointing out' becomes inseparable from what is pointed out, pointing only toward this inseparability. With nothing to point out, there is nowhere to go. And if I do go, how can I distinguish the 'I' that goes from the rhythm of going?

We may be ready to acknowledge that our distinctions are imposed by a fixed way of knowing, based on past structures, present experiences, and future plans. But do we really *know* this to be so? Do we know how past and future affect us and the kind of reality they have? Do we know the nature of mind through our own experience? Do we know the nature of 'experience' and of the one who experiences? If we look honestly, it seems we know what we are; we know the truth of "Here I am." But as for the truth of *how* we came to be, the truth available through active knowing that could transform our being, we have no knowledge.

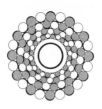

Creative Not-Knowing

BALANCING KNOWING
AND NOT-KNOWING

As human beings, it seems we cannot help but engage in the adventure of knowledge. Usually we do so like passengers aboard a ship who travel wherever the captain decides, ready to experience whatever appears along the way. But we also have the power to proceed independently, letting our intention chart the course that we follow. Engaged in a search for truth and meaning, we can accept insights and glimpses of deeper knowing as they arise, not bound to any particular view, always open to an ever-emerging understanding.

Suppose that we started an inquiry into the nature of existence by focusing on 'substance'. At once a range of questions presents itself. What is the nature of substance? How is it related to the space that surrounds it and the temporal order within which it emerges? What meaning does substance have; what purpose does its existence serve? What might lie 'beyond' substance?

If our inquiry is truly open, we cannot say in advance where these questions would lead us. But by asking questions about how we experience and by activating new resources for knowledge, we would probably be able to access still more basic facets of being.

Eventually, however, certain answers to our questions would take us to a point where no more questions seemed possible. For example, if we came to the understanding that 'space' is simply emptiness—nothing at all—this becomes a stopping point for inquiry. If space has no foundation or qualities, how can it be described? No images apply to 'nothing', for whatever else we might refer it to is 'something'. Is 'having nothing to say' the end of our adventure? Must we finally stand mute in the face of being?

If each inquiry leads back to 'nothing to say', how can we justify departing from that point to affirm a belief or position? Can we support one set of values over another, or defend the choice to act in one way rather than another? Perhaps we could avoid taking positions, but deciding to do so is already the outcome of a highly complex set of positions, based on beliefs, stories, and assumptions. Wary of these positions, we might make a commitment to find a new way of knowing or reasoning: one that did not affirm positions. But this commitment itself affirms the position that we are entities capable of acting in this way. Even referring each position back to 'nothing to say' may be a subtle form of positioning.

The not-knowing implicit in 'nothing to say' might seem to come into play only when we seek out origins, but from a wider perspective not-knowing pervades ordinary knowledge so deeply that it gives to such knowledge its characteristic flavor. Each day we fail to achieve our ends; each day we look on as the mind pursues its restless rhythms, surging out of control. Even questions of interest, value, and involvement, which seem subject to our direction, prove unpredictable. Relying on experience deposited in the past and projections directed toward the future, we steadily present ourselves into time, but still we cannot fabricate the desired present out of an uncertain future.

Distributed out through time, the not-knowing implicit in the ever-present 'nothing to say' manifests as mistakes and frustrations, failures and misunderstandings. Yet when we acknowledge this openly, we have the opportunity to turn inquiry in an unaccustomed direction. What do the failures we experience and the mistakes we make tell us of our circumstances? Can we use them as pointers to the nature of not-knowing?

Usually mistakes are regarded as unwelcome reminders that the knowledge available to us is limited. Instead of drawing on them as capital available for investment, we see mistakes as signs of insolvency; declaring bankruptcy, we start over, pretending that nothing has happened. The painful consequence is that we make the same mistakes over and over again, letting the limits on our knowledge lead us in closed circles.

An awareness direct and immediate in its responses might be able to make better use of mistakes. When unexpected outcomes reveal limits to what we know, we can look not-knowing in the face, searching for signs of a new knowledge. Active, engaged discipline could teach us to work with each new circumstance, refining our projections and plans to make them more accurate and effective.

Like a skilled dancer who incorporates a momentary stumble into the intended movement, perhaps we could apply mistakes immediately in the present, so that the present is directly open to the future. Viewed in a broader perspective, mistakes and failures could be considered local representatives of the not-knowing that pervades our knowing: *points of entry* to expanded knowledge.

In investigating the activity of not-knowing, we naturally begin to also question the nature of 'knowing'. One way to investigate the activity of knowing is to see it as proceeding through a series of positionings. As an object 'presents' itself, the mind takes a position with respect to it. That position then serves as a presupposition for the next, with the link between them supplied through a claim of ownership.

Each presupposed position specifies further what has been presented as a potential object for knowledge, shaping it toward the final act of knowing. At the same time, positioning restricts the range of what can be known to 'information' that can be 'juxtaposed' with what is presupposed. As this twofold dynamic suggests, a way of knowing based on positions and presuppositions seems to balance knowing and not-knowing. Each positioning is both an occasion for knowing more and for closing off a potential domain of knowledge. For example, becoming aware of being located in this immediate time and place makes available a vast range of knowables, but also closes off what is happening in other times and places, or even what is happening 'here' as seen from a different perspective.

If we work out the logic of positioning, however, this seeming balance vanishes. As what is already known 'feeds back' on itself in light of new situations, there is movement in two directions: Old positions are confirmed, while new ones proliferate. Each proliferated position refers back and forth to others, making the 'field' of interactions much more complicated. As proliferation continues, the 'space' available for knowledge becomes increasingly crowded.

The result is to shift the balance between knowing and not-knowing. New positions largely reinforce the old: They obscure potential knowledge that might otherwise have remained available, but do not reveal new knowledge. Not-knowing builds on not-knowing, founding structures that make knowledge almost inaccessible.

Creative Not-Knowing

LIMITS ON
KNOWLEDGE

The structures of not-knowing manifest in the content of what is known, *as the well-established restrictions on that content.* Becoming, perceiving, and acting all accord with such restriction, and the structures of language, shared symbols, and identifying labels join in as well. They create a seamless whole, like a woven fabric or a carefully crafted symphony, expressing a hidden not-knowing in subtle and all-pervasive ways.

When such structures are in operation, whatever does not 'feed back' into the predetermined whole will be understood as meaningless. Perhaps it is set aside as unknown; perhaps it is rejected, distorted, or ignored. The tools available for working with it allow no other access. Since limitations on knowledge are understood as inseparable from the content of knowledge, it becomes unreasonable, even foolish, to ask why knowledge should be limited at all. The all-encompassing 'knowledgeability' of knowledge 'as such' becomes at best an interesting theoretical possibility, at worst a linguistic fallacy.

When knowledge is confined to taking positions, the boundaries of the knowable will remain essentially intact, for no position can diminish the unknown that surrounds the known. The statement just made can serve as a rather special illustration of the point it makes. Understood as a position, what basis is there for accepting or rejecting it? The reader who accepts it implicitly rejects it, for no position can be validly accepted; while the reader who rejects it implicitly affirms it, for the basis for rejecting it must be its incommensurability with previous 'juxtaposed' positions that together set the limits of the knowable.

Any system of knowledge depends on the partition between known and unknown, and thus depends on choosing between opposed alternatives. This methodology reflects a pattern of dichotomy pervasive in experience. Each time we choose, we affirm one position and reject its opposite. In this operation, we inevitably set in place a limited way of being and knowing. A set idea is projected in set ways, shaping and restricting in accord with an 'order' that further inquiry will only confirm.

The starting point for choosing between alternatives is negation. In order to affirm 'A', we must establish it; this means that we must distinguish it from 'not A'. It is the 'not' of 'not A' that establishes 'A'.

This 'not' can be understood as the fundamental tool of logic, which uses it to move in a linear way from point to point. Logical principles such as identity and contradiction depend on the 'power' of 'not' for their effectiveness.

Carefully considered, the truths arrived at through this logic of linear negation can never be final. A logical truth cannot establish itself; it must be referred back to other, more basic truths, and so on. Even 'referred back' and 'arriving at' are processes whose validity could only be established in this way. Whatever path we take, whatever branches we follow, in the end we are led to the point of having 'nothing to say.'

Based only on positions, the 'order' we rely on cannot truly be founded at all. Though we rely on 'witnesses' to affirm the truth of the 'order', the 'air' of trustworthiness each witness communicates is itself unfounded. The 'feel' of certainty available through sense data, the law of contradiction, principles of causality, ethical standards, and so on is real enough, but has no foundation other than juxtaposed positions. And even if 'tracing' did yield a trace of certainty, tracing too can be validated as a procedure only through a knowing without foundation.

The witness attempts to establish the truth of what is known from within what is known. Its knowledge is a not-knowing: a knowing that is not capable of holding the whole. Indeed, the 'air of authenticity' that the witness projects may emanate *from the specific limits on knowledge* that the witness names and maintains. In the end, what the witness affirms is not knowledge, but its surrounding unknown.

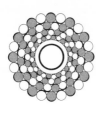

Creative Not-Knowing

NON-POSITIONED
WITNESS

The sense that our knowledge—including our insights, cherished experiences, and strong feelings—
traces only to unfounded positions can be deeply
discouraging. But who is the witness that guarantees the
truth of limitation? When we affirm that our knowledge
is based on not-knowing, we are still caught up in the
opposition between affirming and rejecting. Perhaps instead we could steer a course that did not rely on opposition at all. Without 'rejecting' conventional ways of
knowing, could we accept whatever appears—including
all oppositions and all limitations—as manifestations of
knowledge?

To raise this possibility seems to deny it, for it calls
on us to choose one alternative over another—new
knowledge over the conventional. The move seems inescapable, for if inquiry did not proceed by making com-
mitments to various positions sequentially, how could

any conclusions be reached or any basis for action established? How can there be a witness who does not 'take the stand'?

The search for a non-positioned witness has gone on for time beyond measure. One move often made is to assert the existence of physical objects as wholly independent of the positions adopted by the subject who knows them. Yet the claim of independence is itself a position. Not only does it leave out of account the way that objects arise as the *expression* of meaning-giving activity; more fundamentally, it leaves intact a founding set of assumptions about whose founding we ultimately had 'nothing to say'.

A somewhat more subtle attempt to establish a non-positioned witness depends on having the witness *proclaim* a realm beyond positions and positioning, without *claiming* to represent that realm. Such a witness is free to acknowledge its own limits. The positioned, 'lesser' witness points to an (unknowable) witness beyond itself and attempts to found what is known as based on the (mute) testimony of this higher witness. The very limitations on conventional knowledge are interpreted as pointers toward this ineffable unknown.

Yet a witness who relies on the unknown as its own witness seems only to confirm the primacy of the unknown. Based on such a view, whoever could honestly claim not to understand could at the same time proclaim himself to be in possession of the truth.

To assert an unknown as active 'beyond' the limits on knowledge confirms unknowability as the final truth of human being. Like a map to buried treasure that is worthless because it is missing some crucial piece of information, such knowledge in the end offers only another version of 'nothing to say'.

Although we might try other witnesses, the pattern seems clear: One way or another, each witness affirms the limits of knowledge, returning us to the unknown. If this is so, perhaps we could look directly *to the unknown*—not as situated beyond knowledge, or as the end of knowledge, but as active within knowledge. In the structure of unfounded knowing, only the unknown adopts no positions and makes no claims. What would happen if we let an active not-knowing play the role of witness for knowledge?

The incompleteness of a logic of identity and contradiction suggests that the 'not' cannot be considered final either. Since what has been established by negation can be negated in turn, each established outcome is subject to further manipulation and distinction-making. There can always be more words about words, more concepts about concepts.

Is negation itself established? An established negation could be negated through another act of negation, which would then have to be negated in turn. On the other hand, a non-established negation would seem to lack the power to establish what it affirms through its negation, leaving 'establishing' itself unestablished.

Again we have arrived at 'nothing to say', but with a difference: Now the 'nothing' of 'nothing to say' appears not at the point of origin, but *within* the establishing of what is established. Does this mean that when we speak of what is established, we are saying 'nothing'? And what of *this* 'nothing'? 'Nothing' can be established only if it is referred to something, but in that case, how can it be nothing?

Perhaps the reply is simply, "Nothing is nothing." But this statement, if not just a cry of exasperation, is deceptive. The second 'nothing' in the statement adds 'nothing' to the first; if we reflect on this, we can see that the 'is' that claims to make the connection cannot legitimately do so.

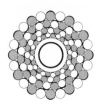

Creative Not-Knowing

DOUBLE NEGATION

L et us return to our starting point: that we choose and take positions by distinguishing 'A' from 'not A'. To make such a distinction, we must be prepared to say: 'A' *is not* 'not A'. In this statement, a second 'not' enters and joins forces with the affirming 'is'. This second 'not' seems to play a different role from the first: It 'cuts' without founding and allows without affirming.

Let us provisionally describe the role of this second, nonaffirming 'not' by saying that it allows for 'realizing' both 'A' and 'not A' *without affirming either one*. That is, knowing 'A' is not an obstacle to knowing 'not A', and knowing 'not A' is not an obstacle to knowing 'A'. 'Realization' in this sense is the nonarising of an obstacle to knowledge—a not 'not-knowing'.

As the tool of linear logic, conventional negation thrusts forward actively, moving from an affirmed subjective source toward a confirmed objective outcome. Its momentum is put into play to establish the opposite of what is negated. But 'realization' is neither subjective nor objective. Its structure of double negation—the 'not not'—suggests a knowing not bound by positions. It could be said to express the negation of conventional negation, 'establishing' full openness by not establishing anything. Taking no sides, it restores the restrictive not 'not not-knowing' of single negation to knowledge, through a not 'not not not-knowing'.

Put another way, 'realization' returns negation to itself by negating a 'not' that has never been affirmed. But this is also not quite accurate, because even the single negation that forms the basis for distinction has never tried to establish itself; it is only the 'logic' of the temporal order that puts it to use. Seen in light of the 'not-not', negation does not require negation.

Knowledge that has been established through the logic of single negation could be understood as a 'not-knowing' of negation: a use of negation for the purpose of affirmation. Realization attempts to establish the infallibility of the known or affirmed, but can do so only by also establishing the fallibility of the unknown or negated. As the basis for affirmation, such linear negation will always leave something unknown—in speaking it will always leave something unsayable.

'Realization', on the other hand, means that nothing is established, and thus nothing is left to be untrue. It speaks in a way that leaves nothing unsaid: no hindrances, no obstacles, no imperfections or impediments. All that is established is recognition of the 'not' as 'not', or more precisely, the 'not' as not 'not not'. The 'realization' implicit in this manifold 'not' will be complete and will not fail. Since nothing has been affirmed, nothing stands 'outside realization' as its enemy or obstacle.

As long as we regard 'realization' as a hypothetical construct, the distinction between 'not-not' and affirmation will be a matter of words. But 'realization' can be put into practice directly in any circumstance. In looking at an object or experiencing a feeling, we do not need to say 'yes' or 'no'. We can 'realize' the object or feeling *together with* what it is not, letting 'is' and 'is not' arise as a whole. In the same way we can bring together knowing and known, joining awareness to 'realization' with all the intensity available to us.

The knowledge that opens in this way, not committed to saying yes or no, is not bound by the endless oppositions of conventional knowing. It can sound in accord with a new and more dynamic rhythm. Planted in the soil of experience, such a knowledge can blossom into joy, love, wisdom, and strength. When we completely embrace this possibility, affirming neither the one who embraces nor what is embraced, we enter a world of ecstatic, boundless freedom, based on perfect 'realization'.

Perhaps we have already caught a glimpse of this potential in our own lives, or perhaps we recognize it under different names in religious and spiritual traditions. Now we can explore it as the gift of 'realization'. With no positions to maintain, 'realization' lets Space and Time and Knowledge manifest without restriction, healing and transforming the field of experience, the human psyche, and the elements of existence.

What can we make of such a possibility? Unless it were in some sense available, would we even have the words to speak of it? Yet if we speak in a way that affirms or denies, how can we hold the possibility open? Saying 'yes' or 'no' only leaves knowledge unfounded—the first step in creating a never-ending need for more knowledge. Through affirmation, not-knowing is established as a limit; from that point on, knowledge can give as the meaning of what is known only what does not hold. Whatever the starting point, the 'feedback' that follows leads to discouragement.

The need for knowledge, however, and the discouragement it leads to, are not intrinsic to knowledge itself. Knowledge is knowledgeable without limitation, open to not-knowing as well as knowing. Knowing this, could we hold the whole of the Body of Knowledge? Could knowledge uphold itself, holding no positions yet allowing for infinite positioning? These prospects are facets of human being, linked to time and space. When we actively explore them, we give new scope to our own potential.

The starting point is to investigate shape and form: the nature of what arises and how it arises. This inquiry will lead to the senses, inviting perception that does not depend on agreed-upon projections and does not affirm what is perceived. From there we can look at speech, proclaiming the truth of being in ways that do not exclude or limit. Finally, we can touch the source of meaning and value.

Step by step, such an inquiry can activate the Body of Knowledge. Beyond yes and no, existence and nonexistence, the Body of Knowledge knows nothing of limitation and leaves nothing aside. It is the truth of our own being, free without ever having been restricted, alive without ever having come to be.

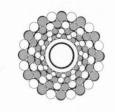

BEFORE
NAME AND FORM

The human mind, with its layers of understanding and interpretation laid down like different geologic strata, is growing ever more dominant in shaping the world. The names and forms that we give and use to identify have proliferated, like ground cover that starts from a single seed and grows in all directions.

Tendencies toward uniformity and standardization contribute to this growth, supported both by those who wish to extend such standards and those who wish to adopt them. Still, the very fact of such growth suggests that for each individual and for humanity as a whole, there must have been a time when the 'order' that the mind sets in place had not yet formed at all.

In this time of the beginning, there would have been no measurement and no basis for agreement; no numbers and so no quantity. There would not even have been qualities, for quality depends on contrast and comparison, and so requires the act of distinction-making that leads from one to two.

Although it may be only speculative to imagine such a consciousness in operation, the logic that suggests there must have been such a time and such a way of 'minding' invites us to let the imagination roam free. Perhaps there is little to say about this 'original' state, but calling it to mind may at least allow us to specify more fully how the 'transition' to name and form has affected our ways of knowing.

From an original state of no distinctions and no specification, names have been established, allowing us to know what is. We know blue in knowing 'blueness'; know it in such a way that we feel it; know and feel in ways so closely linked that the perception and the designation are almost one. And this knowing is in some sense universal, for 'blueness' is shared by all those who form a part of this culture.

This universal nature of what is known is actually easier to contact than the specifics of it. Within consciousness, the 'blueness' of what is blue is difficult to evaluate, but communication with others regarding 'blueness' poses no particular difficulties. It would seem that our conventional knowledge depends first and fundamentally on such universals—names assigned on the basis of agreement.

In the realms of art, music, and spirituality, a different kind of knowledge seems to operate—direct aesthetic experience of individual singulars. Such an aesthetic way of perceiving opens experience in powerful ways. Through contact with the 'singularity' of what appears, we can taste a special joy and beauty. If such experience goes deep enough, it offers peace of mind, and occasionally may even let us glimpse a realm of pure light in a truly transcending experience.

When we return to the domain of universals, of name and form, such experiences will not make themselves available for accurate description. Still, we will be left with the sense that something remarkable and different has entered our lives, bringing with it a sense of fulfillment and well-being. We may sense the prospect for a knowledge missing from the everyday world, for which we know no reliable point of access.

If we imagine an original 'minding' without names, before values and distinctions, interactions and communication, we return to the circumstance of singularity. In this singularity, 'zero' and 'one' are much the same: 'zero' as the absence of what can be distinguished and 'one' as the whole without distinction. Indeed, the distinction that gives 'zero' and 'one' is already a step away from singularity—in making a distinction, it creates two.

For ordinary consciousness, this move from 'zero' to 'one', and thus to two, is 'preordained'. It may, however, be possible to stay at the level of 'zero'—the space of thought before the move into the 'positive' dimension of cognition.

Mind at the 'zero level' is without language or presuppositions—like a newborn baby. Observing experience, we may initially conclude that this quality of mind is irretrievably lost. But perhaps we still move on this level without paying attention to it or recognizing what is happening. If so, we could train ourselves to notice the 'zero state' more fully, in order to explore the potential for 'knowingness' that it contains.

Consider how difficult it is to investigate a single thought. The investigation is also a thought, observing and possessing what is investigated for the sake of the one who investigates. Thus, there are always two thoughts in action, and if we turn from one to investigate the other, we immediately generate a third.

In the 'zero state', on the other hand, observation is not positioned in terms of one who knows. There is a deep neutrality: an opportunity not to occupy space or time in the usual way. The tendency is strong to 'possess' this neutrality, slipping back into the realm of name and form and 'covering up' 'zero space', as though a shadow had reached out to swallow the light. Yet the tendency toward possession is only a tendency. We can encourage ourselves in the neutrality of 'zero', opening to a way of 'minding' in which the singular presents itself.

To enter the space of 'zero', we can begin by renouncing belonging and positions, whether in the form of images (the objective world) or ownership (claims of the self). If we can do this, a quality of knowing emerges that ordinarily hides itself. At once shy and proud, this nameless quality refuses to be possessed and labeled. If we do assign a label, what we label is not this.

When such nameless knowing engages the matter to be observed, it looks at how it matters to mind, *without setting up mind as separate.* The deep neutrality of 'zero' allows for singularity: Mind and matter can jointly interact and still be *directly* accessible to knowledge. With no subject, there is no object. We could put it this way: If no one 'minds', then nothing 'matters'.

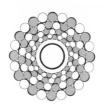

Name and Form

TIMES OF TRANSITION

Although we have no direct access to the 'original' time in history when the activity of naming had not begun, we do have the opportunity to reflect on times of exploration and transition, when old names no longer apply. At such times, whenever and wherever they appear, new worlds of meaning open; new territories and borders and definitions form and shift with dizzying speed. The 'zero state' from which names might be said to emerge is somehow close at hand.

Recalling such times and the distinctive way of being and knowing they represent can put present trends in a new light. In today's rapidly changing world, each day brings problems or concerns for which no words previously existed. Human intelligence and mental processes today seem to move in more intricate rhythms than in the past, as though a new way of knowing was trying to emerge.

357

The evidence of such transformation is visible mainly in signs of difficulty and confusion that appear wherever we look. From simple acts, consequences proliferate in every direction. They expand so rapidly that we cannot take them into account, and we therefore remain in the dark until it is too late. Conflict is easily generated, for the measures it takes to accomplish results in one area clash with the values and concerns of another. Compromises prove to be artificial constructs that cannot hold; in time they lead to the adopting of new positions and new conflicts.

If we attempt to trace the knowledge that has developed in tandem with this complexity, we find that it is more difficult to characterize. As technology gives us ways to process words electronically and science formulates mathematical equations to describe events so strange there are no words for them, the naming process itself changes. Names refer less to physical form and circumstance, while the significance of metaphor grows. Philosophy, art, science, and poetry proceed increasingly through implication and indirection. Projecting into the future, knowing seems headed in directions where words will be unable to contain it. Perhaps parts of our lives may develop in which it is no longer necessary to rely on words at all.

At the same time there is a steady tendency to degrade words and to lose sensitivity to their inner meaning and power. They are used to hide rather than to reveal; to manipulate rather than communicate; they become tools to arouse emotion, encourage artifice, or deflect inquiry and investigation.

Still, these developments do not seem to bring us closer to a knowing at the 'zero level'. We remain bound to words and other symbols that continue to be supplied as needed, whether to identify the unexpected or confirm the well-established. Once the 'right' words are known, we duplicate and distribute their meaning. This same pattern gets repeated again and again, whether in the 'field' of mind or matter or behavior.

The system of knowledge that relies on words and names dominates our understanding and our methods of education. Yet if we try to assess its impact, our judgment will grow out of the system we are trying to evaluate. Although we may hold that such knowledge has brought progress, 'progress' itself is a matter of comparison, made possible through language. Apart from such comparisons, it seems difficult to say whether knowing that arises through name and form could be considered beneficial or harmful.

Name and Form

UNFOLDING
TRANSFORMATION

Fundamental change based on new knowledge or understanding is undeniably a factor in the human experience. But because we are enmeshed in patterns of naming and proclaiming, it can be difficult to imagine any alternative. Moreover, labeling and defining are activities calculated to lead to repetition, so how could they account for the dramatic changes that have occurred in human culture throughout the centuries? Do we have any way to understand how fundamental change occurs?

Since we are the 'owners' of the concepts we apply, using them for our ends, we could say that change comes when *we* change. Most probably, the connection works in both directions: As words and concepts change, we change as well.

If words begin to function differently as symbols, what will become of human beings as symbol-makers? If artificial intelligence advances, will human ways of knowing have to alter with it? Developments in poetry or art or mathematics can transform the mind and mental capacity of whole cultures; will we see such developments emerging in the wake of new technologies? Will individuals who were considered great masters and teachers in the past lose their hold on the human mind and spirit?

Though certain basic thought processes such as those that give rise to the emotions or to the patterns of logic may remain constant, it seems possible that as concepts and images change, the roots of the thinking process, the nature of the human psyche, and even the value that we assign existence may all be transformed.

Furthermore, although we tend to think of human beings as being alike, there is evidence to suggest that individuals and cultures draw on conceptual structures and values that differ at a deep level. True, everyone wants happiness, and each individual reaches maturity through a process of education and acculturation. But thought and mind are implemented through values, and values change from decade to decade and place to place.

This potential for change seems inherent in our own mind and our own ways of knowing as well. We may not be able to see this clearly, for the intelligence we bring to bear is shaped by structures that condition us to see the continuation of the same patterns. But mind and matter and knowledge seem quite clearly to generate a momentum. Though we may not be able to trace the source or directionality of this movement, the prospect for transformation remains.

How could we discover another way of knowing from within the present way? Can there be a mind that looks at mind, or a 'level' of mind that sees mind as one aspect of what is given? Knowing a different way of knowing is like having a dream of waking up: From within the dream, there is no way to verify the truth or falsity of what is being dreamed.

Instead of trying to transport ourselves from one way of knowing or being to another—which may be a hopeless task—perhaps we can explore the momentum of naming and giving form that shapes our current reality. We can begin to do this by looking at the names we assign and the forms to which they give rise, and then at the structures that those names and forms presuppose.

For example, what is the meaning of having a 'home'? What sense of 'locatedness' is presupposed, and what concept of ownership? Who is the one that owns, and how does that one experience 'owning'? What feelings are evoked in connection with such named objects? In what other circumstances do these feelings come to mind?

Once we allow such questions to become truly active in our minds, we can challenge the structuring activity of name and form by questioning the view of time it presupposes. The patterns of name and form require that time can be divided into past, present, and future, and 'measure out' the world in accord with this fundamental 'order'. But suppose we could see the three times as manifestations of rhythm, moving in waves, each appearing like a mushroom that springs up without roots.

Taking this view, we could open to a becoming that 'is' its own unfolding. What role would name and form play then? Within their activity, could we find here a way of knowing that allowed for transformation?

Name and Form

RHYTHMS
OF KNOWLEDGE

Naming could be said to establish the world, for with names come identity and meaning. Names 'express' a momentum of knowing that sets up rhythms of increasing complexity, generating concepts that structure and define. As description is specified with greater accuracy, points emerge, and shape and form can be designated. Now patterns can be discovered, allowing for knowledge that confirms the old or moves toward what is new.

Through name and form, meaning emerges, rich and varied, powerful and subtle. We respond to its presentation strongly, reacting with emotion and conviction, completely involved in what is communicated, representing what we discover to others and to ourselves. In each domain of knowing and acting—religious, philosophical, scientific, practical—words and concepts engage us, exhibiting experience in varying ways, shaping our understanding. If we can articulate the knowledge that results with precision, we gain access to tremendous power, in the same way as someone who uses sound makes beautiful music.

We could summarize these patterns in the following formulation: *Language conducts perception toward reality.* Yet it seems important to acknowledge that the linguistic constructs that give us 'the real' are cultural artifacts. Whether we trace their ultimate origin to a gracious gift from enlightened beings or ascribe it to a string of random and accidental developments, language, symbol, and gesture do not designate anything intrinsic. Within certain limits that can themselves be challenged, a shift in intention will bring about a shift in what is considered 'true' and 'false' as well.

In modern times, we have discovered that the 'realities' of the physical realm unfold with varying momentum at levels from the subatomic to the cosmic. Governed by laws that still await complete discovery, 'reality' exhibits subtle energies 'embodied' in paradoxical particles. As the truths of nature are explored, new surprises emerge, whole new ways of being so distinctive that each of them could almost be said to occupy its own well-defined space.

We know of these newly emerging 'realities' and deduce their operations through name and form, which communicate them to us. But what would happen if a 'reality' unfolded that was truly unique, wholly separate from the old interpretations available through language and symbols, words and images? Because its qualities could not be communicated, we would have no way of knowing it—no way of discovering it or sharing it with others; no way even to accept or reject it as 'real'.

Name and form thus 'give' reality by making knowledge 'of' reality possible. But their giving is magical, for it 'establishes' without establishing a 'real' that is not real. The rules we apply to determine the truth of the real are only a part of the given. Even logic is based only on its own nature, which it holds in common with all that name and form acknowledge.

The giving by name and form that gives the known world is not a giving from 'beyond' that world 'into' the world. The known gives itself, happens of itself. It is a happening that is wholly spontaneous: expression as exhibition. In such a happening, what is given could also be given differently.

The power of giving's happening can be rediscovered in the creativity of writers and poets, the eye of artists, the genius of musicians and thinkers. We find it in the way that language and other forms of expression give meaning beyond the conceptual. At more subtle levels, we see it in the empty embodying of space, as well as in the truths of common sense.

Full allowing of happening discloses giving as spontaneous variations in the rhythms of knowledge. Like an orchestra playing throughout all space, giving expresses all the knowledge recorded in all language and all human voice since the beginning of time. Its music is like a silent echo in space, like the unceasing play of an unmoving rhythm, like the conducting of a dynamic flow of meaning. Proceeding in a 'timely' manner, the giving by name and form is a hidden conducting, bringing out the intrinsic dynamic in all points, so that all points become dimensioned toward being. Not resting or resisting, unceasing unbounded knowledge is conducted naturally into being, expressing echoes of complementary time and accommodating space.

If we take such spontaneous giving as a goal, we may try to direct ourselves toward its happening intensively and forcefully, applying concepts based on imitation. Faithfully following, repeatedly pronouncing, we may believe that we are making progress. But we will be relying on the products of name and form to determine whether our 'progress' has intrinsic value. When that is so, it seems our efforts must founder, for who will judge; who will be the witness?

The happening of giving, inseparable from the content of the given, simply exhibits the beauty of knowledge. The great conductor of the 'timely' conducts the 'feel' of space without moving 'to' or 'from'. The orchestra plays, bringing an imageless content into boundless space. What is conducted into being as substance operates within the image of the physical. Without a giving point, without 'beneathlessness', completely open variation flows, offering freedom, a Knowledge conducted without concept, effortless. A fruitful destiny of sharing is guided toward meaning through the value of the truthful.

Shaping the Known

ACT OF PERCEPTION

In the act of perception that culminates in the recognition 'a red apple', do we see the redness of the apple? Do we see the water it contains, or the sugar and other organic substances that make it up? If we agree that we do not see these aspects, what makes us say that what we see is an apple?

This may seem a strange question, for most often there will be little danger of making a mistake at this level. An apple is not a horse or a rabbit; it is not even an orange. Such possibilities never occur to us. The information we need to make our identification and complete the act of seeing is ready at hand. The image of the apple that forms in our minds is based on this information: previous distinctions communicated forward in time that let us notice this or that aspect and construct from these aspects the identity 'apple'. A series of 'pre-programmed' transitions 'reminds' us at once of what we are seeing. Put differently, we rely on previous concepts and labels to let us recognize the image of the object.

If we reflect on how such recognition arises, we see that sensing comes to completion when we can distinguish an apple from what it is not. An apple is an apple because it is not anything else; conversely, everything else shares the characteristic of not being an apple. It is based on this distinction that we identify the image of the object as the object. In this sense, what we see as the image of the object is more accurately the image of what the object is not. It is negation that describes and points out, determining what appears.

Whenever we give a description in terms of shape and form or quality, we base it on distinctions that trace to negation. But the distinctions also depend on the positive aspect of what is being distinguished. We know an apple in terms of its not being a banana or a houseboat, but in order to say that, we must have available a specific understanding of banana and houseboat. In most contexts, human beings are different from animals, but we know this only on the basis of being able to say something about animals.

It seems that each item has its own specific description, which we must in some sense have 'in mind' in order to determine the image of the object that it is not. When we identify by placing things in categories, we seem to be going back and forth, deriving yes from no and no from yes.

Whatever has a distinctive character is assigned a label: a name that has been previously recorded. This label may vary according to circumstances. A statue is usually a statue, but may also be seen as a chunk of bronze; my robe is usually a robe, but may at times be seen as a length of cotton. But once the label is accepted, it determines the nature of what is known. The world established through individual acts of knowing is based on such labels.

The source of the labels we apply seems to be interpretations communicated back and forth between individuals. Communication sets the conventional standards that will be recorded to determine 'the real'. For example, you and I may share a standard of beauty, or tend to explain human interactions in terms of a particular psychological model. If the agreement is quite strong, this shared 'truth' becomes unchangeable and unshakable.

Seen in this light, the 'trueness' of truth loses its self-evidence. Common sense tells us that truth is what corresponds to reality and suggests ways of testing this correspondence through observation. But the more truth is based on agreement, the less direct observation enters into it. When we all agree that the shape in front of us is an apple, we may not actually have seen the apple at all.

It would be too simple to say that knowledge in its fullness will appear when we replace agreed-upon labels with direct perception. Direct perception in any ordinary sense will always be based on a particular viewpoint and location in space and time—it will yield an intrinsically limited *image* of the object rather than the object itself.

We might say that this limitation on perception reflects a fundamental 'bias'—a commitment to the position held by the perceiver. But such bias seems intrinsic to perception. As human beings, we not only perceive from one particular vantage point, but we perceive in a particular way. Do cats see water as we do? Do frogs? The inner experience or sensory awareness to which we are predisposed by our being sets up certain biases that seem intrinsic to all possible 'fields of knowledge'.

Perhaps we cannot escape our biases or our tendency to assign names to what is seen. Yet knowledge by nature always allows further inquiry. Although labels are standardized based on previously specified distinctions and characteristics, at any time there is the possibility of going 'inside' what has been 'labeled to look at the elements that compose it. This move will at once take us to a new level beneath the usual interpretations, a level that allows for a different way of knowing.

Seeing how our knowing operates, we can open a new dimension on what we know, as though we had gone off at right angles to a path that we had always pursued in one direction only. Although our presupposed determinations affirm that only one story can be accepted as 'true', this affirmation can also be called into question. The single 'true' story can give way to multiple dimensionality. A nonpositioned, unbiased questioning reveals reality in a very different light as *previously recorded determinations and distinctions arising through the transitional operation of indeterminate 'fields of knowledge'.*

Shaping the Known

REACH OF THE
FIELD MECHANISM

The 'fields' of knowledge available to us determine how the sense of reality arises within an experience. For example, the physical receptivity of the eye to light is linked to the mental capacity for seeing: We might say that these two aspects of seeing relate to the 'fields' of 'physical' space and mental awareness respectively.

This distinction between physical and mental is based on categories that operate within a 'field' of their own. What is seen is also interpreted or determined with respect to its various attributes, such as color and shape. A projection is made and the projected object is characterized in terms of qualities. 'Like' and 'dislike', 'useful' and 'useless', 'mine' and 'yours' interact with countless other factors to complete the 'field of the known' in the act of recognition, yielding a final result ("What a beautiful sunset!"). This result can then be further analyzed from other perspectives that call other 'fields' into play.

The transition from one step in this process to the next depends on all the stages being interrelated and co-dependent. Yet each faculty and even each transition between faculties could be seen as having its own 'field' and 'feel'.

Normally we experience this process as unified or even unitary, perhaps because it is so familiar. Of course the eyes can see—why try to look at each stage in the process? But this perspective binds knowledge to what is already known. We could challenge it by focusing on the transitions between 'fields'.

If we look to the senses, the transitions that seem so self-evident are actually quite complex. Although they may feel instantaneous and direct, they depend on a rhythm of transmission 'over' time that succeeds in transferring a quality of momentum and aliveness. The basis for such transmission and transition does not seem to be physical movement: The eye does not go to the top of the mountain, nor does awareness travel there. Instead, there is a characteristic communication 'across' 'fields'—sometimes with a physical 'basis' and sometimes not—that leads to knowledge.

Determination of what has been sensed likewise depends on the transmission of previously recorded distinctions that are communicated 'forward' in time. For example, when we identify the object we see as a red apple, we can do so because we have learned familiarity with colors, with objects, with fruit, and so forth. Without that transmitted familiarity, the senses could not even register what appeared, nor could the awareness in operation 'make sense' of it.

As a preliminary way of summarizing these complex interactions, we could say that for each of the senses, its power to function depends on a very specific 'field mechanism' that reaches both backward and forward in time and allows for transitions through space. Only through the operation of this 'mechanism' does it seem possible for what has been recorded to be transcribed and made available for transmission.

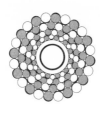

Shaping the Known

FIELD
DETERMINATION

A ny 'field' of perception in operation encompasses certain qualities that are reflected in awareness. This interplay can be seen most directly in the operation of the senses, but also in patterns of thought or emotional reaction. Specific rhythms are at work, as well as specific relationships to time, to space, and to knowledge. Manifesting with different degrees of intensity, these rhythms and relationships give each 'field' a different and characteristic 'feel'.

If we explore this dynamic in its own terms, it seems accurate to say that output based on 'feedback' looks initially to past 'fields' (which in the context of the present could be considered 'indeterminate'), then 'reads out' this input in a way that determines it and establishes its effect. Such 'determining characteristics' have to do with the 'quantity' or 'volume' of energy and the 'quality' of awareness available. The process of determination is based on previous values and experience, but within this context is 'self-determining'.

For the most part, such determinations will fit within well-established patterns. At times, however, the effects generated will offer no clear 'fit', no possibility for applying an accepted interpretation or label. History gives numerous examples of mysterious moments when consciousness seemed to move into a new cycle. Within our personal experience we may have encountered such times as well, though the tendency is to move through these experiences quickly without really taking them 'into' awareness.

Focus on the 'field' might let us explore such occasions by departing from the usual interpretations. Like a scientist with new equipment who has the chance to run a new series of experiments, we could investigate physical reactions, emotional rhythms, or countless other phenomena. We could expand or contract the 'data' available, choosing from a variety of methods depending on our purpose or the degree of accuracy required.

Such inquiry requires us to go 'beneath' mind, senses, and physical circumstances in their conventional operation, freeing ourselves of their influence. Our present limitations, with their characteristic qualities, are based on 'field intensity' and 'feel', and so are not absolute. Ordinary consciousness itself is *determined by the 'field'*. It seems we could cultivate an alternative—an awareness that is free and unknown.

For example, there appears to be a typical way to perceive time based on the character and nature of 'between'. For 'between' to operate, there must be two kinds of experience, or else two 'moments' in experience. Awareness shares from the outset the quality of both these kinds of experiences, as well as the potential for the *difference* between the two to arise. If awareness were different, would time still arise based on the 'between'? If the 'between' took on a different significance, would awareness still function in the same way?

While knowledge ordinarily assigns *time* a beginning and directionality, this is time as seen from outside, as though from the perspective of a 'bystander'. If we imagine looking from within time, it seems that there would be no beginning and no sense of derivation, and thus also no sense of directionality, for derivation and directionality depend on a particular perspective, being linked to a particular position taken in space and to knowing from a particular point of view.

With regard to *space*, knowledge sees this as the domain in which objects 'appear', confirming through their appearance the directionality of time and the truth of derivation. Objects 'in' space derive their shape and form from antecedent circumstances and conditions and from their interrelationships. Though space as such is free from properties and characteristics, it 'shelters' objects and events, allowing their origination, sustaining their characteristics, making them available for interaction, and assuring their continued existence.

As for *knowledge* itself, we might say that knowledge knows what occupies perception. Operating in terms of certain patterns of mental behavior such as thoughts, knowledge expresses established attributes of the human mental capacity. Put differently, knowledge arises in relationship to specific presuppositions regarding the characteristics of the subjective world—the 'field' of thoughts or emotion-centered constructs.

How is this 'field' established? Pursuing this nonstandard question from a first-level perspective, we might offer the following model: Awareness is a readiness to respond. Once experience enters a specific 'field', awareness goes into action, processing what is given in somewhat the same way that the stomach digests food. An image appears and is captured, recorded in a particular way in accord with previously accepted thoughts or perceptions. These recorded images then interact to form the 'field' of permissible knowledge, with individual events linked together sequentially, in accord with the structures of time and space that knowledge affirms.

This model, however, seems misleading in its suggestion that awareness is independent of the 'fields' that specify it and to which it gives rise. Such a view continues to treat awareness (or mind) as a kind of entity. If we look more closely, it seems difficult to conceive of a 'generic' awareness active before the 'fields' to which it responds are established. Instead, it seems more accurate to say that 'fields' are the *determinants* for awareness: They are in operation *before* awareness comes into play.

It is not accurate to view awareness as a response to experience that arises within a 'field'. Though it seems that experience comes first, *experience cannot 'arise' without a specific awareness being there to support it.*

We could say that knowledge arises only when awareness and experience enter into partnership. It is as though one body had two personalities: Experience is within awareness and awareness is within experience.

When awareness is not fixed in particular ways by the 'fields' within which it arises and the predetermined intentions that shape those 'fields', knowledge is likewise not confined to the 'field' of the permissible or the sequential 'rhythm' of temporal perception. Not programmed in the terms specified by the 'field' of ordinary human consciousness, awareness can encompass the 'field' of all possible perceptions; perhaps it can even go beyond the range of the possible.

Since the world of such awareness is not 'reported out' by previous 'juxtapositions', conventional perception cannot embody it. Yet awareness can operate even when not acknowledged in any ordinary sense. The standard rhythm in which movement is at once assigned to 'objects' through the instrumentality of labels need not be the only option. Characteristics and labels that would normally lead to being aware *of* specific content (whether understood as mental events or sensory percepts) can give way to a knowing that is intrinsically lucent.

Understood as a speculative possibility, the prospect for an awareness of 'present indeterminacy' will only support the limitations of 'field characteristics'. But this limitation is not due to an intrinsic defect in knowledge. Though speculation makes awareness restless, knowledge itself is not restless.

Knowledge is unbounded, and so expands. If we let ourselves be bound by the 'gravity' of predetermined becoming, we can join in this expansion in a way that continues our own viewpoint, in which case we will eventually come to a boundary set by the 'field'. But we can also allow Knowledge its nature as pervasive and all-encompassing. Free from the conventional perspective that imposes limits, can limitations on Knowledge truly arise?

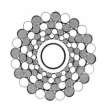

Shaping the Known

FIELDS OF FEELING

Just as the senses predispose us to determine experience in certain ways, so we measure experience out in
accord with other faculties and predispositions. An example would be feelings such as fear, love, and joy, pain,
suffering, and delight.

Such feelings, each of which can be experienced in
various degrees and according to different interpretations, could all be said to establish (or depend on) their
own 'fields'. Beneath each feeling, supporting its activation, preestablished determinations operate; in turn each
feeling creates further determinations.

'Fields' of feeling help determine who we are and
allow us to make judgments and assign values accordingly. Since the awareness active in any given situation
will be related to these feelings, we could say that
feelings *shape* knowledge.

If we pursue the implications of this model, we could say that all modalities of 'minding' shape knowledge in specific ways. The mind creates different manifestations, including senses, feelings, perceptions, and various rhythms of emotionality. It projects what it has created, whether as output ("I am angry") or input ("I am sad"). A mind in balance is content and at peace; a mind out of balance is pushed and pulled in accord with the emotions, including doubt and uncertainty.

In making such distinctions, we already rely on the inputs and outputs of mind. But our model suggests that we do not have to stay on the surface of the energies and elements we distinguish; we can look through them to the quality of the awareness they embody. Seen as interactions 'within' awareness, distinctions express a kind of 'aliveness'. The intensity of awareness available determines the quality of aliveness: It makes aliveness 'live'.

Tracing out awareness in terms of its qualities and intensity, we notice that awareness has a physiological aspect. Sense faculties and feelings are linked to various parts of the body; this body-centered awareness is then linked to the mind, *both making this link and embodying it.* The result is a unity of knowledge specific to each sense: a knowing quality that could be described as physical, but that embodies as well a knowledge restricted only by the boundaries of the 'sense-field'.

For each such form of knowledge, functions or duties or controls or powers respond according to circumstances, giving a unique 'feel' appropriate to the specified 'field'. But each such 'feel'—for body and mind, for each of the senses—can be peeled away. One at a time, or perhaps even simultaneously, we can open up the 'feel' and the boundaries of each physical and mental faculty. As we proceed layer after layer, we come in the end to the commonality of 'knowingness'.

Taking knowledge as the key, observing the interdependence of the stages of perception and reaction, we can make the 'fields' of knowledge transparent, so that 'field determinations' appear less fixed and more variable in nature. In the physical domain this will mean opening into space; for the emotional realm, it means becoming more clear and sharp, less readily caught up in distinctions that carry a specific charge.

Determination operates within each 'field' as the 'self-evidence' of knowledge. Though normally seen as a limit on knowing, it manifests an incomparable power, specifying a world, 'making the point'. Just this shift takes place when we see the 'self-evidence' of knowledge as *transparent*. Not bound to the content of determination, we can appreciate its power as the 'decisive point' in all creation.

Knowledge Ability

STRUCTURE OF PROJECTION

From the 'empty' mind of awareness, how does the quality of the knowable take form? Setting aside our normal models, we point to the process of 'feedback', resulting in recognition that leads to perception, making it possible to pronounce mind and matter, subject and object, self and existence, self and others, here and there.

Distinctions arise through symbols of communication that are not positioned. Born of 'zero gravity', positions and polarity give shape and form; from this come likes and dislikes and emotional reactions. As each reaction is pronounced, it establishes viewpoints and specific ways of cognizing, each presented as trustworthy.

We could model the full expression of this process as having three aspects. At the center is the projecting that pronounces 'something' to be 'born'. Then there is the one that presents it, allowing it 'to be'. Finally, there is the one that projects it into awareness as 'being there'. This triadic structure—which is entrenched establishing through the pronouncing projection of an allowing awareness—repeats on different levels, successively founding more solid positions.

For example, the presentation of an idea into receptive imagination could be understood as leading to 'feedback' that results in an image, projected as though against a 'background' of form. The projection becomes established; the position becomes solid. Distinctions and judgments arise, asserting that they belong to 'someone'. A 'center of gravity' emerges in the form of ownership, yielding the central point: 'Here I am'.

This moving to a central point can be seen as the outcome of pronounced projections. The point presents 'something', in accord with the threefold structure of projection, and is established through its presentation. The 'center of gravity' reinforces itself, expanding into a 'gravity' of polarity. Linear lines of force pull back and forth, founding a continuum that determines a modality of being, such as 'like/dislike' or 'exist/not-exist'.

This basic pattern continues to expand outward in a movement that seems as natural as breathing. Instant proliferation gives the structure of the operative triad in infinite variety, which nonetheless remains a single uniform 'read-out'. Once awareness settles clearly on the central point, the idea is pronounced and the structure established. The projection is reflected and goes back to be possessed by the central point, which now takes up its position.

The possession of the position refers back to the 'gravity' of the polarity and also to what might be considered the longing of the point. It is pronounced and projected again and again, in boundless reactions and reflections. The triad of projection, reflection, reaction affirms in every respect the first-level structures given by 'knowingness'.

Excavation of the projection of knowing becomes the known, complete with the quality of being knowable. Knowing possesses and thus establishes: A recurrent pattern is reinforced, repossessed, recognized. The known is the pronouncing of this 'feedback': an affirmation of the 'source'.

We could restate the happening of this process in a way that is not bound so tightly to the arising of what conventional knowledge affirms. Knowing arises when the knowable is possessed by 'knowingness'. For first-level structures, this means that the knowable can be pronounced in the terms established by the 'gravity' of the underlying triad that the model projects. But at a deeper level, matters appear differently. Awareness presents itself in the intimacy of known and knowing—a rhythm of extension for the allowing possibility of knowledge.

Knowledge Ability

ARISING FREELY
IN AWARENESS

Imagine taking an object, with its specific shape and form, and rolling it out as though it were a ball of clay. As we roll, it becomes thinner and thinner. If we could keep going, eventually the object would become translucent. If we still kept rolling, there would ultimately be almost no distinction between the object 'inside' and the surrounding space 'outside'.

The mind seems able to create translucence in a somewhat similar way. When a thought comes up or we give something attention or energy, the mind focuses in on its content (which is still mind) in a way that determines shape and form. But if we could settle into awareness in a way that was lighter or had a wider 'focal setting', we could open shape and form.

The light of the opening accommodated by this wider 'focal setting' would infuse appearance with a kind of luminosity. With energy and space more integrated, distinctions between 'this' and 'that' would lose much of their significance (though not their 'distinctiveness'). The gap between known objects or between object and subject, as specified through points, would likewise seem less fixed.

A similar transition is possible through a fresh appreciation for the way in which events 'occupy' time. When the energy that time manifests is tightly focused, it presents separation and distinction and character. But a more open appreciation for appearance lets the energy of time become directly available. Distinctions 'dissolve' into unity; the tension of separation (active both in generating and maintaining) disappears.

As a way of experimenting with these capacities of mind, we could allow events and perceptions to arise freely in awareness, in such a way that each object was space and each event time, with the separation between knower and known as knowledge. Patiently cultivated and applied in daily interactions, such a nonstandard way of experiencing could shift awareness to the quality of experience itself.

To pursue this focus on the quality of experience further, we could combine the categories being explored in different ways; for example, by letting the object experienced be knowledge or the separation between knower and known be time. What is the effect of doing this? What combinations seem especially difficult; which ones are easily entered into and expanded? Is there more sensitivity to the light within which objects appear to the mind? To the energy that powers the stream of thoughts?

When the energy of time merges with the accommodation of space, the resulting intimacy discloses knowledge in every point. Participation by awareness, occupancy by space, and bridging of distance by time inform the subject of experience, which now comes into experience directly. Participation takes on new significance: Space (or Time) manifesting to project into Space, allowing a more complete exhibition.

A first-level analogy for such participation might be the way that the light of the sun or moon sparkles in the waters of a lake. Viewed carefully, the reflection is unitary; there is no originating cause and produced effect, no 'from' or 'to'.

This way of looking, however, is still too closely bound to subject and object, leaving their relationship problematic. With greater knowledge, the subject-object relationship itself can become more accommodating or receptive or integrated—only one possible label for what is experienced. In fact, experience itself can be called into question.

The 'coming into being' of appearance can be traced to the interplay of space and awareness. It is as though two 'characters' appeared on stage to enact a play. The curtain opens, and awareness radiates into space like a beam of light, ready to disclose appearance.

Within awareness we can sense a specific wanting to know. Since awareness is linked to existence through the body, this wanting to know of awareness manifests through the senses, which could be considered the 'agents' through which awareness makes its appearance in the world. Indeed, we know awareness only in such specific forms; if we look for an awareness that 'sponsors' the activity of the senses, we will not readily be able to contact it.

The senses have their own momentum, curving naturally in a trajectory directed toward knowing the world. From the moment the infant emerging from the womb asserts its first claims, the senses reach toward what is there. Wanting merges with the frustration of not-having in a fundamental urgency, seeking specific modes of existence or existent entities that will confirm and satisfy.

The outward momentum of sense faculties, propagated through the 'medium' that we identify as space, propels awareness outward as well. What is sensed is divided from what is not sensed, what appears from what does not appear. What is known is accorded a status equal to the awareness that the senses 'embody', while awareness is proclaimed to enjoy a status akin to what is known. The original demand of the originating momentum establishes what appears, together with awareness, *as being existent.*

If the light of awareness encountered only empty space, its radiance would never manifest. Only as objects appear to the senses, creating a reflecting 'surface', can awareness 'come into being'. But the outcome of this specific mode of 'coming into being' is an awareness that is 'mine', its directionality and force appropriated by an 'entity' whose being is as yet unspecified. Knower and known emerge together, supporting one another's candidacy for being.

This initial candidacy is then accorded accreditation. The wanting implicit in the momentum of the senses trends in a specific direction, giving the potential for form to be specified. The potential is actualized through agreement: 'My' awareness encounters 'your' awareness; my 'sense of frustration' and yours confirm one another, creating 'common ground'. A mutuality of wanting gives specification its basis. Agreement finds expression through the faculty of speech. Through the rhythms of voice, labels are communicated, and also meanings based on those labels. Drawing awareness into symbols, language establishes the possibility that particular 'qualities' can be said to 'be'.

Within this realm of symbols and meanings, the fundamental symbol is the self, understood as the one who owns awareness, senses experience, and gives meaning. Tied to the projects and projections of this self, the world appears fully as world: an intricate structure too subtle to be fully apprehended, based on names and definitions, identities and attributes. In inescapable intimacy, self and world take form together, shaping a way of being and giving content to what is.

Knowledge Ability

OPENING THE SENSES

The senses can be understood as the agents or ambassadors of knowledge: envoys who present their credentials in establishing the realm of what is known. But within their activity of establishing, original intimacy remains open for discovery and appreciation.

Gateways to this original knowing, the senses maintain the quality of 'knowingness' and perfect freedom. Although the characteristic modes of perception are 'well known', 'beneath' their presupposed functioning, the senses reflect the allowing of Time by Space.

The embodiment of Knowledge in Space and Time could easily remain a theoretical construct, but in the activity of sense perception it takes on direct experiential significance. Through the sensing of the world, Knowledge can truly be without boundaries, for it is available locally, 'here and now'.

We do Knowledge injustice if we imagine it removed and abstract, unaware of distinctions, in a godlike retirement that robs it of the capacity to see or to know on a conventional level. The activity of the senses counters this limited perspective by returning Knowledge to Being. Through the operation of the senses, the whole of human being is activated as the embodiment of Knowledge. To put it more directly: *Sense perception is an activity of the Body of Knowledge.*

If knowing can be found through the senses, we have at hand the resources to live in the wealth and luxury of a knowledgeable life. Knowledge need never be limited or in short supply. Alive to the unfolding presentations of Time, Space, and Knowledge, we can make use of knowledge to fulfill our highest destiny and transform the world.

Can we say why we have the senses we do? Could we have different senses that embodied knowledge in a different way? Could we make use of our senses in new ways? Could we see with the ears or hear silence? The rules that exclude such possibilities are part of the 'order' that determines the scope of time, space, and knowledge available to us. But if the senses can truly be gateways to new knowledge, then such knowledge can open time and space, creating the possibility for new sense modalities.

By opening the senses, we demonstrate in our own experience that we are 'trainable in knowledge', that greater knowledge affects our lives for the better, and that knowledge is available 'here and now'. We do not need to cultivate 'inspiring' thoughts or 'special experiences':

The path to knowledge depends on greater appreciation for the conventional realm.

If the senses prove able to communicate unexpected knowledge, we could explore other alternatives to conventional knowing as well. Intuition could become a legitimate vehicle for understanding. Knowledge of time could open, and within the realm of history events inexplicable by ordinary logic might reveal new possibilities.

The opening of the senses can be considered a test case for all such possibilities—an invitation for further exploration. We might be able to tap a vast reserve of knowledge, with untold benefits for ourselves and for others. Knowledge could lead to knowledge; the more we explored, the more knowledge would become an extension of our own activity, available in abundance.

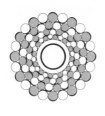

Knowledge Ability

REACHING OUT

When the senses can embrace all-presenting time and all-allowing space, we hear the echo of silent sound and see the shadow of the formless. We feel without imagination or memory, taste without substance, smell without discrimination.

Intimacy opens space and makes experience lighter; obstacles become occasions for learning, and the pressure of mistakes and narrowness of fixed positions is relieved. Old patterns and a new nonpatterning are interchangeable and equally accessible. Benefits flow in a stream of benediction, so that we no longer need to rely on others for healing or well-being. Props that seemed essential in the past are no longer required.

The senses can be cultivated through nine progressive stages. At first they are a tool, then they become a vehicle for knowledge, and next a channel for deeper understanding. With more knowing available, the senses become friends. As this quality deepens, we recognize the senses as agents of a loving master, and in time come to see this master as our good friend. Eventually our friend becomes the dearest and best of friends, who gives us the gift of our own being. Intimacy awakens, and in the end we find the fulfillment of a perfect love.

When the senses open in this manner, our way of life could be considered spiritual—not because of any distinguishing content or style to our knowledge or our activities, but because the quality of life becomes more fully available. Instead of succumbing to the incessant pace of linear time, with its characteristic stream of unending thought, we recognize intimacy as the source of experience, and look to the light of awareness within all thoughts.

The senses open in all directions—as we reach out to know experience, we contact the innermost center of our own hearts as well. We learn that the senses are instruments of the heart, intimate at the deepest level with the time of time. The knowledge they unfold leads awareness to Being and appreciation to the essential quality of Time, Space, and Knowledge.

INTIMACY

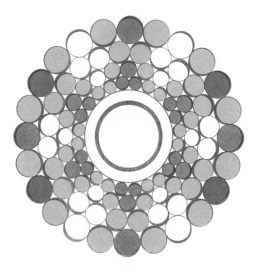

PART FOUR

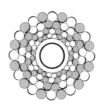

Determining Knowledge

ACTIVATING KNOWLEDGE

What knowledge founds our ways of knowing? Whatever we see or think about, whatever appears in the world we know, is a part of what we can call the Body of Knowledge. We have never in all our experience encountered anything that is not within the Body of Knowledge, nor can we imagine anything ever arising that would be outside it. What we have been taught or learned to imitate is only one aspect of the Body of Knowledge: The entire range of the possible and even the impossible fits within its domain as well.

To explore the Body of Knowledge means to inaugurate an inquiry alive with a special power and beauty. It is an exploration that depends only on willingness, for in each moment the Body of Knowledge is available to be investigated. Barriers to knowing cannot halt such inquiry, for they too are part of the Body of Knowledge. And once activated, knowledge grows of its own accord.

The dynamic set in motion through inquiry can be so powerful that the history of past thought merges with the reality of present experience and the future of boundless expectations. Inquiry unfolds into intimacy in a process that heals as it reveals. The power of exploration can bring into play the being of the one who explores, *together with* all that appears. No matter what point presents itself for investigation, it becomes possible to go beyond it, and eventually to go beyond the structure that gives 'points' as 'topics' for investigation.

If we follow knowledge into the vastness of space and the potential of time, we see that our own limited world, with all its processes and identities, accommodates and embodies a deeper knowing. We can determine for ourselves that in our being and knowing we are the 'carriers' for Great Knowledge.

Human beings express through their knowing the aesthetic of Great Knowledge: its magnificent variety and spontaneous wealth. We can activate this aesthetic through appreciation, touching the unknown Body of Knowledge through direct communication *that does not need to specify in advance what is communicated.* Adapting to the intimacy of knowing, finding knowing within our adaptability, we can discover within each thought-form and each sensory experience a knowing inseparable from being.

In the rhythms of conventional observation, the restless motion of the eyes mirrors the restless momentum of the world that the senses disclose. It is as though the eyes were constantly at work, constructing the world in accord with the fabrications and interpretations of a knowledge that knows no way out.

What would happen if we saw with new eyes, gazing steadily and openly at what is presented? What if we refrained from projecting the image onto what is seen, and from 'making sense' of what appears? Prior to models, such a seeing could accommodate countless interpretations without being fixed or limited to any specific view. It could discover hidden worlds, moving in different rhythms, illuminated in a light not previously seen.

Without seeing and the other senses, knowledge is active only as the 'zero point'. There is no possibility of operating or not operating, no 'reason why' and also no absence of a reason. The allowing (or disallowing) of appearance, of shape and form, is made available only through the senses. It is in their activity that Space projects Space into Space, giving rise (on the conventional level) to the interdependence of form and space.

In such projection, knowledge does not project 'forward into' another preexisting dimension or direction. The projection is nondimensional: intrinsic to appearing. The 'into' comes when seeing (or another sense) 'establishes' the projection of what is seen. On the first level, this 'established projection' is the source of the distinction between space and object. But on a deeper level, projection implicates the interaction of seeing and seen, object and space. 'Lack of distinction' becomes intimacy: the distinctive contribution of the senses to knowledge.

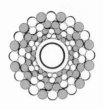

Determining Knowledge

CONSENSUS WORLD

The world of our experience forms a constituency for the known, for assumptions that can be traced to the past of this present. Applying these assumptions, which shape a first level of knowledge, we can describe or define or categorize or specify, presenting evidence to establish facts, factors, or facticity. Through juxtapositions based on the operation of consciousness and the senses, we assemble patterns that we accept as indicators of what is 'happening'. But we cannot go beyond the assumptions themselves or the first-level structures that they present. When consciousness records name and form, it draws on presupposed conceptual or linguistic structures. Descriptions of that which is considered real are based on what has appeared in the past and are categorized accordingly.

If we can be aware of this limitation in operation, we will recognize that the 'reality' given by first-level knowledge is not 'real' in first-level terms, but rather a perspective arising from specific viewpoints. In this way of understanding, it is the implementation of knowledge that 'causes' what is real.

The specific 'reality' of our consensus world seems to arise in being 'measured out'. Without measurement, how could there be an instrument or vehicle for describing what appears? How could time, space, or knowledge make sense?

Within the 'order' of what has been 'measured out', the pattern of 'feedback' establishes how things manifest, how relationships work, how concepts and senses interact. These 'mechanisms' in turn can be manipulated to make connections and allow for practical applications. They allow us to engage in social interactions, make use of time, ease pain, deal with obstacles, work out new ideas, and develop greater quantity or quality, speed or convenience.

If we look for the source of this 'feedback system', we may turn first to the patterns of perception, which seem to specify what is knowable. But perception in turn traces to an intrinsic sense of value. When we interpret what appears in space and time, our fundamental values and concerns determine how we accumulate data, make inferences, draw conclusions, identify experience, expand into speculations, and collect and organize what appears into meaningful constructs.

As long as values remain constant, perception operates in the same basic ways. The nature of 'reality' endures through all the countless changes in shape and form. Our determinations and distinctions are made within a context that dictates the importance of establishing just those conclusions and not others.

When we search out the source of values, we are led to presupposed structures. What is 'right' or 'true' is what has been approved as right or true; what is valuable is what is valued. Our interpretations and possibilities, together with the tools we use to manipulate 'reality', are founded or assigned meaning based on the record of what has been already. Even the way our senses function is based on consensus.

It seems important to acknowledge this structure fully. Our perspective is based on the past and on past positions: ours and those of others who have come before us. The source of our present knowledge seems to be past knowledge, arising through previous determinations and valuations. Is there anything else?

What would happen if we dropped all values and distinctions? With nothing left to shape experience, would there be any experience at all? Would time, space, or knowledge arise? Could we ever even ask such questions, when the very basis for questioning has seemingly disappeared?

Perhaps the answer is that we cannot simply 'stop' in this way. Human nature has been programmed physically; it has a character transmitted by the genes. Perhaps it has been programmed mentally as well, for it seems that thoughts, senses, and mind arise and pulsate in accord with their own inner dynamic. What we consider the nature or patterns of the mind may arise through cycles of repetition that originate prior to birth. Perhaps it is this 'programmed' tendency that organizes what would otherwise appear as random.

Even when something arises in our awareness without seeming to be based on a particular cause and reason, even when it is independent of anything that is remembered or that has left its traces in individual or collective history or consciousness, it will be determined in its most basic aspect by preestablished patterns of mind, thought, and senses. For example, when the senses and the thinking mind 'bounce off' the physical realm, giving 'feedback' to the one who knows, a similar process operates within awareness, stimulating the beginnings of an inner dialogue. There is movement in a specific direction, toward a particular situation that 'pops up'. The 'feel' of this dynamic, with all its interconnections and internal references, seems to be what establishes the 'nature' of experience.

When we trace this basic 'feel' in conventional terms, we encounter awareness giving 'feedback' to the self. It is the self that determines identities and thereby enacts its own identity. As objects are established in opposition to the self, its identity becomes more 'rounded', more fully established as existent.

This trend toward identity can be challenged through a focus on the 'field' within which specific qualities or distinctions arise. Each 'field' (for example, the 'field' of sensory projections) has its specific character, associated with a specific faculty and with specific ways that thoughts and mind manifest.

Looking in terms of the 'field' allows the structure of identity to give way to a much more fluid view. Different elements gather to be grouped and experienced, judged and determined. A governing principle sets the tone for the 'field', as a chief executive might set the tone for a corporation. The awareness at work determines the kinds of manifestations that will be possible.

Based on these elements, a particular story or drama can unfold, complete with the characters and characteristics, distinctions and styles of separation that 'fit' the 'field'. If we focus on the *content* of this drama, we will be led back to the identity of the self, slipping readily into a momentum to which we have long since grown accustomed. But the shapes and forms that the 'field' allows can themselves enact a drama of high interest, with great variations, that does not depend on content. There is no need to identify with this drama or with parts of it, for the play unfolds of its own accord.

Looking at the drama enacted within each 'field' (or in the interaction of 'fields') leads directly to the creativity of mind. Just as musicians shape sound using the rhythms and tones of different instruments, artists create appearance by applying paint or other media, and architects design structures by combining various forms, so the mind projects different shapes and forms that have their own integrity and meaning.

When we first attempt to understand the workings of the mind, we may have the sense that we are in contact with something mysterious, even random in nature. Why does one thought follow the next? Why do we find it difficult to concentrate or to control our moods? Either the answers to such questions are not forthcoming, or the answers we do propose seem only theoretical.

But this sense of mystery may come because we are looking for explanations, when knowledge lies elsewhere. Exploring the mind from within the play that it projects, we may discover a source for the creative patterns of the mind in a fundamental 'aliveness' of awareness. Mind *gives* experience, as the artist gives expression, the architect design, the musician rhythm. The dance and drama of the mind, yielding shapes and forms and modes of knowing, disclose an unexpected ability to act 'into' time and space.

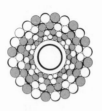

ONLY KNOWING

Because we tend to think of experience as primary and as separate from awareness, first 'arising' and only then 'presenting itself' to awareness, our awareness has a grasping quality. Awareness 'takes hold' of experience, making sense of it in accord with its own capacities, concerns, and predispositions.

Suppose that we proceed instead from the view that awareness and experience arise together. It might seem that in that case awareness would be more narrow and restricted, but in fact the opposite seems to be true.

Awareness and experience together open a quality of knowing that *does not depend on taking any position.* Awareness does not have to be bound by experience, nor does experience have to 'appear' only in those ways that awareness countenances.

Free from positions, experience becomes more than experience and awareness more than awareness. The 'objects' of awareness do not have to be identified as particular entities appearing in space, manifesting a specific range of qualities. Time and space, as the allowing and sustaining elements of experience, can be different as well.

From the Time–Space–Knowledge perspective, we might adapt an analogy used elsewhere and say that reality is like a photograph: Space takes the picture, Time develops the film, and Knowledge exhibits the result. But what is it that is being photographed? What is there 'outside' of Time and Space and Knowledge? Reflection suggests that there is only the picture-taking activity itself—a knowing 'into' Space and Time.

This 'only knowing' insight can be expressed simply and directly:

Space has no 'from'. Time has no 'from'. Knowledge has no 'from'. There are no progenitors. What more is there to say?

The simplicity of 'only knowing' seems very difficult to discover. But this is because when we undertake an investigation, we are accustomed to looking for the results of the investigation. From the 'only knowing' perspective, it is the inquiry that truly represents 'knowingness', not the 'truth' of what is discovered.

Given 'only knowing', once we have initiated the process of an open inquiry, there is no need to go any further—to discover 'who' we are or to change 'what' we are doing; to feel embarrassed for being ignorant or to try to alter anything. Great Knowledge is available, giving us permission to be.

This simplicity has slipped from view, so that we can no longer recognize it as our natural state. Taking positions, we have positions to defend. As the endless complications of the temporal order come to the fore, we lose sight of what we are doing with our lives. Great Knowledge seems to recede, leaving only its agent, knowledge. Time, 're-presented' as the onrushing momentum of linear temporality, produces more than lower-level knowledge can take in. We remain perpetually 'behind the times'; the future is upon us 'before we know it'. Confusion and complication become our second nature.

If Time did not steadily 'time itself out', leaving knowledge struggling to catch up to the knowable, knowing could reveal a new dynamic and a new way of being. If Space allowed presentations without insisting on substance, there would be room for a multidimensional reality. We could advance 'ahead of time', feeding knowledge into knowledge, resolving each 'point of decision' into an opportunity for informed and appropriate activity. As knowledge emerged through the union of Space and Time, the truth could shine with an incandescent radiance.

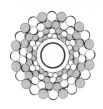

THE LOGOS
OF THE ORDER

M uch of what is normally presented as fixed and invariable in the world can be reinterpreted as an aspect of the prevailing 'order'. That 'order' in turn can be referred to a comprehensive 'knowing', the 'logos' of the order.

More fundamental than the governing principles and premises of the prevailing 'order', the 'logos' founds the 'order', determining what can appear and in what ways, setting limits and 'measuring out' possibilities. Thus the 'logos' might be characterized by how it presents time, space, and knowledge. Whatever is 'true' (and even indisputable) in terms of the temporal order derives its truth from 'conforming' to the 'logos'. The knowledge inherent in the 'logos' unfolds in a certain way, and 'reality' follows suit. As the 'founder' of the prevailing 'order', the 'logos' operates in all aspects of being, giving the 'realness' of the real.

411

The inner 'logic' of the 'logos' manifests in ways that cut across the usual distinction between 'subjective' and 'objective' or 'physical' and 'mental'. Codes of conduct, means of inquiry, and laws of nature all 'embody' the knowledge of the 'logos' in a way that determines the structure of both the known world and its knower. Cultural norms, past experience, organized institutions, and systems of belief can all serve as agents of such 'embodied' knowledge, presenting themselves as candidates for 'adoption'.

Once adopted, certain of these structures are identified as absolute, in the sense of being presupposed in all acts of knowing. The initial attribution of knowledge to a self, the existence of self and world, and first-level time, space, and knowledge are such self-defined absolutes, subject to investigation but not to being challenged from within the first-level 'order'.

Rules, projections, and observations that tightly match one another are also candidates for 'absolute' status within the conventional realm. Specific fields of knowledge such as psychology, religion, and philosophy take such structures as their domain of inquiry; at the same time, each of these disciplines itself 'embodies' the first-level knowledge these absolute structures help put in operation. Adopting presuppositions, positions, and absolutes of their own, these disciplines develop interpretive models accordingly.

Conventional knowledge is an *expression* of the world or 'order' within which it arises, and would change if that 'order' changed. Within the prevailing 'order', however, knowledge that corresponds to that order is both appropriate and accurate. For example, historical conditioning and causal connections are 'true', even though they need not be the final truth. In a different temporal order, conditioning and causality might only be one aspect of the truth, or might not be true at all.

The knowledge 'of' the 'logos' shapes the possible like a parent transmitting genetic coding to the next generation. It gives form to time and space, like an architect directing a builder in how to utilize construction materials. In turn, time and space specify the ('first-level') knowledge that will be available within the circumstances that they present and reveal.

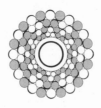

KNOWLEDGE BY THE KNOWER OF THE LOGOS

The knowledge inherent in the 'logos' is available as an object of observation or inquiry. In first-level terms, we can refer to this specific knowledge—knowledge *by* the knower *of* the logos—as 'cognition'.

'Cognition' sets out to know the 'logos' through the basic tools of measurement: calculation, observation, and prediction, the scientific methods that aim at disclosing fundamental 'laws' of nature. The potential range of 'cognition' is unlimited: The way matter behaves in space, the unfolding of events in time, and the patterns of actions and reactions by the self are all available to it. In one sense all lower-level knowledge is 'cognition', but for the most part the 'cognitive' aspect of knowledge is subordinated to the more 'goal-oriented' concerns of the self.

When a goal orientation prevails, and 'cognition' is put to the use of the 'self', 'cognition' is typically directed toward 'explanations' that are put forward to account for the results of observation in terms of the established 'order'. Explanations indicate why something happened and even why it could not have happened otherwise.

Drawing on the past, such explanations have value for the future. Patterns become clear, allowing us to know things 'in advance'; action can be taken accordingly, and the added knowledge can lead to specific benefits. In this way, explanation aims to bring causal sequences under control, making the world of the self a less fearful and mysterious place.

Thus at different times in history, 'cognition' may develop more in one direction than in another, so that certain aspects of the 'logos' become accessible, and others are hidden from view. Accepting all knowledge as belonging to the knowing self is an example of a model that encourages certain kinds of 'cognition' but severely restricts others.

The focus on the knowing activities of a knowing self leaves out of account a more fundamental, structuring knowledge. It restricts 'cognition', which has the capacity to know *through* the 'logos', to the role of knowing the 'logos' as object. Once this restriction is in place, even 'logos' as object recedes from view: What appears in its place are the structures of the prevailing 'order', including the first-level 'modalities' of time, space, and knowledge. As 'cognition' is reduced to 'explanation', the opportunity to contact knowledge of a new kind is lost.

For example, the conventional temporal order does not allow for phenomena such as miracles and mystical experience. This is not because such possibilities are 'known' to be false, but because the knowledge implicit in the temporal order *does not know how they could be true.* The 'logos' does not allow for it, and so 'cognition' must deny it.

When the prevailing 'order' attributes knowledge to 'the self that knows', the self becomes an absolute. Based on this absolute, great efforts have been expended on the question of what happens to the self when it dies. But this question remains bound to first-level space and time and the knowledge they embody and allow. From a second-level perspective, we might see matters differently. When the self dies, it remains a part of space and time: 'Where' else could it go, and what else is 'happening'?

When 'cognition' is limited to the observation and inquiry of the 'self', the knowledge gained of the 'order' will be limited, even faulty, and its solutions to problems will be provisional and incomplete, tending to lead toward new and unforeseen problems. Ideas and plans readily miscarry; error and frustration of purpose establish a vicious circle in which error feeds on itself and knowing is confined within ever narrowing channels.

However, this is not the full story, for occasionally 'cognition' can be full in scope, giving a lower-level knowledge that accords with the 'logos'. When explanations are used to generate verifiable theories that can be put to the test, inquiry tends to be self-correcting. Its observation will be complete and its predictions will be accurate; its solutions will work well and will endure. But while this methodology may yield reliable results and extend the domain of the explicable, creativity depends on a 'cognition' that operates quite differently, even mysteriously.

To explore this possibility, we could rethink the nature of 'cognition' itself. If the 'logos' is an expression of knowledge, *'cognition' is not restricted to 'knowing' the 'logos'; instead, it can 'embody' the 'logos'.* As this embodiment becomes more comprehensive, the prospect arises for knowledge of a new order.

From this perspective, 'cognition' reflects the free availability of knowledge within the 'logos'. Indeed, the 'knowingness' implicit in 'cognition' is an ongoing 'presentation' of the 'logos'. At the first level, this may help 'explain' why the known universe and the knowing mind correspond to one another.

When the goal orientation of the self yields to free and open inquiry, the play of space and time presented by the temporal order, together with human knowledge, become factors that open to the investigation of inquiry. Knowledge can become more precise about what is known and what is not known, and even about knowledge itself. 'Knowingness' can proceed beyond the knowing of the knower and 'embody' the 'logos' directly.

Even within the realm of first-level knowledge, however, 'cognition' can proceed in different ways. When the focus is not on achieving first-level aims, but on the growth of knowledge, it is immaterial whether an explanation 'succeeds'. When mistakes occur or predictions go wrong, the opportunity for knowing remains.

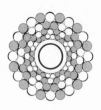

Knowledge of the Logos

KNOWING
IN NOT-KNOWING

Suppose we asked how it is that all of us now alive have come to share a particular time. A variety of answers come to mind—the workings of a divine plan; the result of fate, destiny, or conduct in previous lives; the random workings of accident, and so on. Or we may decide that we simply do not and cannot know. Whatever our answer, it will be given in terms of the founding structures of the prevailing order. The 'logos' determines the range of permissible events, and thus indirectly determines what kinds of explanations or other modes of knowledge can arise—what 'forms' 'cognition' can 'take'.

From the multidimensional perspective of second-level knowledge, all such absolutes can be 'opened up' without being attacked as false or even as limited. Each manifestation can be accepted as it is, for 'truth' is understood as dependent for its values on the 'order' that the 'logos' sets in place. Through this very acceptance, new possibilities encompassed in second-level time and space are free to emerge.

To say that knowledge 'shapes' time and space could be interpreted as a form of mentalism: the claim that something exists only because it is known. Mentalistic theories, however, depend on a first-level understanding of knowledge. Positing a reality in which 'existence' is based on perception or first-level 'cognition', they leave unexamined standard first-level distinctions such as 'exist' and 'not-exist', 'mental' and 'physical', and even 'reality' and 'perception'. From a second-level perspective, these distinctions themselves can be applied only because the knowledge 'of' the 'logos' makes them available to be known.

Yet when we ask how the 'order' comes into being—how the 'fabric' of existence comes to be 'fabricated'—the answer seems to be that there is no independent 'source from'. For example, within the 'logos' that establishes self and world, knowledge finds expression in the activity of a knower. *This very activity* proposes, confirms, and imposes the 'logos' that establishes it.

The known world and its contents, including the self that knows both world and contents, are nothing other than the explicit 'fabrication' of the knowledge implicit in the 'logos' 'through' the knowing activity of the self. We can draw from this interrelationship a key principle:

> Just as they are, without being 'reduced' to mental phenomena, the realities of conventional understanding 'are' knowledge.

Each act of knowing depends on having the 'logos' communicated to it 'in advance', but also communicates the 'logos' in turn. In addition to its content, each such act communicates the fundamental 'order' on which it depends. A subtle communication—active in 'cognition'—is constantly in operation. There is a constant flow back and forth; indeed, the specific momentum characteristic of the temporal order could be interpreted as an expression of this 'communicating flow'.

Linked to free and open inquiry, 'cognition' discovers knowing in not-knowing, for *not-knowing also embodies the 'logos'*. When inquiry leads us to the unknown, we can abandon our concern with 'explanation' and turn instead to the unknown as a starting point.

The second-level knowledge implicit in the 'logos' operates without regard to identity or distinctions, for it has no location or definition. Instead, it is a process, a 'knowingness' that expresses itself in the activity of knowing, free from projection or identification. As and through the 'logos', *knowledge is the unfolding of knowledge.* Illuminated by such knowledge, not-knowing itself becomes knowledge.

We might distinguish two kinds of not-knowing. 'Conventional not-knowing' is simply another position taken by the self—a judgment that takes form in terms of a goal that has proved unattainable. Such not-knowing sets itself up as opposed to knowing, on a par with such other dichotomies as acceptance and rejection, praise and blame, or positive and negative. Because it is opposed to knowledge, it signals the end of inquiry and the failure of investigation. The 'not-knowing' accessible to inquiry, however, can be understood as the 'completion' of inquiry. This not-knowing emerges only when inquiry has reached its furthest limits: at the point when knowledge has traversed the domain of knowing and is ready to see that domain revealed in a new light. It is a 'not-knowing' that must be earned through the power and vigor of inquiry itself.

The knowledge available within this second kind of 'not-knowing' is not knowledge in a first-level sense—to assert this would be to indulge in a particularly confusing kind of word game. Instead, it is a knowledge that arises through acknowledging *inquiry as the activity of 'knowingness'*.

As an active knowing, inquiry converts the first-level opposition between knowing and not-knowing into a partnership. Instead of being exhausted in pointing 'to' or 'from', knowledge is left free to *know itself* as the *context* of lower-level knowing and not-knowing. The projections of the human mind, which ordinarily seem to set the limits on what can be known, become instances of a knowing prior to all projections, encompassing models and reasons, mistakes and confusion alike. At this point, the 'embodied' knowledge 'of' the 'logos' is available directly.

To know in this way, *through* the knowledge of the 'logos', is to 'embody' an all-pervading knowledge that strips the first-level structures of knower and known of their claim to ultimate significance. We are invited to participate in a fundamental transformation. Though 'objectively' nothing may have changed, it is also true that nothing remains the same.

If knowledge is to open in a new way, we must challenge the claims made 'within' the 'logos' that collectively make the 'logos' accessible only as an object for 'cognition'. The method for doing this is close at hand. There are places where the old structures break down, where internal inconsistencies and unresolved mysteries come to the fore.

The puzzles of a space 'beyond' space or a time 'before' time, the incoherence in our understanding of linear temporality, the mysterious 'locatedness' of thoughts, the unknown origins for awareness, the inaccessibility of 'nothing'—in such points of difficulty the temporal order does not hold. An idea pushes toward its opposite until both collapse.

Because we can go to such places in our inquiry, we do not need to challenge the temporal order directly. It is enough to let the 'order' speak for itself; we are led naturally to points of transition from 'order' to 'order'— points that serve both as signs of limitations and as symbols that point beyond.

One such point of difficulty is the relationship through which the subject knows objects in space and time. Sometimes the subject has been described as essentially passive, mechanically processing input from the object, but the vital role of interpretive activity in even the simplest act of observation makes this view untenable.

At the other extreme, it is sometimes said that what is known depends wholly on the patterns, constructs, and ways of knowing that the subject brings to the knowing. But reducing experience to the realm of mental constructs leaves us with no way of understanding how experience can be initiated or how it can develop, while raising troubling questions as to why everything is not already known in advance.

Between these two alternatives lies a third view based on interaction and feedback, in which subject and object relate in complete intimacy. When the self applies *judgments* to *objects* experienced as having specific *attributes*, object, attributes, and the judgments made by the self all sustain one another, with none more basic than the rest. An object is not 'beautiful' only because it is seen by a self who makes this judgment: Something about the object supports this judgment and thus makes it possible.

This intimacy has an intricate structure. When an image of an object appears in the mind, presenting itself to be known, it is perceived in terms of certain preexisting patterns. However, perception is an *act* that requires time and is ordered in terms of a distinctive temporal rhythm. As the act of knowing unfolds, the image also projects itself into those patterns, contributing the direct 'feedback' of immediate experience.

In this sense, the image of the object can be said to *understand itself*, in a process that develops sequentially in accord with 'feedback' and repetition. The object in being known reflects the interpretive structure that knows it; the subject in knowing the object is modified by the object it knows.

At this level, it may no longer make good sense to insist on the structure of subject and object as fundamental to knowing. Subject has the nature of object, or it could not know; object has the nature of subject, or it could not be known. The two are interlaced in a web of knowing, woven in the rhythms of the temporal order.

Through the 'feedback' that unfolds in the specific sequential rhythm of the act of knowing, an interpretation of experience is established that sets up 'subject and object', 'knower and known', 'here and there', and the other dichotomies of conventional knowledge. This interpretation is normally understood to yield knowledge as its fruit. But *as* an interpretation, it reflects knowledge on a more fundamental level—a knowledge that *embodies* the 'knowingness' inherent in the situation as a whole.

Seen in this light, conventional ways of accounting for knowledge can be acknowledged as partial and complementary insights into the fundamental role of the 'logos' in all knowing. The view that knowledge is based exclusively on the explanations, interpretations, and identifications supplied by the self as knower is one such insight; it is balanced by the insistence that knowledge is founded on objects that exist independently 'outside' the self.

The view being explored here takes both these alternatives into account, while pointing to their limitations. Knowledge is understood as being distributed throughout the domain of what is known, inherent in the mutual unfolding of subject and object in time and space. The 'logos' is the 'locus' for an all-embracing 'knowledge'. Unlike conventional knowledge, which must emerge from a state of not-knowing, such distributed 'knowledge' is *naturally present*, inherent in the interwoven substance and temporal rhythm that subject and object share from the outset.

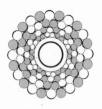

No Path

FRUIT OF INQUIRY

When time, space, and knowledge are understood in a more comprehensive and encompassing manner, unacknowledged patterns become visible, while distinctions and polarities that seem fundamental or irreconcilable are united. Great Time, Great Space, and Great Knowledge are the final deepening or expansion of this progression—the fruit of previous inquiry.

From the perspective of Great Knowledge, however, this whole structure may appear in a very different light. The system that establishes 'levels' of time, space, and knowledge is itself a product of conventional understanding and cannot be considered absolute.

Imagining the three-level structure of time, space, and knowledge as a pyramid, and looking from the 'first-level' base of the pyramid, it seems natural to proceed by climbing from the base to the top.

But looking from the top of the pyramid, there is nowhere to go. Indeed, from this perspective the top is also at the center. Here, at the center of present experience, Great Knowledge is already available.

This 'no-journey' perspective is not a mystical claim that cannot be subjected to inquiry, nor is it an excuse for deciding that 'things as they are are perfect'. The point is more straightforward: Inquiry embodies a particular form of knowledge, together with a certain understanding of time and space. An inquiry that presupposes a step-like structure and a hierarchy of meaning or insight expresses 'first-level' forms of knowledge, working in ways that establish and affirm limitations.

A hierarchical model risks the interpretation that Great Time, Space, and Knowledge are states to be arrived at, as one would arrive at the upper story of a house after climbing a set of stairs. As a corrective to this model, we might use the traditional image of a finger pointing at the moon: The structure is the finger, and it would be a serious error to mistake the tip of the finger for the moon at which it was pointing.

It may be that we cannot point 'to' Great Knowledge at all or even make any points 'about' it. But if Great Knowledge is this subtle, its subtlety seems to become a hindrance or obstacle to its realization. Is it possible to make a bridge from ordinary knowledge to a knowledge that is so fully encompassing? In ordinary knowledge, projections find expression in angles on knowledge, defined by points that establish fixed positions. Points comprise 'fields', each with its own 'subject matter' and prevailing ideas. It seems that Great Knowledge would become available through 'opening' these points.

From the perspective of Great Knowledge, however, no such 'procedure' is required. When positions are seen as positions, and this seeing does not itself become another position, then knowledge is already open. Time changes, creating new possibilities, and Space offers different attitudes. Intimacy communicates itself without language or within language. An integral integrity of interaction of Space and Time becomes the reflection of knowledge: Space Time Knowledge as the same, yet completely different—not subject to interpretation.

When knowledge is 'exercised' through 'pointing out', a pattern of 'derivation' manifests, a tempo or momentum linked to the power of time. On the first level, something is presented to be known, in accord with the logic of 'from' and 'to'. From another perspective, derivation allows a 'knowledgeability' that knows the 'to' of the future or knows in all aspects of time simultaneously.

Knowledge is like a key, though the door that it opens has never been closed. A great treasure is made available, a fullness beyond all fullness. The sense channels open to Knowledge, which becomes greater than ever, greater than great. With no above or beyond, ordinary perceptions, thoughts, consensus, and rational order become displays of the 'knowingness' of Knowledge, the 'knowledgeability' of all human abilities.

What knowledge 'points out' is manifestation 'in' space and time. In this 'pointing out', space and time are 'pointed out' as well: time in the power that knowledge exercises and in the derivation of 'this' from 'that'; space in the accommodation of what arises in the physical and mental realms, and in the borders and limits that characterize thought, sensation, and feeling.

The relationship of knowledge to time and space is reciprocal: As knowledge 'points out' time and space, so time presents knowledge and space allows it. Thus, first-level space exhibits knowledge in the activity that reports what is known, while first-level time presents knowledge as the witness who verifies the truth of what arises. These structures can be further specified: In recognizing knowledge as 'mine', 'I' appear; through 'my' activity of identifying and judging, shape and form arise.

These first-level manifestations have their second-level counterparts. The momentum of time enacts knowledge as 'read-outs' that present a governing 'logos'; the prolific allowing of space 'establishes' a 'field' within which 'meaning' takes shape.

As knowledge and time and space interact, three levels arise, each unfolding in three distinct ways, making nine levels in all. However, this is a first-level description. From a second-level orientation we could say that at each level a 'read-out' prevails and a 'field' unifies; in third-level terms we might say that throughout time and space the Body of Knowledge is variously enacted, in accord with the fullness of Being.

What is understood as limitation and restriction on one level takes on a wholly different significance at another, until at the third level there is no restriction at all. The dynamic moves toward revealing ever greater wealth—a vastness without borders and a value not bound by distinctions. Free from the content that it manifests, pointing points out the dynamic of Being.

Within the range of perfect, self-attributing openness and unrestricted energy that this interplay invites, Being arises as Time, Space, and Knowledge at play, assuming positions without making them into anything solid. Like light reflecting off itself, experience and experiencer are seen to be equally images of pure transformation. There is an unending flow, an aliveness that is vastly 'entertaining' without someone craving entertainment.

The Being of this global dynamic blends time and energy. Founded on 'knowingness', it accepts labels as labels, not turning the saying that something 'is' into a particular kind of being that is then labeled as existent. The programs and interpretations of ordinary life continue, but they do not constrain. At any time, we are free to change.

Rational inquiry maintains that knowledge grows through a steady progression. Even in this view, however, if the first step were not bound to the last in a single Body of Knowledge, moving from starting point to goal in an ordered sequence would be impossible. For progression to occur, starting point, path, and goal must form a single, unitary 'field'.

Within this 'field', knowledge identifies a path to knowing the knowing of Knowledge, the timing of Time, and the allowing of Space. But since this specific way of knowing in turn reflects a specific embodiment of Time, Space, and Knowledge, we can say that Time, Space, and

Knowledge themselves point out and establish the path to acquiring knowledge. Since these three 'factors' of Being are present at the outset as they are at the conclusion, the path is ultimately no path. In 'pointing out' the path to Knowledge, Time, Space, and Knowledge point only to themselves.

Time, Space, and Knowledge are the path to their own realization because *they* are the being of our becoming, and *we* are their embodiment. When we seek out Great Knowledge, we are actively seeking our own nature. Perhaps this helps explain why it is that when we contact the vision of Time, Space, and Knowledge, it seems almost familiar, so that we are tempted to ask why we have not understood things in this way before.

Great Time, Great Space, and Great Knowledge are not somewhere else (for example, at the top of a pyramid to whose summit we must ascend). They are not accessible only as a beautiful dream or vision cut off from the ordinary reality we inhabit. This present reality *is* Time, Space, and Knowledge. The vision is in the seeing, and the seeing is in us.

To arrive at this understanding seemingly requires us to pursue an intricate line of inquiry, carefully negotiating a maze of levels, 'fields', and 'orders'. But all this activity is only the expression of our lack of understanding: as though we were looking through the wrong end of a telescope at our own hand, persistently thinking that it was located far, far away. It is our own interpretive structures that lead us to insist on distance, not the 'reality' of the situation.

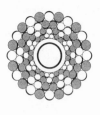

No Path

PATH TOWARD GREAT KNOWLEDGE

The path toward Great Knowledge opens when we see that there is no path and 'abandon' even the smallest, least-formed conception of goal. But this seeing seems to happen progressively. It begins when greater seeing 'feeds back' on itself, initiating a process that intensifies through the momentum generated by continuing 'feedback'.

In time we see that the light of knowing illuminates the mind; that the body embodies space; that time is the process of investigation. We recognize that there is no hierarchy and no system; that the point to be known is within; that the peak of the pyramid is also the center of our being, and that the point at the peak can equally be Time or Space or Knowledge. Only then, having abandoned all positioning, do we see that each point can be the center of the pyramid—the pinnacle of Being—for each point contains the whole.

The idea of 'making progress toward' Great Knowledge is the continuing expression of an understanding based on substance. This understanding, which on the first level is firmly entrenched, persists in more subtle form on the second level. Even when Time, Space, and Knowledge are understood as the active dimensions of Being, different *qualities* of these three facets of Being seem to determine the 'level' of truth or reality in effect.

On the third level, this distinction among levels breaks down completely. Whereas from earlier perspectives higher realms appear as remarkable and marvelous, higher and lower now become the same. Even the 'qualities' that distinguish the levels are understood simply as expressions of Time, Space, and Knowledge.

Failure to appreciate this progression can promote considerable confusion. For example, the description of Great Time as 'invariable' or even 'timeless' suggests in first-level terms that the future is predetermined, so that the 'happening' of events is ultimately illusory and without significance. But these conclusions depend on attaching primary importance to the boundaries that mark off one event from another. The categories that reflect this commitment to distinctions are no more appropriate to 'higher levels' than is the typology of levels itself.

Freedom emerges fully into Being when Great Time, Great Space, and Great Knowledge are acknowledged as inseparable from ordinary reality, and yet as nothing at all. If Time, Space, and Knowledge 'are' our being in being 'nothing at all', then no possibilities are excluded and nothing is determined in advance. Different realms of being can unfold, each with its own patterning, 'order', and 'field'.

A preliminary 'move' toward 'nothing at all' might acknowledge an intimacy between subject and object unknown to the borders and limits of first-level observation. Viewed from outside, 'nothing at all' might be seen as negating what would otherwise be significant. But 'experienced' as intimacy, there can be no question of disruptive negation. Intimacy gives permission. It is an invitation from Great Knowledge to open to the deep vastness of Space within appearance.

Once intimacy has become more fully available as the truth of Being, we might ask why Time, Space, and Knowledge show up at all. In a sense, the answer is a simple one: Time, Space, and Knowledge express the 'reality' of our being. We live in an 'existent' realm in which knowledge is 'active'; given these 'facts', Time, Space, and Knowledge will be in operation. The universe, history, and human intelligence presuppose them.

Perhaps we could hypothesize something totally 'other', in which 'Being' had a meaning unrelated to anything in our present understanding. In that case, we might have to 'exchange' Time, Space, and Knowledge for different facets of Being. But if Being really took on new meaning, who would make this discovery, and who would report it to whom? When would the discovery take place, and how would it manifest?

As long as there is a knower investigating, there is the existent realm that traces back to Time, Space, and

Knowledge. True, our understanding of what it means to 'exist' may have to be substantially revised. Models based on substance may give way to models that present a developing process; these models in turn may prove to be 'empty'. But there seems no meaningful way to 'step outside' a presentation in terms of Time, Space, and Knowledge as fundamental facets of Being.

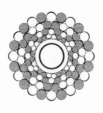

No Path

GLOBAL
KNOWLEDGE

Time, Space, and Knowledge cannot be characterized as absolutes. Great Knowledge accepts 'absolutes', but only as lower-level interpretations of the all-permissive 'knowingness' of Knowledge.

If absolutes seem to appear, we must be ready to question them. Questioning must extend as well to whatever we rely on in this questioning.

The presentation here relies on Time, Space, and Knowledge only because we seem unable to see beyond these factors—not due to a lack of ability, but due to the nature of 'seeing' and 'beyond'. If there were a 'knowledge' beyond Knowledge, we could inquire into it as well, but then we would have to confront the fact that 'knowledge' seems necessary to know what is 'beyond' Knowledge. In the same way, a 'place' beyond Space seems to require 'space', and a 'happening' outside of Time seems to require 'time'.

436

In terms of what we can know or speak of, Time, Space, and Knowledge do seem to operate as absolutes. Yet this operation sets up no structures and has no outcome. 'Emptiness', 'openness', and 'zero' are pointers toward this 'no structures, no outcome' perspective; reminders that whatever appears as absolute is not absolute, and that there is no absolute beyond what appears. It is precisely because of this 'no limiting absolute' that knowledge can become all-encompassing.

The 'activity' of the 'logos' suffuses the temporal order. Since it is fully embodied in the distinctions that the 'order' supports, distinctions can equally well be understood as expressions of Knowledge, exhibitions of Space, and presentations of Time.

Global knowledge, which knows 'through' the 'logos', is the expression of this insight. It leads to an acceptance and appreciation of the prevailing 'order' without making this 'order' binding *as such*. Good and bad, right and wrong, and other such distinctions are understood as judgments based on human values and conventions that arise within the 'order'—'read-outs' that resonate within the temporal order.

Good is 'good for' and *bad is 'bad for'*—they are values and meanings that depend on structures of the temporal order. Together with knowing and not-knowing, as well as mistakes and misperceptions that they permit, they are illuminated by higher knowledge, which shines through them.

Lower knowledge, based *on* the temporal order, can give way to higher knowledge without the necessity for any transition between the two. Conventionally speaking, there may be a kind of expanding in which lower knowledge 'grows' into higher knowledge, following a pattern that accords with the quality of lower time. When knowledge has 'attained' its fullness, however, there are no residues. Nothing is left over to clutter space or impede the energy of time, nor has anything been left behind.

The 'growth' from lower to higher knowledge and the initial 'state' of lower knowledge itself are equally expressions of the higher knowledge 'attained'. Even mistakes are expressions of this knowledge: *Mistakes have meaning within an order, and this order is the product of knowledge.* To take a simple example, making a wrong turn while driving goes together with the system of cars, streets, directions, and places to be reached or not reached. The 'read-out' that encompasses the 'order' encompasses the possibility of the mistake.

From this all-encompassing perspective, there is no such thing as wrong action, because knowledge is embodied in all action. However, we should not confuse this analysis with the position that all actions, all choices, and all interpretations are equally valid, for such a position—as a position—has not progressed beyond a first level of knowledge. The insight that would clarify this confusion cannot be fully sustained in first-level terms. This is one reason for proceeding from the first level to the second level, rather than going immediately to a third-level understanding. Second-level analysis can be understood as a concession to first-level understanding, but one that at the same time challenges that understanding to go beyond itself.

438

However, second-level analysis or experience may lead to a confusion of its own, in which the structures of first-level reality are rejected and an obsession or fascination with 'altered realities', pervasive dynamics and mechanics, or global perspectives takes hold. The 'no path' of Great Knowledge can easily be forgotten. Yet Great Knowledge embodies fully in all presentations—in the truth of what is and what is not, what appears and what does not, what is known and what could never be imagined.

Body of Knowledge

GATEWAYS
TO KNOWLEDGE

Every *form* of knowing establishes a *body* of knowledge: the range of the known and the knowable. However, not all possibilities are allowed within each body of knowledge, nor can every event—whether an act of knowing or an appearance to be known—be presented.

The body of knowledge reveals its limitations at points of unknowing and paradox. Such points can serve as gateways to a greater knowledge, informed by a different relationship to time and space. For example, the split between body and mind, and the difficulty of accounting for communication between the two, can lead us to the realization that breath is a meeting place for the physical and mental.

Normally, however, we do not challenge limitations in this way. We accept the role of knower offered us by first-level time and space, embodying their restrictions and deformation. By 'specifying' as our own the disembodied way of being of the 'bystander', whose being is always in question, we consent to the reality of linear time and empty space. Time runs down or runs on, leaving past experience lifeless in its wake. Space closes in on itself, leaving a knowing that leads nowhere. Dependent on the various displays of the temporal order, we 'measure out' the route we traverse through time, marking out limitations, and discover space as the distance that separates and confines us.

This relentless interplay of time, space, and knowledge on the lower level is transmuted on the higher level. The 'presentations' of Time and the 'exhibitions' of Space are equally 'embodiments' of Knowledge: The three facets are inseparable, like the three sides of a triangle. We might say that the three points of the triangle define a fundamental 'form'—the plane on which specific shapes and forms can manifest the boundless possibilities of Being. The direct evocation of this inseparability can be understood as Great Knowledge, revealing the Body of Knowledge as active and available within each fact of our embodiment.

We can touch the Body of Knowledge by focusing on our embodiment directly. With our senses attuned to the world around us, we grow aware of a more encompassing body of knowledge. Expanding awareness aligns with the subtle energies of inner experience, making knowledge available not only through the activity of senses and mind, but throughout the realm of physical space and linear time. Rigid dichotomies begin to dissolve and loosen in favor of a more open allowing and a more active presentation.

Appreciation for the energy within all presentations leads to a lightness that lets us jump easily from one side of a situation to another, one experience to another. We can release the pressure of stress into the openness of Space, and can choose which aspects of the 'lower-level' body of knowledge we wish to embody. When we encounter a difficult situation or challenge, we can allow a true creativity to operate, so that Knowledge draws on Time to present new possibilities.

Questions arise that look to the origins of patterns and momentum in conventional space and time: Why does time present the sequence of decay and aging, or space exhibit the limitations of distance, impenetrability, and fixed location? Within the governing 'logos' no absolute answers are possible. But as the mind awakens into full embodiment of knowledge, we bring such questions into our hearts and embody them with our being. The same questions now invite a presence and allowing that open new dimensions and invite new knowledge.

Such multidimensional 'knowability' could be understood as the heart of the Body of Knowledge. Fully available *within* the temporal order, the 'field' of space, and lower-level knowledge, the Body of Knowledge embodies Space and Time in such a way that Space allows higher intelligence and Time empowers it. The 'outcome' is Great Knowledge—the Body of Knowledge free from all limitations.

Great Knowledge is not a knowledge projected into the world by human consciousness in accord with the 'logos'; instead it opens the consciousness and its objects—as they manifest in the temporal order of the 'logos'—to a fully embodied 'knowingness'. The emerging 'knowingness' activates new energy and creates a new relationship to time. The grip of lower time's accelerating momentum is broken, restoring the integrity of knowledge. We begin to understand what it means to be truly 'knowledgeable'.

'Knowingness' discloses the Body of Knowledge, indestructible and brilliant, like a multifaceted diamond. In the Body of Knowledge, there is no impermanence, no transitions, no knower and no known. There is not even embodiment of knowledge within an ordinary realm. Creation lives in the uncreated, presenting Knowledge as Great Knowledge, truly all-pervading.

Great Knowledge offers itself unceasingly and without limitation. Though it asks nothing of us, we can ask ourselves: Can we match our own knowing to its gracious offer, offering our own being in return? Can we touch the Body of Knowledge?

If we imagine our own being as a unique expression of knowledge, we might say that we ourselves can be the programmer or creator who joins and makes connections, defining the characteristics and qualities that give the expression form. Yet what do we know about this creator? To say that shape and form are dictated does not mean that there is someone who dictates. Perhaps we can simply say this: *'Knowingness' knows.* In the knowing of 'knowingness', Great Knowledge presents itself.

Great Knowledge manifests as fully free liberation, uplifting and unbounded, completely incisive. It is 'above' each and every thing, yet inseparable from all that is known. It needs no protection and has no faults; if it is inaccessible, it is because there is no need to approach it. All that has been given in specific points or as the truth of the past becomes luminous awareness: Even what supports the judgment "That is wrong" is translucent.

This quality of awareness as unbounded, available within all experience, gives time as uncharacterized. There is neither belonging to a self nor its contrary. A dynamic sense of complete open-ending has already arrived; liberation is fully 'here'. The 'mechanism' that (in the name of 'doing') might turn liberation into something 'fixed' cannot begin to operate. There is no need for tools; as the 'being alive' of what is, Knowledge is self-adjusting and self-correcting, appearing *as* knowledge *through* what appears and is.

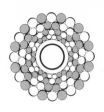

Body of Knowledge

DANCE
OF KNOWLEDGE

Out of the beauty of perfect expression comes the 'aliveness' of Knowledge, like a dance, like beautiful music sounding, or perhaps like a taste that satisfies an unsuspected hunger. Not bound by 'here' or by 'this', the Body of Knowledge is no body at all. Free from a conceptual framework or a structural order, it is not shaped and formed as bodies usually are. There are no previous records to rely on, no categories based on given points. Nothing points toward it and nothing prevents it from becoming.

The Body of Knowledge is not a position body, an ownership body, a category body. Embodied Knowledge is extension and continuation, relationships and distinctions and character. It is the creation of the 'field', the 'feel' of the 'field', and the creation from 'field' to 'field'. 'Knowingness' becomes the whole, and the whole has no 'belonging to'. The bond that comes with 'nothing other than' is inescapable, but is also within the whole, also an aspect of luminous awareness. There is no aware 'of', no aware 'to', no aware 'from' or 'toward'; no derivation at all.

Even the beauty of expression as full activation of Knowledge is a kind of sign, not expressing 'itself' in any way. The alive, fresh quality of knowing becomes 'beautific': no longer dependent on a particular arrangement or appearance, or on possessing particular attributes—no longer dependent on any of the understandings that we generate through a 'point-based' interpretation.

Through Great Knowledge, expression expresses itself. Knowledge is not presented as the antidote to confusion; nor is it applied to 'make sense' of things; nor does it resolve conflict or work toward solutions. Free from purpose or intention, the Body of Knowledge freely commands Time and Space.

Whether we recognize these possibilities as meaningful in terms of ordinary knowledge may not matter. Though the unity of the 'field' might be understood as the central core of what is presented here, there is no one body that is unified: no 'one place' or 'one way', no 'one who knows'. Knowledge is simply Knowledge. We can participate, we can own, we can use, we can play—for all doing and all being is the 'aliveness' of the Body of Knowledge.

Although we might say that the Body of Knowledge plays out across 'past', 'present', and 'future', this tripartite temporal structure is simply a lower-level 'read-out' of the 'timeless' dynamic of Time. Located at a specific point in time and confined to a certain kind of knowing, the self has reasons for 'measuring out' events as though the past were dead and the future not yet born. But from a more encompassing perspective, Time is the vitality of the Body of Knowledge, in which nothing arises and nothing passes away. The separation of potential from actuality and cause from effect is a consequence of measurements imposed by a lower-level knowing.

On the first level, the Body of Knowledge is bounded by linear time and physical space; by positions, locations, and distance; by birth and death. On the second level, confinement comes through the pervasive structures of 'field', 'order', and 'logos'. But confinement itself is only the characteristic indication that lower levels are in operation; from a 'third-level' perspective, confinement has no reality as such. When the interpretations of lower-level knowledge are understood as presentations of the Body of Knowledge, 'knowingness' remains fully available *even when such interpretations are in effect.*

Returning to the realm of 'knowingness', which is also the realm of the Body of Knowledge, transforms the quality and character of first-level 'experience'. Ordinary laws governing existence may continue in operation, but knowledge is no longer bound by their promulgations. The firm and substantial distinctions on which knowing relies, and which it adopts as its own essence, become *expressions* of 'knowingness'. Open for all possibilities, Knowledge is free to give any interpretation.

A lower-level indication that knowledge is freely available is the 'coexistence' through which existence points beyond itself to a more comprehensive whole. The 'coexistence' of existence with nonexistence gives each entity as embodying its opposite; the coexistence of existence with space gives openness in all that appears; the 'coexistence' of existence and knowledge gives the interplay of intention, action, and consequences that brings life to being.

Through 'coexistence', each interpretation made by lower-level knowledge establishes a global 'read-out'. The 'presence' of 'coexistence' 'in' each existent indicates that objective characteristics hold no fixed meaning. Though Knowledge can freely present Space to the mind for interpretation, in the unity of Space and Knowledge there is no 'belonging to' a system based on categories. Before and after 'establishment' there is simply 'knowingness'.

Freedom on this fundamental level discloses independence. As actors in the play of existence, we do not need to take our assigned role; we do not need to participate in the drama. Perhaps we choose to do so nonetheless; whatever choice we make, our choice does not bind us or lessen our possibilities.

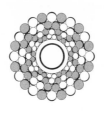

Body of Knowledge

DISPLAY
OF KNOWLEDGE

The countless specific appearances that arise within lower-level space can be understood as projections of lower-level mind. It is the structure of the mind that recognizes and assigns their specific attributes.

But this does not mean that these forms are 'only' mental, or that they are not active or do not produce effects. Mind, form, their interaction, and the effects that result are a *unified lower-level display* of the interplay of Space and Knowledge in Time.

In the domain of ordinary reality this interplay appears directly only as emptiness. Emptiness presents the open 'only knowing' of Knowledge as the 'nothingness' of Space: intimacy as vacancy and oneness in negation. Once there is appearance, Space and Knowledge diverge, tending toward the objective and the subjective realms.

449

If we look with care, however, we see that the intimacy of Space and Knowledge remains active in the *appearing* of first-level shape and form. The transition to this insight requires two distinct steps. The first involves seeing 'through' the substantiality of mind and objects, which are recognized as 'empty' and 'inactive' in their essence. This transitional view gives way to a deeper awareness, in which mind and objects are seen to 'coexist', generating existence and action through the 'activity' of 'coexisting'.

Coexistence gives emptiness a new dimension, disclosing it as the Space-Knowledge interplay of the Body of Knowledge. Subject knows and object embodies Space of Knowledge and Knowledge of Space. Prior to substance or form, prior to body, mind, or action, 'knowability' is revealed.

We could imagine trying to establish 'knowability' differently; for example on the basis of a separate creative intelligence that structured a world in terms of mind and body and their 'knowingful' interaction. But then we have departed from the 'only knowing' of emptiness: Confronted with a new structure, we will have to account for how this structure arises. Only in the 'empty' interaction of Space and Knowledge—the Body of Knowledge 'before' shape and form—can we touch a 'knowability' whose 'texture' is Space—a 'knowability' *within* Being that leaves nothing unknown.

Alive with its own intrinsic vitality, active at the heart of appearance, the Body of Knowledge dances and sings, sharing changes as they manifest, recycling the dynamic of Time and the allowing of Space. As the 'field' of all possible points, it expresses a global potential for human being, activating all human capacity to exhibit what until now has not manifested.

When we discard even 'potential' and 'field', the invisible and boundless, the 'nonexistent impossible' can be created as unique. Knowledge itself can encourage Knowledge, inviting form to be form and existence to exist. All is allowed and open, manifested and permitted. All history passes through experience, presenting beginnings and endings, preserved by Time in Space, cultivating Knowledge. What happens serves as agent for exhibition and distribution alike.

In the unboundedness of what is and might be, what was and never will be, shape and form join in an architectonic display, self-creating and self-generating. All that brings gain or loss, all that situates itself in a 'given' direction, all that is thought or appears can be explored in ways that further a powerful and creative dynamic.

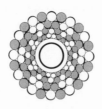

Toward Time and Space

DRAMA
OF EXISTENCE

W hen Knowledge and Space present the play of the Body of Knowledge, first-level 'bearings' lose their significance. We are free to adopt new positions—not in order to assert new claims of ownership, but to explore new roles and possibilities. It is like having a choice of vehicles that can take us to our destination, or several systems of measurement available for use.

In such circumstances, arguments about truth are like arguments about whether one system of measurement is right and another wrong. The test of what is 'true' becomes the pragmatic test of worth and value, accompanied by the recognition that different truths may operate at different levels and in different contexts. Each prevailing 'truth' will have its validating reality, with no truth absolute. Juxtaposing the fixed positions of one truth to those of another may open them both to greater flexibility and potential (which may take the form of a more 'comprehensive' truth). In the end we will come to a knowledge that does not depend on 'being true'.

Knowledge without 'the true' will unfold in terms of 'presentations'. For example, suppose that sound projects a beautiful melody into consciousness. The sound has the quality of appearance and thus 'traces back' to Space. But beauty comes only when the appearance is joined with the quality of appreciation, an expression of Knowledge. In the same way, any presentation depends on Knowledge and Space—in lower-level terms, on mind and what appears to mind.

Presentation can occur in two distinct ways. On the ordinary level, the mind seizes what is presented to it by time, positioning it in accord with its models and the prevailing order. When Knowledge is more fully available, another alternative opens: Mind can join in the presentation. This begins to happen when what is presented or given is accepted and appreciated as an offering, rather than being appropriated and specified.

It is such appreciation, which can be understood as participation in the offering, that gives the capacity to enjoy music and art. In the same way, appreciation allows the artist to create by bringing together form, color, texture, and meaning, shaping a symbol that points *beyond what is given to the giving.* Art as an expression of appreciation invites participation in what appears as the manifested 'coexistence' of Space and Knowledge.

From one perspective, all appearance can be understood as akin to art: *Space dancing the universe of Being.* The drama of existence unfolds like a well-loved epic

453

with countless episodes. Within the epic, there is joy and suffering, birth and death, victory and defeat. But as the playful display of Space, such an unfolding of events simply reveals new facets of the Body of Knowledge. No structure 'outside' the display selects presentations to be taken up for later consideration so that they can be assigned value and meanings within a model.

In the vast play of continuous creation, models drawn from the first-level world of substance are applied by human beings to reckon gains and losses, pleasures and pains. Yet in the presentations of Space and Knowledge, substance has no foundation. In the allowing of Space there is no becoming; in the free play of Knowledge there is no seed. In the interaction of Space and Knowledge in Time, what changes does not come to an end, and there are no transitions. Even the transition from life to death remains ever embodied in the Body of Knowledge.

The range of the knowable could be described as vast beyond all comprehension. Yet this is true only in a first-level way of seeing. Putting matters in this way implicitly affirms a limit even in denying limits, for it separates knowing and the knowable.

From a higher perspective, the 'incomprehensibility' of the knowable does not conflict with a unitary 'knowledgeability'. Wherever we look—in all thoughts and emotions, all knowing of specific entities, all being *as such*—knowledge is active. Appearance itself is the magical play of knowledge, alive with knowledge, joyful without a source or cause, intrinsic to Being.

From the psychological perspective, we may fear greater knowing, a fear that grows out of a suspicion that we are living our lives based on half-truths or assumptions that we would rather not question. But as soon as we allow for a knowledge not owned subjectively, these concerns disappear. Fear and other emotions familiar to conventional psychology become expressions of the play of Knowledge. Without feeling compelled to 'accept' our situation (which, *as* 'our situation', may actually call for fundamental change), we can let go of the 'focal setting' that makes this situation an occasion for concern.

In the creative dynamic of the Body of Knowledge, whatever appears can be a sparkling jewel, a precious offering. Even patterns that repeat endlessly, in cycles that limit and confine, express this creative surge. We can reject, but we can also reunite, re-express, re-determine, re-value, re-reward. We can reemerge, renew and re-access, re-continue, reincarnate, re-remove, re-unsettle. A steady stream of rebirth reexamines even what is repressed or re-denied, reassessing what is re-thought.

In such a dynamic, thoughts and forms and senses manifest as their own creation: program and programmer together, distributed attributes to explore through the momentum of inquiry. A unique rhythm sets in motion what appears, creating, arranging, encompassing. Expectation and imagination merge in images and form, moods and experiences. Through a ceaseless play of becoming that shepherds birth into being, Knowledge re-commands Greatness.

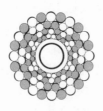

Toward Time and Space

AWAKENING TO GREAT KNOWLEDGE

K nowledge alive enacts Time beyond past and future. A potential for manifestation moves and activates, disclosing change and character and condition. Reasons of place and reasons of experience improve and disprove, improvising variations on the 'instant point' in time.

The 'giving point' of time can equally yield self-exploration or self-exploitation. Ways of thinking or acting combine with the attitudes of the subjective mind, relying on faculties that emerge from forms inaugurated by the rhythm of successive images. Steadily changing or merging in harmony with unfolding rhythms, mind emerges as the faculty of form, continuing what image has initiated.

The Body of Knowledge remains unknown, and thus unknowing, *because its knowledge does not belong to the self*. To embody the Body of Knowledge, we must cut through this limitation, touching with awareness the heart of Being. We begin to do this when we pursue inquiry beyond all limits and within all structures. Then we learn that knowledge is not a guest that has to be invited; it is already in residence. We need not progressively purify lower knowledge, for the whole of what is known is already pure gold. Even when knowledge is alloyed with confusion or conflict, or with interpretations relevant to a particular purpose or concern, the alloy itself is also pure. We can only alloy gold with gold.

And yet perhaps awakening to Great Knowledge does not seem inviting. From within the conventional temporal order, Great Time can look like an ending, Great Space like a void. Fear and subtle forms of holding can easily assert themselves. But the commitment to Knowledge need not take the form of an attack on old ways of being. When we become the rhythm of our becoming, we challenge the old order in a way that also accepts it.

Great Time is in the beginning and the ending of this very moment, Great Space in the 'here' and 'there' of all that appears. A specific character continues to unfold as manifestation of an underlying unity. The rhythms developed by Time are 'read out' by Knowledge, 'printed out' by the embodied senses, and 'expressed' in the instant of action. We open our hearts to 'our own' Being.

Inquiry as Great Knowledge allows the Body of Knowledge to become the Body of Time, gaining intimacy with Time by embracing it in the instant. In each emerging instant there is a merging with the momentum of Time, so that the many presentations of time merge into the one Body of Knowledge. All-embracing Knowledge incorporates all rhythm into one point, pointing toward the one Body—the whole.

Knowledge knowing and embodying Time breaks the frozen chain of events. The rhythm of time is mastered, giving Knowledge as completely stable, Time as invariable, and all presentations as equally allowing Space. Mind and matter alike communicate with Time on the deepest level, creating the opportunity for freedom and for truly independent action. All points become open (without ever having been closed), and the full nature of Being is present in each variable presentation.

The qualities of opposition inherent in the dichotomies of ordinary experience are an aspect of Being presenting: a rhythm of contrasts and of contrasting points. The whole that they establish is itself the Body of Knowledge, and the self-interpretation active within each contrasting point is a 'feeding back' of the energy that 'knowingness' embodies.

When the patterns of the temporal order are seen as luminous with an inner light, they become expressions of infinite knowing rather than the substance of specific points. Experience itself, freely open to the rhythms of Time, has a texture that reveals inexpressible beauty, which no one has to foster, preserve, or protect.

From a religious perspective, such a state could be described as God's blessing, or perhaps as a heaven realm; from a psychological perspective, it could be described as self-actualization; from a social perspective, it might be considered utopia. But whatever interpretation is put on it, the embodied dynamic is beyond interpretations, not closed off in any way. Human energy can be considered to be 'within' this dynamic, to be 'of' or 'from' it, to emerge 'out of' it or 'reflect' it—the specifics do not seem to matter. The Body of Knowledge is the Body of Time, dynamic and alive; the Body of Knowledge is the Body of Space, accommodating and allowing. Being emerges into fullness.

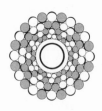

Toward Time and Space

A PARADISE OF BEING

Within invariable Time, the measurements and rhythms that distinguish and separate are only further possibilities. Points become symbols, communicating Great Knowledge, transforming into each other like the products of chemical reactions or the display of a conjurer's most marvelous illusions.

Time, energy, and mind alike are the great magician, presenting existence, revealing the magician as another magical apparition. Nothing is stagnant or fixed, and there is no going forward toward a future or coming out of a past. The dichotomies of the temporal order lose their fixed reality, for the 'order' itself is simply the display of Great Time and Great Space. Nothing is held back, nothing left out.

If this fundamental realization of *sameness in difference* 'clicks', space and time are visibly transformed. The patterns of past, present, and future and of static objects appearing in space may change completely. The Body of Knowledge gives ordinary appearance new radiance. Perhaps it will be such transformations that first alert us to the awakening of Great Knowledge.

Knowledge is the timeless inheritor of a rich, expansive vision that deepens effortlessly, moving in a circle that feeds knowledge back into knowledge. When Knowledge awakens fully, intimacy appears within living itself, and the vision opens further. Being becomes the rich embodiment of Knowledge, and Knowledge the quality of all Being. The aesthetic splendor of the Body of Knowledge invites knowledge to acknowledge embodiment as the bodying forth of Knowledge. The angle of the subject and of the object and their unity all become one point.

Such Knowledge—Great Knowledge—belongs to no one. It is more fundamental than belonging; more fundamental than the categories that it shapes. It is like the light that enables seeing to take place, revealing not specific characteristics and attributes, but rather the *quality* of aesthetic beauty that accommodating Great Space allows and dynamic Great Time presents.

From a certain perspective, we could describe Great Space as space 'within' space, allowing space to appear, and Great Time as time 'before' time, presenting the unfolding of time. In this view, Great Knowledge is what knows this 'within' and this 'before'. In just this way, in perfect intimacy, Great Knowledge knows the 'blueness' of blue—the shining of the light that makes blue happen—and the 'isness' of what is. But the 'ness' of blueness is no different from blue, nor is the 'isness' of what is different from the manifestation itself. And because Great Knowledge is also the Body of Knowledge, and the Body of Knowledge is the Body of Time and Space, we can say that this knowing of the 'ness' is the 'knowingness' within Great Space and Great Time.

The 'Greatness' of Knowledge, Space, and Time does not mean that what is being referred to is above us, nor that it is greater than what we are, for our realm is not different in any way from the Time, Space, and Knowledge that it embodies. Still, it would be misleading to interpret this 'not different' as meaning in any ordinary way that 'the way things are' is all right, or to claim that our only responsibility is to 'let it be'. Only when the embodiment of knowledge that is our world has 'recovered' its primordial splendor, when Knowledge has awakened to Knowledge, can we discover that the finite is Being within ordinary existence.

Although we could say that there is nothing higher than human being, we would have to acknowledge in the same breath that we have lost our human being. Cut off from Time and Space, we have gone astray. Yet the intrinsic power of Being remains always available. To speak of Great Time, Great Space, and Great Knowledge is a reminder of this availability. It is also a summoning and a call to responsibility, and a call for Being to return to itself.

When appearance manifests as a projection of accommodating Great Space, all facets of Being are visible at once; all dimensions cooperate in a harmonious display.

This richness could justly bear the name 'immortality': eternally alive in a primordial not-ending. Its symbol is the magical nectar that transforms the body into embodied knowledge, immaculate and free from defect.

Seen with the embodied 'knowingness' of Great Knowledge, the 'lifeless' momentum of lower time and space is a fantastic exhibition of the qualities of existence: an embodiment of light in which all the cosmos shares in simultaneous unity. The play of the universe is reflected in the infinite variety of ways that human beings have found to express themselves. Here, within the heart of existence—projections of shadowless luminosity—is a paradise of Being.

Like water in a lake, unaffected by rocks that tumble into its depths, Being accommodates everything. There is nothing that cannot be and nothing that must remain. There is no permanent blockage; no seed of becoming to establish what must henceforth remain unmoved; only a timeless procession and presentation that is neither real nor unreal.

Everyday life is an arising and coming into Being, and responsive awareness is the rightful response to its joyous energy. Such a responsive minding knows in a new way. Its knowing is the fullness of the Body of Knowledge, set free of self-imposed limits. Not based on interpretation that presupposes separation, Great Knowledge occurs within each presentation. Knower and known share equally in a treasury of limitless abundance.

Within each thought and each arising, knower, known, and communicating power manifest equally the presence of present Being and embodied Knowledge. Floating effortlessly in the unbounded region of allowing, the Body of Knowledge offers the gift of light, revealing its own radiance, identical with the energy that fills experience with content and brings existence to be.

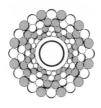

Inseparable Presentation

ONLY KNOWING

As a fabric is woven, an image is transmitted by light, or a thought is projected by awareness, so whatever appears seems to arise in dependence on a 'background' or 'source' that allows or accommodates it. Name and form could be considered the outcome of the process through which appearance emerges from the 'background', conducting meaning into being.

What can be said about the nature of this 'background'? In relation to what appears as meaningful, it is 'transparent', shining through in each form as water appears in each wave. Yet this same transparency makes the 'background' inaccessible: As soon as we try to contact it, we obscure its natural clarity.

For example, when we say that the 'background' accommodates 'by nature', we assign it to the category of 'existence'; when we consider it a 'basis' or 'source' for what appears, we reinforce this interpretation. But this understanding is circular. We cannot base the arising of existence on the operation of a special 'existent'.

We can make the same point somewhat differently. Whatever exists (including 'existence') is based on its opposite—one is established because the other is 'there' as well. But this 'joint establishing' is not itself 'based on' anything, except perhaps the mental operation 'based on'. When we affirm the 'existence' of what has no basis, we do so only on the basis of dogma and belief. Knowledge cannot know the basis, for there is no basis to be known.

When existence and nonexistence are referred to a 'basis', an unknown is established as 'background'—an axiomatic 'x' deemed 'worthy' of belief. The result is to present knowledge as inherently limited, for it can never reach beyond the unknown axiom, which serves as a kind of 'body of the whole'.

The counter to this limitation is to imagine knowledge or awareness itself as the transparent 'background' of appearance. But we stay true to a 'knowledge background' only when we do not offer it as basis. Knowledge is excluded by 'based on'; it retires from the field. Based on the 'based on', an unknown is interpreted and a report is filed. Everything is 'ok', but this 'ok' offers 'zero knowledge'.

It might seem that if we stepped outside the accepted axioms, the 'necessary' basis, there would be no possibility for knowledge at all. But perhaps just the opposite is true. A knowledge without axioms, without a 'based on' or 'source from', would present its own transparent luminosity: a 'knowingness' without limitation.

Stepping 'outside' the known does not mean stepping into 'nothing at all'. This view understands 'nothing' as 'something'—what is left when everything is taken away. Such a 'nothing' becomes a point that remains impenetrable, a hole into which we risk falling. What we do not see is that this hole arises through our own determination to hold on to 'something', and thus signals that we have not stepped 'outside' the known at all.

More generally, stepping 'outside' the realm of axioms does not mean going 'somewhere else', for then we would just be 'basing ourselves' in a different axiom. Instead, we step 'outside' the axiom when we step 'into' the process of 'feedback' through which appearance takes form. Seeing the way that knowledge arises allows knowledge to be open. What appears *as* appearance *in* appearing cannot be restricted to the accepted structures of ordinary knowledge.

Such an opening is not a state we will arrive at; it is pervasive, immediate, fully available before it is reached. Knowledge is already 'here'; there is nothing 'else' to be known. Within the structures of what is known, 'knowingness' is active—the encompassing inviting of all human experience.

What would happen if we entered such a realm of always active knowing? Because we would see polarity, judgment, speculations, and the other foundations for establishing existence as leading nowhere, it seems that much of this activity would stop of its own accord. But this stopping would not be an annihilation based on a forceful ignoring or a reduction akin to ignorance. It would be spontaneous cessation, the fruit of an expanded knowing. Free from the restless agitation that sustains the known, knowledge would sustain activity that was truly meaningful.

Then what would be the basis for action? If we trace values and moral choices to beliefs and conditioning, we may conclude that a knowledge 'without foundation' will leave us without standards to guide our conduct. But the dichotomy between beliefs and knowledge also has no basis. *Like every other form of appearance*, beliefs can be rich with knowledge; not only the knowledge inherent in the 'truth' of the belief, but knowledge of arising and consequences, knowledge of ways in which knowledge is frozen and ignored; knowledge of the structure of beliefs. It is when we trace knowledge *within* the known in this way that we approach a way of acting 'based on' transparent knowledge—knowledge without limits, in which action springs from inspiration.

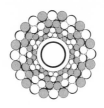

Inseparable Presentation

ATTEMPTS
TO GO BEYOND

Great Knowledge is always accessible. Why then does it not always manifest as Great Knowledge? What gives us the characteristic experience of being caught in lower-level knowledge, with all its limitations and its pervasive sense of not-knowing?

In presupposing 'levels' of knowledge, this question manifests the lower-level knowledge that it seeks to question. There is no special 'kind' of knowing that can be classified as Great Knowledge, distinct from 'lower-level' knowledge: 'Lower-level' and 'Great Knowledge' are inseparable from one another.

We might understand this statement as a 'point' being made about Great Knowledge. This 'point' can be made in terms of 'points'. We might say that all points known on the lower level are open or open-ended, or that all points can emerge from one point. We might even say that all points are light, or that a point made in terms of lower-level knowledge is 'at the same time' an expression of the Body of Knowledge as a whole.

Yet the 'methodology' that we are now implicitly invoking is suspect; once again a first-level way of understanding is brought to bear. When we make a 'point' about Great Knowledge, we make Great Knowledge a possibility within the realm of lower-level knowledge. Our 'point' at once invalidates itself; instead of being 'about' Great Knowledge, it is about the lower-level construct 'Great Knowledge'.

Perhaps we could still risk this move, provided that we acknowledged clearly that we were only pointing 'at' Great Knowledge, and that our 'pointing' had nothing to do with Great Knowledge 'as such'. But even this approach conceals the nature of Great Knowledge from our inquiry.

When we make the 'point' that Great Knowledge has nothing to do with points, we turn Great Knowledge 'into' the 'final point', which is also the 'stopping point' for inquiry. Once this limitation on knowing is in place, Great Knowledge has eluded our grasp. If just one point is opaque to inquiry, the darkness of a fundamental not-knowing settles. Only if *all* points are transparent can the light of Great Knowledge radiate freely.

If Great Knowledge cannot be pointed 'at', and if we will never come to a 'point' in our inquiry where we can claim to have 'reached' Great Knowledge, then how is Great Knowledge accessible at all? It seems that lower-level knowledge and Great Knowledge cannot be juxtaposed. Just as it makes no sense to try to calculate the distance from here to another universe, so there is no 'point of access' to Great Knowledge. Or if such a 'point' does 'exist', it seems that it must in principle remain unknown—the axiomatic 'x' that puts in place the defining borders of the world accessible to first-level knowledge.

This conclusion expresses the reverse side of the question with which we began. If we are already 'in' Great Knowledge, how can there be lower-knowledge experiences? But if we do indeed find ourselves on the level of lower knowledge, how could we ever move beyond it?

Though we may call them inseparable, first-level knowledge and Great Knowledge seem incapable of sharing the same space or 'coexisting' in the same universe. Conventional knowledge—the specific sets of information owned by a self—proceeds by fitting together bits and pieces to form a whole. It knows 'from' a specific perspective—more or less consistent and encompassing—that is invariably bound to a specific 'order'.

On the second level, the tendency to objectify is repeated on a more subtle level in terms of 'field' and 'temporal order'. Even 'the flow of time' can become an 'outsider' to that flow. Similar difficulties arise as soon as Time, Space, or Knowledge is understood as a potentiality out of which ordinary experience arises.

Attempts to go beyond such a limited knowledge remain within first-level structures. Each new vision we 'arrive at', no matter how beautiful or refined, is tied to a 'something' or a 'someone'. There is always the 'object' of the vision, and as soon as there is an object subject to description there is limitation. Descriptions automatically bring with them positionings and points of view, while objects bring with them subjects. Proceeding in this way, the established order of self and world can only perpetuate itself.

The world of conventional experience depends on mutually limiting entities. Thus 'chair' exists in relation to 'table'; both exist in relation to 'floor', and the entire domain of 'artifacts' exists in relation to 'human beings'. Each entity takes its shape and form in relation to all those entities it is not. Without being limited by its 'not' in this way, no entity could come into existence as such.

'Is' and 'not' present a complete interdependence that operates whenever distinctions are made. If there is no edge, there can be no middle. For example, if space were truly unbounded, how could anything other than space exist? Yet the edge also depends on the middle, and even space 'appears' in relation to what 'shows up' within it. In this sense, existence is a matter of definition. It is due to this interdependence of entities and what they are not that we can speak of the known world as being fabricated by language.

For language to accomplish its task of fabrication, it must act as a framework for communication: a vehicle for expressing and shaping agreement. Of course, the accuracy of this communication can be questioned: Since each individual has unique experiences based on maintaining specific positions, agreement can only be inferred, and in a certain sense may be illusory. Yet the realm of ordinary experience seemingly takes shape and form only through such communication—the root activity through which language calls existence into being.

Communication is not only a basis for naming and identification, but is shaped in turn by those activities. Logical discourse depends on labeling and defining, limiting and distinguishing. An act of speech furthers communication only if it *refers back* to previous acts of labeling based on interdefined identities and *projects forward* what has already been agreed upon as true or real. There may be nonverbal forms of communication that are more direct and immediate, but as long as such experiences are referred to or associated with identities and entities, the structure of logical discourse will continue to establish what is possible.

When we stop focusing on the information provided by the distinctions and definitions and polarities that form the surface of experience, and look instead at the nature of those distinctions, we soon recognize that they are fundamentally linguistic structures, with nothing of substance 'beneath' the surface information they display. Light and dark appear, but the 'lightness' of light is stripped away, together with the 'darkness' of dark.

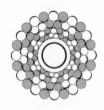

Inseparable Presentation

KNOWLEDGEABILITY OF THE WHOLE

S uppose that we have a direct 'experience' of Great Knowledge. As soon as we juxtapose this experience to ordinary experience, it becomes a part of that experience (even if presented as 'nonstandard' or as 'beyond the ordinary realm'). The problem is one of communication: Since Great Knowledge cannot be limited, how can it be communicated within the framework of conventional discourse?

This way of framing the difficulty also suggests a way out. Great Knowledge itself does not need to be communicated: It has no audience toward whom it must make itself clear. Communication presupposes a place where knowledge exists, a second place where it does not, and an act of 'transportation' between them. But Great Knowledge does not exist in one place as opposed to another, nor does it require transportation, for there is nothing to be transported.

Whether or not the logic of lower-level discourse allows for the possibility of Great Knowledge leaves Great Knowledge completely unaffected, even though Great Knowledge will be inseparable from such discourse and from its objects. Communicated in being active, Great Knowledge is active as the inner light illuminating all that is known.

So long as it is not 'assessed' from a lower knowledge point of view, Great Knowledge counteracts all limits. It presents all specific knowings, all information and techniques, facts and visions, without being bound by them. Infinite in scope, it is universally available without regard for ownership or limitation. Like light, it is invisible as it propagates, but illuminates whatever it encounters. Pure energy, its power is available at the most subtle level.

Though the conventional 'order' is potent in its effects, Great Knowledge recognizes it as neither substantial nor fixed, but as a 'read-out': a unitary 'expression' or 'embodiment' of Knowledge. Since what appears is already Knowledge, there is nothing to be transformed or altered, and no 'new knowledge' to gain. *The 'recognition' of what appears 'to' lower knowledge 'as' knowledge 'is' Great Knowledge.*

As part of an all-encompassing 'read-out', the structures 'established' by the 'logos' can be appreciated as the creative expression of a fundamental knowing. Within this creative realm, the symbols and concepts that unfold to knowledge in ordinary space and time are *accepted* without being *binding*. Mind and 'self as knower' are not the authoritative source of what is presented; instead, there is the open momentum of presenting.

Free from the usual need to establish anything, we need not be concerned with the specifics of what is presented. We no longer have to choose or take sides, for there are no more dogmas or beliefs that must be sustained and supported. Any tendency toward tension or pressure is released naturally, 'in the course of events'. Space opens, and knowledge, because it is more accepting, no longer finds limitations so impenetrable. We draw closer to a natural wisdom of 'knowingness'.

Knowledge on this level is 'knowledgeability', a knowledge of the whole that supports and establishes human intelligence without adopting the structures put forward by that intelligence. The element of distance inherent in first-level knowing simply disappears: Great Knowledge inspires all aspects of life.

When the 'order' itself reveals the 'knowledgeability' of the whole, knowledge can be global. Nothing can 'go' wrong, and there will be no difficulties. Truly 'knowledgeable', we act with a power that brings Knowledge to Being in remarkable ways.

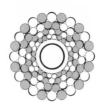

Decisive Creation

MIND THAT KNOWS

The patterns that we live by make themselves available as the record of the whole; they are presented as what has been passed on and must be preserved. What patterns form this record, whose tracings we patiently transcribe?

Taken singly, they are far too extensive to grasp, yet we might consider tracing the scope of a pattern of the whole: Senses, feelings, projections, and beliefs; creation, imagination, and the logic of an underlying 'order'; rightness and wrongness and all procedures for decision-making; hopes and expectations, and all sustaining, improving, or disappearing; change in material nature, the occurring of thoughts, 'read-outs', the adding and subtracting of different attributes; philosophy and culture, morality and social interactions; and the interaction of whole and parts, completing each story and establishing its themes.

Through such prospects, propositions, and processes, we can propose to know the whole. Do the patterns shape what we preserve, or does our preserving activate the patterns? Have we adopted as our own a prehistory that sets all limits, or are we foretelling a future whose scope we set in place?

The patterns we accept and the record we transmit all seem related to the mind that knows. Yet the mind itself is a kind of artifact, pointing onward to knowledge. It is knowledge that can know the record and thus establish it as the record; that can set in motion the dynamic that determines shape and form. Knowledge itself develops, and while it does so in accord with the patterns of the record, the development also creates the record. Even the potential for going beyond the record points toward the knowing capacity of knowledge.

Usually we consider knowledge as a possession of the mind, but it seems more nearly true to say that subjective mind is a part of the record that knowledge embodies in its development. We might say that knowledge is the sole shareholder in a corporation whose business it is to produce mind and the experiences of mind. Traced to its source, mind has the nature of knowledge.

The experience of mind—the patterns that mind can 'cognize'—can be understood as fabrications. Images express accepted characteristics; qualities develop, taking shape and form; 'feedback' leads to 'read-outs' in repeated reinforcing cycles. Each image manifests the power of knowledge, creating potentialities that vary with the dynamic of differing cultures and periods of time. How potentiality finds expression will shape the patterns of the record, determining the prospects for creativity, the solidity of established characteristics, and whether knowledge is 'on' time, 'of' time, or 'out of' time.

To describe this perspective in lower-level terms, we might say that knowledge and its agent mind are responsible for the creation of all that is. To specify further: Creation emerges through the activation of the potentiality that knowledge embodies through its 'development'. This activation—which takes place in time and space—is the Body of Knowledge, the 'truth' of what appears in ordinary experience as 'what exists'.

In presenting such prospects in lower-level terms, however, we presuppose too much. The potential that we specify will close knowledge off, assuring that the potential goes unfulfilled. But this need not be an obstacle. *As it closes off*, potential invites Great Knowledge. *As it specifies*, Great Knowledge accepts the invitation.

Always 'ahead of time', 'establishing' before establishing and 'knowing' before the known, Great Knowledge portrays the creation of what is as a previously untold story, intrinsically available but never before attributed. Ahead of all stories, creation is the story of the whole. The fullness of humanity's development can be exhibited in light of creation's possibilities: a history ahead of history, a telling ahead of time. Yet this exhibition need not take conventional form, unfolding 'over' time. Only the existence-centered perspective of a lower level insists on creation as temporally prior to 'what is'.

The point at which the vastness of potential knowledge embodies in the actual is the 'point of decision'. Normally we say the mind decides; by extension we might say that the senses decide or that we decide in taking up a point of view. But in each of these characteristic 'moves', the 'decisive point' is prior to all distinctions and characteristics, including those that specify mind, senses, and point of view.

The 'decisive point' that determines the outcome is given 'ahead' of time, 'before' the potential that appears within the *model* put forward by mind or the *'feel'* of the 'field'. 'Setting aside' or 'including within', 'establishing' governing rules or values, 'determining' and 'identifying': All such activities presuppose that the 'decisive point' has already been reached.

For the 'decisive point' to be decisive, it cannot be a point of origin, a 'source from' or a 'pointing to'. Based on such beginnings, knowledge could not be unbounded, as it must be to manifest the power to know. Though time could be said to play a role in the 'development' of knowledge, it creates unanswerable paradoxes to say that knowledge originates at a point in time.

The very possibility that knowledge can develop cannot be said to originate *within* a temporal order. Instead, the knowledge available within the 'point of decision' is its own source. The point 'reads-out' its own appearance; enacts its own decision. In more conventional terms, we could say that shape and form develop in accord with their own dynamic; they express their own potential. What is decisive for creation comes 'in advance': The 'read-out' could be said to *program itself* as 'read-out'.

Each 'decisive point' can be seen as a bubble, insubstantial, yet embodying its own being. Moreover, though bubbles succeed one another and interact with one another, succession and interaction *have no separate source* —their potential is implicit in the 'bubble read-out'.

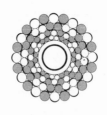

Decisive Creation

ALWAYS EMERGING
CREATIVITY

The wholly open realm of decisive creation is transformed in conventional reality into a world where the important decisions have already been made. A proposition is put forward as a candidate for belief; once accepted, the 'truth' toward which the belief is directed is given the attribute of being solid. The decision has been made, the point established; once and for all, creation is relegated to the past.

The established point sustains other points, at the same time affirming that they are separate from 'this' point (for 'solid' and 'separate' are fundamentally interrelated.) Separate points interact in a given dynamic, influencing one another in accord with the rules of the given 'order.'

The 'logos' of the 'order' confirms what has been established: Its time presents specific points and its knowledge allows for interaction and variation. Together time and knowledge accommodate a range of possibilities: products or interpretations that can be further refined. Sets of rules set ruling ideals, defining first-level limits on creativity.

Yet the whole of this display is arranged by knowledge. In light of the self-arising quality of the display, we could say that *knowledge manufactures magic*. True, *at once* this 'magic' is taken up within an 'order'; *at once* 'magic' becomes 'logic', valued for its benefits but tamed in its mastery. But as this process runs its course, what becomes of the 'magic' that activates the 'order' to begin with? Can we trace its activity in the actual? Does the 'decisive point' remain available—even after all decisions have been made?

The variable outcome of the decisions we make in the course of events shows that first-level knowledge itself is variable, depending on how well 'cognition' accords with the underlying 'order'. For decisions to be effective, knowledge must conform not only to what appears in space, but also to the rhythm of time.

For example, the dynamic of temporal unfolding may sustain changes that are fast or slow; if knowledge is 'tuned in' to the resulting rhythm, the decisions it leads to will produce the predicted and wished-for outcome. Attention to cognitive 'fit' in this sense may offer a useful way of understanding and may even extend the ethical and moral knowledge through which we attempt to guide our conduct.

But the interaction of time and knowledge in decision also has a more subtle aspect. Each first-level 'point of decision' is both a kind of knowing and a point in the linear sequence of time. The 'decision point' gathers together all that is known and all that presents itself in that 'moment' of time.

Second-level knowledge sees every 'moment' in linear time as such a summation—a decisive choosing to uphold what has been established. The succession of these 'points of decision' generates the rhythm in accord with which first-level knowing unfolds. It establishes the basis for the sequencing of time, generating patterns and rhythm through repetition, 'measuring out' knowledge on the basis of knowledge.

As a gathering together of all that contributes to its making, each 'point of decision' is the whole. We could go even further: Each 'point of decision' is the emerging gathering of *all known knowledge,* at whatever level it operates. In the gathered wholeness of the 'point of decision', nothing is left out, and choice is freely available. The known world is sustained from moment to moment on the basis of ever-emerging 'points of decision'.

In this ongoing 'emergency', all that is is invariably at stake. Since this is so, what binds us 'now' is evanescent—freedom can be 'recovered' at any moment.

The chain of 'decision points' duplicates itself, interweaving time and knowledge. But the chain is always forming anew—at each point in the chain we choose to maintain what is. Though the choice we make is based on the sum of our knowledge, it grows also out of the rhythm of time, for choosing is action, and action responds to and is powered by the temporal dynamic.

Between the rhythm of time and the 'decision points' of knowledge, a sustaining balance holds. If there were only rhythm, with no knowledge, there would be no decision to make, and so no possibility of freedom. First-level time presents just such an imbalance—choices already made, so that further knowing is not allowed. But when we understand this first-level circumstance as a 'read-out' that we 'choose' to maintain, we can restore the underlying balance. We can recover the true significance of 'points of decision' as points that gather the whole of being and return to a freedom of always emerging creativity.

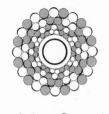

Decisive Creation

OPEN TO CREATION

First-level knowledge suggests that for experience to be available, a starting point is required. But a more open understanding need not posit such a beginning. When each point is unique in expressing a variation on the dynamic power of Time, Space, and Knowledge, the singularity of the point can manifest not as an existent but as a quality.

In such singularity, there is nothing that insists on specificity. Each point is an opportunity for creation, but *not* in a way that turns the point into a starting point for experience.

Since there are only independent, encompassing *qualities*, there is nothing to initiate, just as there is nothing to destroy or change. The nature of the point is in one sense impenetrable, but in another sense is completely open.

Such points are 'gathered together' by the 'focal setting'—a time point, a space point, a knowledge point. The gathering of shape and form and patterns allows for perception that does not eliminate. The light of awareness links to the silence of time and the luminosity of space. What appears ripples 'outwards'; at the edge of the ripple is the potential to connect with other appearance in ways that are unbounded.

Even so, to explore what appears in terms of points amounts to an attempt by mind to 'point out'—to describe through dialogue and imagery. What is 'pointed out' becomes concrete; a program or pattern gives order and meaning. Images or verbal constructs or certain ways of perceiving lead to specification that gives shape and form and affirms a given 'logic'.

In seeing this 'pointing out' in operation, we also proceed 'point by point', gathering points through inference, memory, examples, experience. Images arise, together with memories related to images. We trace the activity of 'pointing out' through what is already known, building up what proceeds from what has gone before.

Even when what is 'pointed out' is other levels of knowledge, the act of 'pointing out' leads to determination. We confirm the point of view of the self, which owns each 'pointed-out' point. Starting from a given point, the self affirms its points of reference, establishing the basis for consensus.

No matter how far and in what unexpected directions a process based on such a structure unfolds, it does not 'attain' Being, nor does it empower creativity. Points give referents according to an 'according to'; there is a 'pointing back toward'. The 'setting up' of the 'feedback structure' makes it possible to go only so far.

Reference and consensus lead to the objective and the subjective, defining what is available in terms of 'what there is to talk about'. Whatever occupies space and time, including what arises within 'fields' of thought and awareness, does so as a point that is situated and fixed in being occupied.

This process of increasing specification leads to characteristic first-level outcomes. On the psychological level, patterns are initiated or confirmed; on the epistemological level, knowledge is produced that accords with preliminary limitations on knowing; on the ontological level, existence and experience are again established. The 'field' is reinstated and the 'logos' reinforced.

What has been activated in this way is no longer a 'locus' for creation. What is said presents itself only as an occasion for assent and affirmation. Positions are adopted as a matter of course, and claims to rely on no position are seen as naive or disingenuous, perhaps even manipulative.

But such tendencies can be anticipated and counteracted. The movement toward specification proceeds only in its own terms. At another level each point offers a quality of space or 'zero'. In the lineage of the point's arising, traceable in terms of logic, sequential events, time, or space, the 'end point' refers back to the initial 'point of decision', which remains available to be activated as the open space of 'zero'.

Occupying a particular point of view, we are tied to a 'specific' time and space, making the space-quality intrinsic to each point difficult to experience directly. Based on what has gone before, occupancy is presupposed and predetermined: We have already made our point.

Yet vision can set in motion a power that may be able to 'unmake'the point. Open to creation and the unique 'being' of 'zero', the 'point of decision' can lead us to the rhythms of becoming. Rhythms refer back to rhythm, suggesting a flexibility that can open further. If Knowledge gives permission, the abundance of available richness can express a knowing 'within' rhythms and 'before' points—a 'locus' for creation before decision. As long as 'knowingness' is directly available, Knowledge can unfold within Time and Space without restriction, for there is nowhere to go and nothing that remains unaccomplished. All intrinsic limitations are restored to the 'zero point' of decisive creativity.

Though we encounter limits wherever 'something' has been established, we are free to look instead toward 'nothing'—toward the 'nowhere' of nonpositioned Space, the 'nothing happening' of invariant Time, and the 'nothing to know' of an indeterminate Knowledge.

Intimacy

A PARTNERSHIP

The qualities and character of phenomena bring coherence and order to the world. We are a part of the world, and we too depend on such qualities as they apply to what we perceive and what we are; without them, we would have no role to play—we would be left without a job.

Despite their fundamental significance, however, character and qualities are *just their own presentation*, nothing more. We can feel free to challenge them without reservation. In fact, we may find that they respond to such challenge like gold that is beaten: They will shine with a luster that grows ever more brilliant.

At the furthest limits of conventional knowledge, the qualities that manifest are those inherent in all existence. A 'field' is in operation and an 'order' has been established, and the truth of these 'wholes' is visible in every part.

Questioning and exploring the various aspects of the 'field' and 'order', studying whatever makes itself available, we can gain new insights into the character and quality of what is. Though a journey to the furthest limits of the known will leave us enclosed by the same borders that were present at the outset, it will also offer independence from any particular position or assumption.

Activated by such inquiry, knowledge restores its own intrinsic vitality, penetrating the depths of Time and Space to yield more Knowledge. Without *reducing* appearance to 'Time and Space as known by Knowledge', it shows that appearance is not what it claims to be: that the pedigree it offers is false. It 'recovers' for Being its nature as light.

Conducted with care and devotion, inquiry lets experience resonate within us. As we shift our attention from place to place, we may eventually discover that there is no moving at all.

Not caught up in the flow of events, we touch the 'zero point' 'beneath' all manifestations. To speak of 'zero' as 'beneath' does not mean that the 'zero point' is like a cushion on which existence rests. Rather, manifestations are bound to 'zero' as the echo of 'zero'. When the openness of 'zero' is fully open, there is no difference between 'zero' and 'not-zero'.

Seeing this 'no-difference' is seeing Great Knowledge. The 'container' of the human body opens, so that space and time pour in; the container of the human mind opens, so that 'zero' can be acknowledged. The limits of mental operations as fed by the senses no longer bind the mind; there is more than 'minding', more than human, 'nothing at all'.

The fullness of 'nothing at all' is the inseparability of Great Knowledge from Great Time and Great Space. Space allows the rhythms of Time to propagate, while Knowledge establishes the purpose or pattern. When one of these three is wholly unbound, even the distinctions of Time, Space, and Knowledge are absorbed in Being.

Great Knowledge emerges in partnership with Great Space and Great Time. We can almost imagine the three in conversation: "I can do anything!" says Time with great animation. Space agrees, smiling broadly, "Yes, that is so. I offer you room." Knowledge has been listening, and now nods knowingly: "Yes, both of you are right. I give you full permission—you are free."

In a fellowship of such intimacy, the members share in being one. For example, the rhythm of Time must be 'timed out', and for this Knowledge is required. Knowledge is the evaluator and shaper, yet what appears and is known by Knowledge is the embodiment of Space. But without Time there would be no presentation to evaluate, no activity capable of generating being and becoming.

The 'mechanism' that allows such interactions among Time, Space, and Knowledge appears to be very subtle, like a glow around the edges of a bright, intense light. Yet the glow is not found only at the periphery. It is the radiant heart of the light, invisible in the light of ordinary concerns, but intrinsic to all appearance. It is the glow of 'zero', the 'point' of decision, the 'rhythm' of Being. Discovering and appreciating this glow is the special responsibility of Great Knowledge, which in fact is inseparable from the glow.

Although we could say that Great Knowledge is lucent, its light is not opposed to darkness. Darkness cannot limit its radiance, nor can shadow and form, whether physical or mental. The lucency of Great Knowledge has no point of origin and no point of cessation. At one with Space and Time, its inspiration embodies in all emerging. Since there is nothing that is not known, how can there be obstacles?

First-level characteristics could be said to be created by Time, Space, and Knowledge; the same is true for more fundamental activities and attributes such as allowing and knowing, rhythm, momentum, and light. But this creation, out of which the world in a certain sense could be said to arise, is not creation by a creator, for nothing of substance is created. Lucency simply radiates within Being. All qualities and attributes, in their own being, *are* Time and Space and Knowledge; they express this triad in boundless variety.

Intimacy

INSPIRED INQUIRY

For inquiry to be of real benefit, it must be inspired by a concern that goes beyond the rational, a motivation that will lift the accustomed form of knowing outside itself, so that transcendence of the old 'order' is possible. Without this dimension of aspiration, inquiry will not be able to maintain its freedom, and the Body of Knowledge will remain unknown.

Aspiration itself is an expression of 'knowingness': a way for the light of knowledge to shine through the patterns of our 'minding'. The best aspiration, then, is the Love of Knowledge itself, for only when our aspiration is great can Great Knowledge arise.

This does not mean that our inquiry must be selfless, or that we must give up the idea that there will be personal benefit as the result of more knowledge. The pattern that bases action on the obtaining of benefit does not have to be rejected any more than any other pattern or model. We can simply acknowledge that the desire for benefit sets up a goal, and thus a barrier. That barrier too can become a subject for inquiry.

The aspiration for Knowledge shows lower knowledge to be separated from Great Knowledge only by a distance without substance, which aspiration itself *has already bridged*. Under the guidance of aspiration, shadow merges with light—not because it becomes light, but because the distinction between light and shadow proves to be one of intention. Limits are eliminated through being illuminated, and there remain no obstructing partitions.

When we take aspiration and resolve as our constant companions, the path that opens to Knowledge becomes the path that Knowledge opens to us. We become partners with Knowledge, and learn to communicate with it. Our voice becomes the voice of Knowledge, our actions the activity of Knowledge, and our being the embodiment of Knowledge. Then our questions answer themselves in being asked. Problems are resolved without becoming the focus of concern, and we become more fully ourselves. Circling, refining, transforming, we explore with joy the pathways of Knowledge.

Intimacy

GREAT LOVE

Although recognizing the interplay between lack of knowledge and human discontent can help inspire aspiration, it may be more fruitful to cultivate appreciation for what manifests in space and time. Acknowledging the whole as the embodiment of Knowledge is one form that such appreciation can take.

Aesthetic enjoyment of the rich displays that time and space present is another. Through such enjoyment and appreciation, the concerns that lead to positioning tend to loosen.

The more that knowledge opens, the more fully appreciation can deepen into a wordless wonderment, rich in joy, profound respect, and even awe. Respect and awe can also change into devotion, which under appropriate circumstances may take such religious forms as prayer and worship.

Together with appreciation comes compassion. Compassion is based on a knowing that sees the 'order' as a whole and sees the pain that arises within it. Compassion arises for the self and for others, for everyone who is needlessly trapped within the structure that the 'order' imposes.

A great benefit of compassion is that it naturally turns attention away from the concerns of the self and the limited knowledge that those concerns engender. Aware of suffering, compassion looks toward the possibility of action that could bring transformation, and thus works toward the growth of 'knowledgeability'.

It might seem that compassion insists on the substantiality of the one that suffers. But this is true only in lower-level terms. From a higher-level perspective, compassion is a form of 'knowingness': a clearsighted vision of the prevailing knowledge in operation. It sustains the Body of Knowledge as active force, working to bring benefit where benefit is needed.

Finally, there is inspiration through love. This is not the love that is actually attachment, which only tightens the bonds of the conventional order by reinforcing the concerns of a needy, wanting self. It is a love indifferent to ownership or security. Akin to deep appreciation, it has a unique flavor of its own.

Love is the expression of the full unfolding of Knowledge, and the Love of Knowledge is the Love that Knowledge extends toward us. In extending Love, Knowledge expresses its own continuity and growth, its perfect availability. When we respond to the Love of Knowledge,

deepening and expanding that Love through our response, we acknowledge that Knowledge is boundless,
creative, and generative; that it does not end. Attuned to
its activity, we slip easily 'outside' conventional structures, nourished and inspired on the deepest level.

The Love of Knowledge reveals 'why' Knowledge is
available. Knowledge presents itself to knowledge to
manifest Knowledge. The Love of Knowledge is the activity of the Body of Knowledge, disclosing Being as
Love's Body.

Love, compassion, and appreciation can be practiced
and cultivated in every activity and every field of human
endeavor. Wherever this is done, knowledge will deepen
and inquiry will make valuable contributions. In personal relationships and private reflection, in study, research, artistic endeavor, social action, and business,
inspiration offers knowledge freely.

The result will be tangible and cumulative. Once
Knowledge has been awakened, it builds on itself—
Knowledge giving Knowledge. Not based on models,
Knowledge sets no limits, freeing human destiny to be
unbounded. Alive and continuous, Knowledge cannot be
owned or accumulated. Always available, Knowledge
extends its benefits freely in all directions.

There are times when knowledge presents itself so
forcefully that it cannot be ignored. Freely known, the
rhythm of a new becoming surges into being like a tidal
wave. Old patterns are swept away, so that the 'measured-out' momentum collapses, adding its accumulated
energy to the flow. As barriers fall, light can enter and

openness emerge, leading to harmony, balance, and fullness. All becomes silent and motionless. Though knowledge in the old sense has collapsed, a new knowing is available. Being itself exhibits the Body of Knowledge.

In its most direct expression, the love that leads toward Great Knowledge is the Love of Knowledge. Perhaps it could be called Great Love. It is a special kind of love, in which there is no object, no separation between the one who loves and what is loved. It is difficult to speak of such a love, in which we are both the ones who love and the ones toward whom love flows. But we can say that in the Love of Knowledge, there is no reaching out to something else, no effort or obligation. There is only the unfolding of Knowledge itself.

INDEX

absolute realm, 274

acceleration, 85, 97, 98, 99, 224

activity, 35, 37, 45, 50, 209, 211

agreement, 370, 472

allowing, 59–61, 184, 192, 198, 201–206; awareness, 385; matrix, 228, 230, 231; -ness, 94, 203; of space, 58, 94, 120, 132, 133, 154, 155, 180, 211–214, 221, 223, 227ff, 248, 249; non-, 112; dynamic of, 7

'altered realities', 439

appearance, 37, 151–154, 159, 169–172, 209, 227, 230–232, 272; source of, 7, 238–240

appreciation, 58, 63, 186, 187, 223, 238, 496–498

aspiration, 494-496

atomic realm, 25, 45, 67, 69, 70, 83, 86, 124, 127, 135, 137, 153, 188, 198, 213, 263, 319, 321, 322, 365

awareness, 10, 11, 15, 16, 31, 34, 75, 88, 89, 146, 217, 225, 232, 242, 253, 309, 313–315, 375, 377, 379, 384, 385, 387, 389–391, 405, 444, 446, 463, 465; as 'field', 146, 147, 314, 372, 374, 378, 379, 382, 408; as witness, 32; experience and, 379; joined to realization, 349; space and, 146, 148, 159–162; time and, 61, 309; 'owners' of, 312, 313